TEAM LEADER'S PROBLEM SOLVER

◆ ◆ ◆ ◆

CLAY CARR

PRENTICE HALL

Englewood Cliffs, New Jersey 07632

Library of Congress Cataloging-in-Publication Data

Carr, Clay.
    Team leader's problem solver / Clay Carr.
        p.   cm.
    Includes index.
    ISBN 0-13-409970-2 (cloth)—ISBN 0-13-409962-1 (paper)
    1. Work groups.   2. Self-directed work groups.   I. Title.
    HD66.C368   1995   95-39795
    658.4'036—dc20   CIP

Printed in the United States of America

10   9   8   7   6   5   4   3   2

ISBN 0-13-409970-2   ISBN 0-13-409962-1 (PBK)

PRENTICE HALL
Career & Personal Development
Englewood Cliffs, NJ 07632
A Simon & Schuster Company

On the World Wide Web at http://www.phdirect.com

Prentice-Hall International (UK) Limited, *London*
Prentice-Hall of Australia Pty. Limited, *Sydney*
Prentice-Hall Canada Inc., *Toronto*
Prentice-Hall Hispanoamericana, S.A., *Mexico*
Prentice-Hall of India Private Limited, *New Delhi*
Prentice-Hall of Japan, Inc., *Tokyo*
Simon & Schuster Asia Pte. Ltd., *Singapore*
Editora Prentice-Hall do Brasil, Ltda., *Rio de Janeiro*

INTRODUCTION

Self-managing teams have become one of the most promising organizational developments of the last two or three decades. Hundreds of organizations are experimenting with them. If you're a team leader in one of these organizations, I've written this book for you and your team.

I've been working with teams in one way or another since the late 1960s. In 1968, I led a successful multifunctional team—quite a few years before the word "multifunctional" was even coined. In the years since then, I've not only led multifunctional teams but created effective management teams in organizations that had never used them before. During the week that I wrote this introduction, I also facilitated a cross-functional team attempting to resolve the tensions between two functions—and at the same time mediated between that team and my management team to ensure that everyone supported the direction that the cross-functional team was taking. In short, I understand teams, not from reading books but from working with them for over twenty-five years.

As you might guess, I believe in teams. My purpose is to share what I know about them with you—to help you and your team resolve problems and become more effective. And to help you avoid some of the mistakes that I made through out the years.

Teams face many problems that traditional work groups never encounter. *Team Leader's Problems Solver* will help you deal with a wide range of these problems. For example, Chapter 2 will help you identify and solve a variety of problems caused by poor interpersonal relationships among team members.

Not all problems that teams encounter, however, are unique to teams. For example, Chapter 4 describes problems caused by the performance of individual team members. Many of these problems, such as the individual with a negative attitude who doesn't produce much work, are the same kinds of problems that traditional work groups face. But teams need to solve these problems more creatively than traditional work groups do (as you'll see).

The book refers to you as a team leader. That may or may not be what your organization calls you. It may still call you a supervisor, or it may call you a coach. You may be a more or less permanent leader, or a you may be a leader for a certain period of time, or for a particular project. Don't worry about the title. If you have or share responsibility for helping the team achieve its goals, this book will help you.

The book also assumes that your teams is self-managing. Whether or not this is true, you can still use most of the information. Just adapt it as necessary to your won situation. Remember, though—the more you can help the team move toward true self-management, the stronger and more effective the team will be.

How to Get the Most From This Book

Don't even think about sitting down and reading the book through from cover to cover. It's not that kind of book. Instead, it's designed to help you deal with specific problems—when they come up.

But you can take some steps to familiarize yourself with the book and its contents, so that it will be easier to use when you need it. Here are some of the steps you might consider:

- Look through the Table of Contents to get an idea of the kind of problems the book covers and how they're organized. Then read the introduction to each chapter. The introductions are short—about a page a piece—and they'll help you put each chapter in perspective.

- Read a few of the cases. If you want to be systematic, pick a case from each chapter and read it. But you don't need to do that. Just find a few cases that interest you and look at them. When you do, you'll get a feel for the format that's used to present each example. Then, when you need to use the book to help you solve a problem, you'll understand how it approaches problems.

- Each example ends with a section entitled "Tips to Help You Strengthen Your Team." These tips cover the broad spectrum of what a team leader needs to know. If you can schedule five minutes a day, you might want to read a tip and think about how it applies to you and your team. I can promise you that if you do this, you'll need to refer to the problem situations much less often—because you'll solve a lot of problems before they occur. (By the way, you don't need to read the tips in any particular order to benefit from them.)

The Heart of Effective Team Performance

As I mentioned, I've worked with teams for over twenty-five years. Sometimes teams work, and sometimes they don't. I can tell you why they work: Teams are effective when they find ways to draw on each individual's strength—and create the opportunity for individuals to contribute that strength.

You've probably read that before, or perhaps heard it in a training course. It sounds very simple. Take my word for it—it isn't. Each of us creates stereotypes of the people we deal with. Tom is kind of slow, while Mabel is very quick. Esther is good problem solver. Juan is good at details. And Gordon is a great negotiator.

Use those skills, but remember something: Individuals can contribute far more than your stereotypes would let them. Tom may be slow, but if the team gives him time, he may have the most effective solution to a problem. Mabel is very quick, but the team may sometimes benefit if she holds back and helps others develop their ideas. Esther may need to spend some time helping others solve problems.

Juan may want to work the details most of the time, but occasionally he'd like to lake the lead in developing the overall design of a project. And Gordon, who's a great negotiator, may want an occasional break where someone else does the negotiating so he can spend his time just working on a project.

In short, every one of us—yourself included—has more to contribute than others think. If you want to be a successful team leader, always leave room for the members of your team to realize their full potential.

A Final Thought

When they're used correctly, teams are more effective than traditional work groups. They're also more challenging and often more fun. I hope this book helps you and your team work more effectively, deal with the challenges you face more successfully, and have more fun. Good luck.

CONTENTS

Introduction
iii

Chapter 1

Interpersonal Problems Within Your Team
1

1-1. The Problem:
      The team doesn't trust one of its members   2

1-2. The Problem:
      The team shuts out one of its best workers   5

1-3. The Problem:
      The team wants to get rid of one of its members   7

1-4. The Problem: The team won't accept a member of a different
      ethnic group   10

1-5. The Problem:
      A member wants to leave the team   13

1-6. The Problem:
      A new team member won't relax and be "part of the gang"   17

1-7: The Problem: A small clique within the team insists on
      always working together   19

1-8. The Problem: Some members of the team won't work with
      other members   22

1-9. The Problem: Two team members are constantly fighting   25

1-10. The Problem: The team doesn't know what to do with
      a new team member who's weird   28

1-11. The Problem: A new female team member files a sexual
      harassment charge against several team members   31

1-12. The Problem: Several members of your team tell you that
      they believe another member has AIDS and they won't
      work with him   34

Chapter 2

Interpersonal Problems That Affect Your Team as a Whole 40

2-1. The Problem:
      Team members compete with one another when they need
      to cooperate   41

2-2. The Problem:
      The team members don't appear to like each other   44

2-3. The Problem:
      The team doesn't work together effectively   47

2-4. The Problem:
      The team keeps fighting over trivial matters   51

2-5. The Problem:
      The team can't handle serious disagreement   54

2-6. The Problem:
      Team members won't bring up their differences   57

2-7. The Problem:
      The team compromises instead of working problems through   60

2-8. The Problem:
      The team makes decisions that members then won't support   63

2-9. The Problem: Team members keep blaming one another for
      mistakes   66

2-10. The Problem:
      The team is very discouraged   70

2-11. The Problem: The team spends too much time socializing   74

2-12. The Problem:
      Sometimes the team acts just plain silly and you don't know
      how to handle it   77

Chapter 3

Problems With the Behavior of an Individual Team Member 79

3-1. The Problem:
      A team member tries to hog the credit   80

3-2. The Problem:
      A team member is extremely dogmatic and won't compromise   83

3-3. The Problem:
      A team member quickly backs off from her ideas if anyone
      disagrees   86

3-4. The Problem:
      A team member rejects everyone else's ideas   90

3-5. The Problem:
      A team member won't bring his problems up openly   92

3-6. The Problem:
      A team member refuses to do what the team has decided   95

3-7. The Problem:
      A team member criticizes fellow members to other teams   98

3-8.   The Problem:
       A member of the team has stolen several dollars from the
       team coffee fund   100

3-9.   The Problem:
       The team suspects that one of its members has been going
       through others' desks and personal belongings   104

3-10. The Problem:
       A team member has lied to another member about
       completing a task   108

Chapter 4

Problems With the Performance of an Individual Team Member 112

4-1.   The Problem:
       A team member has an excellent attitude but doesn't
       produce much work   113

4-2.   The Problem:
       A team member doesn't keep her commitments to the team   116

4-3.   The Problem:
       A team member who is a good performer keeps disrupting
       the team   119

4-4.   The Problem:
       A team member is an excellent individual performer
       but won't work with the team   122

4-5.   The Problem:
       A team member goes around the team to the next level
       of management when the team makes a decision
       she doesn't like   125

4-6.   The Problem:
       A team member performs well only when the
       rest of the team "gets on his case"   129

4-7.   The Problem:
       A team member performs well only on tasks she enjoys   132

4-8.   The Problem:
       A team member will perform only tasks he enjoys   135

Chapter 5

Problems With the Performance of the Team as a Whole 139

5-1. The Problem:
The team doesn't have enough to do to keep it busy 140

5-2. The Problem:
The team has more work than it can accomplish effectively 142

5-3. The Problem:
The team isn't performing its mission effectively 146

5-4. The Problem:
The team doesn't want to do administrative work 149

5-5. The Problem:
The team's decisions often aren't very good 153

5-6. The Problem:
The team doesn't have enough time to do quality work 156

5-7. The Problem:
Team members won't help one another 159

5-8. The Problem:
The team refuses to do anything about a nonperformer 162

5-9. The Problem:
The team refuses to get feedback from its customers 165

5-10. The Problem:
The team refuses to accept feedback from its customers 170

5-11. The Problem:
The turnover on the team is too high 173

5-12. The Problem:
The team gets sidetracked instead of concentrating
on its mission 176

5-13. The Problem:
Different functions within the team won't work together 179

5-14. The Problem:
The team functions poorly because members have
different statuses 184

5-15. *The Problem:*
      The team wants to ignore its next-level manager   189

5-16. *The Problem:*
      Team members are discouraged and performance has
      begun to decline because there is little career progression   191

5-17. *The Problem:*
      The team wants to give up   194

5-18. *The Problem:*
      The team wants to split into two teams   197

5-19. *The Problem:*
      The team keeps violating its norms   199

Chapter 6

Problems With Individual and Team Work Practices 202

6-1. *The Problem:*
      A team member refuses to use new technology   203

6-2. *The Problem:*
      A team member refuses to consider new ways of working   206

6-3. *The Problem:*
      The team refuses to use new technology   209

6-4. *The Problem:*
      The team refuses to consider new ways of working   213

6-5. *The Problem:*
      The team won't conform to company procedures   217

6-6. *The Problem:*
      The team keeps trying new methods that no one has approved 220

6-7. *The Problem:*
      The team always seems to be disorganized   223

6-8. *The Problem:*
      The team is very creative but not very productive   227

6-9. *The Problem:*
      The team is very productive but not very creative   231

6-10. *The Problem:*
The team is always wrangling over how to do things   234

Chapter 7

Problems Among Your Team and Other Teams 238

7-1. *The Problem:*
Another team that should be cooperating with your
team is competing with it   239

7-2. *The Problem:*
Your team doesn't want to work with other teams   242

7-3. *The Problem:*
Other teams are constantly trying to take over some
of your team's functions   244

7-4. *The Problem:*
The team often argues with other teams over who should
do what   248

7-5. *The Problem:*
Another team keeps blaming your team for mistakes   252

7-6. *The Problem:*
Another team asks you to tell your manager that they
gave you a report two days earlier than they actually did   255

Chapter 8

Problems With Team Leadership 258

8-1. *The Problem:*
The team wants to be told what to do instead of deciding
for itself   259

8-2. *The Problem:*
The team permits only two members to assume
leadership functions   262

8-3. *The Problem:*
The team constantly defers to one of its members 266

8-4. *The Problem:*
The team is ready to be self-leading, but your boss wants
you to perform all the leadership functions 269

8-5. *The Problem:*
When you encourage others to lead the team, they
don't do very well 273

8-6. *The Problem:*
The team won't support the leaders it picks 276

8-7. *The Problem:*
A team member won't take a leadership role but
constantly criticizes those who do 280

8-8. *The Problem:*
The team won't accept leadership from anyone 283

8-9. *The Problem:*
The team has a very rigid approach to leadership 286

Chapter 9

Problems With Your Team's Mission 289

9-1. *The Problem:*
The team's mission isn't clear 290

9-2. *The Problem:*
The team doesn't think its mission is important 293

9-3. *The Problem:*
The team's mission overlaps that of another team 297

9-4. *The Problem:*
The team's mission is too broad 300

9-5. *The Problem:*
The team has trouble establishing short-term objectives 303

9-6. *The Problem:*
The team isn't challenged by its mission 307

9-7. *The Problem:*
The team doesn't get any feedback on how it's doing 310

9-8.   The Problem:
        The team's mission keeps changing   314

9-9.   The Problem:
        The team is consistently assigned special projects that
        detract from its mission   317

9-10.   The Problem:
        The team doesn't have any customers or doesn't know
        who they are   320

9-11.   The Problem:
        The team is caught between its customers and its
        next-level manager   324

9-12.   The Problem:
        The team can't control the factors critical to its success   327

Chapter 10

Problems Caused by Higher Management
331

10-1.   The Problem:
        Higher management gives a project to another team that
        you think should have been yours   332

10-2.   The Problem:
        Higher management won't let you increase the size of
        the team, even though the workload is increasing   335

10-3.   The Problem:
        Your next-level manager insists on rating all the team
        members without input from anyone but you   339

10-4.   The Problem:
        Your next-level manager has unreasonable expectations
        for the quantity or quality of work the team can produce   343

10-5.   The Problem:
        Higher management refuses to support team decisions
        that are controversial   347

10-6.   The Problem:
        Your next-level manager keeps overruling your team's
        decisions   351

10-7. The Problem:
Your next level manager "micromanages" the team
and won't delegate 354

10-8. The Problem:
Your manager is pressuring you to tell her who made
the mistake that resulted in the team's missing a deadline 358

10-9. The Problem:
Two unnecessary members have been forced on the team 361

10-10. The Problem:
The team wants to change its mission and your next-level
manager won't consider it 366

10-11. The Problem:
Your next-level manager doesn't think much of the
team's performance 369

10-12. The Problem:
The team isn't recognized for its good performance 372

10-13. The Problem:
Your next-level manager doesn't believe in teams
and won't support your team 375

10-14. The Problem:
Your next-level manager is talking about breaking
up your team and reassigning its members 378

10-15. The Problem:
The team is expected to act as a traditional workgroup 382

Chapter 11

Problems With Computers and Support Systems 385

11-1. The Problem:
The computer system ties the team into rigid, inefficient
work methods 386

11-2. The Problem:
The team constantly has to use "workarounds"
to accomplish its work effectively 389

11-3.   The Problem:
        The computer system constantly makes mistakes
        that the team can't control   392

11-4.   The Problem:
        The team has to reenter data it gets from other teams   396

11-5.   The Problem:
        The team can't get the data it needs from the
        computer system   400

11-6.   The Problem:
        The team doesn't get the information it needs   403

11-7.   The Problem:
        The team has to keep its own production records because
        the formal system isn't accurate   407

11-8.   The Problem:
        The team can't get the supplies it needs   410

11-9.   The Problem:
        The team can't replace members quickly enough   414

11-10. The Problem:
        The team can't get the training it needs   418

11-11. The Problem:
        Team members are still being appraised as individuals,
        not as team members   421

Chapter 12

The Final Problem 426

The Problem:
The organization has just decided to abolish its teams   427

Index

431

CHAPTER 1

Interpersonal Problems Within Your Team

In a traditional workgroup, not everyone has to work well together. Someone who wants to be an independent worker can often be assigned a job that doesn't require him or her to work with others. Two or three individuals can sometimes work together and pay little attention to other workers.

Unfortunately, teams don't have that kind of flexibility. Team members must be able to work together. Even more important, each member must feel valued as a member of the team, and the team as a whole must value each member. Without this cohesiveness, a team never really becomes a team.

Chapter 1 contains 12 cases that present some of the kinds of interpersonal problems that can arise within a team that threaten team cohesiveness. The team may not trust one of its members or may shut out an individual. Two team members may constantly fight. The team may have problems with a new member.

To be effective, the team must face and deal with problems such as these. It cannot afford to ignore them in hopes that they'll go away. This chapter explains how to deal with these kinds of problems in ways that will both solve the problem and make the team stronger.

The Problem
The team doesn't trust one of its members

The Scene

One of your key people asks you: "Did you let Jeremy negotiate the agreement with Supply?"

"Yes. Shouldn't I have?"

"No! Don't you know by now that Jeremy puts a spin on everything that makes him a hero and the rest of us dum-dums. I'll bet you he's convinced Supply that he's the only one on the team they can deal with, so he can make points with the rest of us when he gets us something we can't get for ourselves."

Possible Causes

Jeremy has been an individual "wheeler-dealer" for so long that he doesn't understand what it means to be part of a team.

Moving from a traditional organization based on individual performance to a team-based organization can be a painful change. Some people have worked closely with others before, so for them it's not quite as dramatic. Others have built their whole career on their ability to produce by themselves. Performing as part of a team is a whole new world for them, a world they may not understand very well.

Jeremy didn't want to be put on a team.

He might have done his best to be a good team member anyway, which means this problem wouldn't exist. The fact that it does exist means that he hasn't made his peace with being on a team. In all probability, he still resents it.

Jeremy is untrustworthy.

Cures

If Jeremy has been an individual "wheeler-dealer" for so long that he doesn't understand what it means to be part of a team:

The team needs to take three steps, preferably all at the same time.

- It needs to continually demonstrate the benefits that come from working together. Perhaps if individual team members make a point to have Jeremy work with them on a project where it takes more than one person to succeed he will get the message. Perhaps the team might create situations where he is responsible for a project that he can't accomplish alone. Whatever it does, the team needs to "sell" Jeremy on the advantages of teamwork.

- It needs to notice and recognize every step Jeremy takes to become more of a team player. Don't let the team fall into the error that it should to wait for him to make a major move before recognizing his progress; he'll never become a team player in one bound. Instead, in the *One Minute Manager*'s words, try to "catch him doing something right" at every chance. This will communicate what the team wants and expects better than anything else could.

- Whenever it has sufficient data, it needs to confront Jeremy with his "wheeler-dealer" behavior and discuss it with him. For instance, you might contact Supply. If you find that Jeremy did attempt to make himself the only point of contact, this can be brought up in a team meeting and the team can make it clear how it interprets this behavior.

Don't be discouraged if Jeremy doesn't respond right away. Be patient and keep at this three-pronged approach for a while. Don't give up unless he absolutely fails to respond or, even worse, produces the surface behavior the team wants but continues behind the scenes with his wheeler-dealer ways. If either of these happens, assume that simple lack of knowledge isn't the problem and move to one of the next two solutions.

If Jeremy didn't want to be put on a team:

The team should make at least one attempt to bring up the problem at a team meeting. It shouldn't require great subtlety: "Jeremy, we get the impression you don't really like being on a team" should be adequate. If he discovers the team is genuinely concerned about what he wants, he may start to change and decide that he likes being on a team after all.

If Jeremy won't discuss the situation, or if he strongly prefers to be an independent worker, the next step is straightforward. Try to find him an independent job he qualifies for. You'll help turn a disruptive team member into a productive solo worker.

If Jeremy is untrustworthy:

Confront Jeremy with the team's perception of his untrustworthiness. Make it clear that it won't be tolerated, no matter what. Give him every chance to respond; the shock of the confrontation and/or of being forced off the team might be enough to make him reevaluate his behavior.

It's not enough for him to say the right words. The team should insist that he change his behavior and then watch his behavior closely. If it starts to change, move to the three-pronged approach mentioned in the first cure. If it doesn't change, take the situation to the next level of management and give them a chance to move Jeremy. If they won't or can't, keep the pressure on Jeremy until he really changes or decides to find himself a new job.

Team Strengthener

There are individuals who have chosen to be dishonest, untrustworthy, or otherwise unwilling to be open with those around them. In most cases, the team should make an honest effort to give them the chance to change. Knowing that others care about them and expect straightforward, open behavior from them is sometimes enough to turn these individuals around. But deal with them with your eyes open; unless they're genuinely willing to change, there's no place for them on the team. Teams require honest, open, trustworthy behavior to function. Insist on this from every member, and if you don't get it help the individual in one way or another to find another job.

The Problem
The team shuts out one of its best workers

The Scene

As you walk down the hall, you notice Walter and Miguel talking. You slow down, and hear the following:

"Hey, Miguel, I hear some of you are getting together for drinks tonight."

"Well . . . yeah . . . I guess so."

"I'd sure like to join you."

"Well . . . uh . . . It was really Elaine's idea. You really need to ask her."

"OK—where is she?"

"Gee, I don't know. Oh, hey, I gotta go."

"They're at it again," you think to yourself. "This is the third time this week they've deliberately shut Walter out. I wonder why...."

Possible Causes

Walter has done something that's offended the team.

Perhaps Walter refused to pitch in and help on a high-priority project, or he talked about one team member's personal life to another member, or he committed any number of other actions that the rest of the team resented.

The team has taken a dislike to Walter.

In this case, what bothers the team isn't a specific action Walter has taken but something more generally characteristic of Walter himself. Perhaps he won't listen to others, or he won't keep his commitments, or he simply isn't very likeable.

Cures

If Walter has done something that's offended the team:

Ask discreet questions to find out how he offended the team. Then leave the situation alone for a while, and expect it to resolve itself when the team concludes that Walter has suffered enough and it's time to readmit him to team membership. The team is making a point. Let them make it. If the team is mature, they'll ensure that Walter gets the point, then they'll welcome him back in.

What if the team isn't mature, or for some other reason they continue to exclude Walter? You need to find out all you can about what happened. Then you need to meet with the team or several key members, without Walter, and find out just what they're trying to accomplish. If they're too wrapped up in what happened, you need to gently change their focus to the present, to what they're accomplishing (or not accomplishing) by what they're doing. You can't control the team, but you can encourage them to look at what's happening and what the consequences are. If you can get them to focus on what's best for them and for Walter, they'll probably decide that they've made their point and get on with their business.

If the team has taken a dislike to Walter:

You need to discuss the situation with the team or two or three of its key members directly, without Walter there. Confront them with your perception of what's happening, then give them the opportunity to explain themselves. (Always listen carefully before deciding what someone else's motives are.) Then, as forcibly as you can, make it clear that this kind of exclusion has no place in an effective team, that it stunts the team's growth and holds it back from being what it could become. Everything here depends on your persuasiveness, which depends on your understanding of what's important to them.

It may help you to look at Case 1–4 in this chapter, where a team discriminates in the hiring process against someone in a different ethnic group. That may give you a somewhat broader perspective.

Team Strengthener

When a team becomes mature and effective, it develops the power to discipline its members. Neither the team leader nor higher-level management needs to interfere. But any team leader needs to keep the team focusing on what it wants to accomplish, not on excluding or punishing a member because of something that happened in the past. Help the team free itself from hangups based on the past and move on to attack and overcome its current challenges.

1–3

The Problem
The team wants to get rid of one of its members

The Scene

One member of your team sticks his head into your cubicle. "Are you busy?"

"Not for you, Rocco. What's on your mind?"

"Martin just isn't working out. We want you to get him reassigned to another team or something."

Possible Causes

This is a passing thing. The team is angry with Martin and is overreacting.

This could result from the kind of incident described in the previous case, or from a variety of other causes. Whatever Martin has done has upset the rest of the team, and they're reacting strongly to it.

The team hasn't given Martin a chance.

Perhaps Martin is new, and the team's first reaction to him is negative. For some reason, he's not what the team expected. Perhaps he's too casual or too talkative, too formal or too casual. Perhaps he made a serious mistake soon after he joined the team. The team has decided he won't fit in because of what he did.

Martin isn't fitting in.

Teams have personalities of their own, and the stronger the team the stronger its personality will probably be. Martin's personality is too different.

Cures

If the team is angry with Martin and overreacting:

Talk with Rocco and then with the entire team (preferably without Martin). Find out what happened. Give the team a chance to blow off steam and get the incident out of its collective system. Then gently guide the team toward closing the book on the past and taking Martin back in the team.

If there is a serious issue, don't try to sweep it under the rug to get Martin accepted by the team once again. Perhaps he betrayed someone's trust or failed to carry out an important task he'd promised to accomplish. If anything like this happened, the team needs to deal with it. You may have to encourage them here; they may have wanted to get Martin off the team as a way to keep from having to face the issue with him. Such an approach will always be harmful to the growth and effectiveness of the team. One of your functions as a leader is to lead the team to deal with its problems and keep growing.

If the team hasn't given Martin a chance:

Again, talk with the team. Get the best feel you can for what the issue really is. If Martin is relatively new, or if he's very different from other members of the team, the team may have reached a snap decision about him. (This happens particularly when the team has just begun to see itself as a team and doesn't want to think of anyone new becoming part of it.)

If this is the case, your foremost goal is to get Martin and the team talking with one another. Encourage the team to voice its concerns; just why does it believe Martin won't fit in? Then make sure that Martin has the chance to reply and that the team really hears what he has to say. If he and the team can become open in what they say and can truly listen to each other, the problem will almost always go away. When it doesn't, you can be confident that Martin really doesn't fit, and he may well make the decision to leave for himself.

If you have a good team facilitator available, this would be a good opportunity to use the individual's services.

If Martin isn't fitting in:

Don't conclude this until you've exhausted both of the previous alternatives. In particular, try not to reach the conclusion until Martin and the rest of the team have talked. If you're forced to the conclusion that he doesn't fit in, you and the team need to do whatever you can to help the organization find a place where he does fit.

An important point: Neither you, the team, nor Martin has been successful unless he leaves without anyone feeling that he or the team has failed. Some marriages don't work even when both parties are decent people and try hard. And some individuals just don't fit on some teams, even when both the individual and the team try hard. Lead the team in working through any issues it may have with Martin, and vice versa, and then let the parting occur with a clean slate on every side.

Never jump quickly to the conclusion that someone won't "fit in" on a team, and never let the team do so. Diversity really does strengthen a team, and diversity is far more than simply race, ethnic background, or gender. As this book states, the more a team is open to new experiences and different kinds of members, the stronger it will become.

Team Strengthener

Most of us are brought up to avoid controversy. We're told "If you can't say something nice about someone, don't say anything at all." That may be good advice when it comes to talking *about* someone, but it's misleading when we need to talk *with* someone. Teams grow only when they face their problems, not when they try to avoid them or have them reassigned elsewhere. One of a leader's primary functions, whether you're the permanent leader or just exercising the role in this situation, is to see that problems are faced, worked through, and solved. The first time or two that the team faces significant problems individuals may get very emotional, and the whole situation may become very strenuous. After it works through a few situations successfully, however, the team will develop the ability to confront and solve even serious problems without becoming overly emotional.

The Problem

The team won't accept a member of a different ethnic group

The Scene

Paul comes into your office. "You said we'd get a voice in selecting the new team member. Do we?"

"Sure, Paul. I think the team is well enough along. What's up?"

"I saw that list you got from personnel, and one of the guys on it is Vietnamese or something. Now I don't really have anything against him or his people, but he just wouldn't fit in here. And I know that several other people on the team feel the same way. If we really have a voice in this, we don't even want to interview him."

Possible Causes

Prejudice against someone from a different ethnic group.

Paul or someone else on the team may have had an unfortunate experience with someone in that ethnic group, he may be working from hearsay, or he may just not want someone that different on the team. No matter. It all adds up to prejudice.

Clannishness.

When a team first develops real cohesion and begins thinking of itself as a team and not just as a collection of individuals, it often goes to an extreme and becomes very clannish. Any outsider becomes a problem, perhaps even a threat. Your team may be going through this stage now. If so, it may make the thought of someone from a different ethnic group joining the team much harder to take than it would be in other circumstances.

Hint

No matter what else is true, whether the team is just starting or is experienced and mature, don't ever take the word of one team member in a situation as touchy as this one. If the team is just starting, you don't know whether the individual speaks for the team or has just appointed himself spokesperson. If the team is mature, it doesn't need a spokesperson to deal with you. Whatever solution you choose, it has to involve getting more information than just Paul's opinion.

Cures

If the team is prejudiced:

This may be the first real test of the team's maturity, and you need to let them either make the choice or significantly influence your choice. But discrimination against someone from another group is not only illegal but repugnant; you need to express this as loudly and clearly as possible. The team needs to understand the risk it takes if it rejects a candidate for no better reason than this. You'll hope that at least some team members feel the same way and will support you. Ultimately, though, don't force your convictions—as right as they may be—on the team.

If the team ultimately decides to reject someone primarily because of his or her ethnic background, it has set a terrible precedent. Even if no one files a complaint, the team has broken the law. It has chosen a dangerous path, even if it never has to make this kind of choice again. This means that one of your goals must be to help the team develop insight into the meaning of the choice and understand the seriousness of what it has done.

Is there an even worse alternative? Yes. Should you and others on the team go through the charade of considering the individual and then construct a bogus reason for not selecting him or her, you would have set an even more dangerous precedent. Honesty is an absolute requirement for effective team functioning. A team cannot be a little bit dishonest any more than someone can be a little bit pregnant. To practice discrimination and dishonesty in the same action is as destructive a step as the team could take. If the team is mature enough to make its decisions even if you don't agree, you have a major problem. Don't rule out the possibility of disbanding the team; you may not want to recommend that, but the situation is serious enough that disbanding may be the lesser of two evils. (This should motivate you to work even harder to prevent both the discrimination and the dishonesty.)

If this is a sign of team clannishness:

You still face a serious problem, but a different one. Here, your number one goal is to help the team become aware of their situation. How do you do that?

- If the team has developed openness and some ability to deal with conflict effectively, put the matter before the team as you see it. Present it as what it is, a challenge for the team to grow. By closing off this alternative, it harms itself. The discussion will be lively, but if the team really is maturing it will probably see the logic in your ideas.

- If the team uses a facilitator, he or she can be extremely helpful here. Even if the team has reached the point that it seldom uses its facilitator, this may be the place to make an appropriate exception. Remember, the team is facing a critical growth point here.

- What if the team has started to perform as a team, but hasn't yet learned openness and effective conflict-resolution methods? You have to take the lead, but the goal remains the same. Help the team to see that it faces a significant choice between growing and remaining safely in its little niche.

No matter what the cause is:

Don't go to the other extreme and select (or propose to select) someone simply because he or she is from another ethnic group. That's just as discriminatory. The team needs to make selections on their merits, not because someone is or isn't a member of another group.

Now that I've said that, let me add quickly that it can be a very responsible decision for the team to select someone from a group of well-qualified candidates because he or she is very different, *and because it believes it will learn from the difference.* This is the opposite of the tokenism in the paragraph above. A team that self-consciously chooses the path of growth will seldom go wrong; the worst that will happen is that it will learn tremendously from the experience.

Team Strengthener

Teams don't ever mature and then just remain that way. Every team is growing or stagnating. Unfortunately, the more competent a team is as a team, the more it will tend to stagnate. "Why should we change anything," the team asks itself, "when things are going so well?" Then, almost invisibly, it begins to lose its edge. The team can help prevent this by treating every proposed change as a challenge to move back into the growth mode. The greater the stretch that the change requires, the greater the team's opportunity for growth—if it consciously chooses the path of growth. Remember, one of the keys to real creativity and effective problem solving is the ability to find the challenges hiding inside problems.

1–5

The Problem
A member wants to leave the team

The Scene

"Say, do you have a minute?"

"Sure, Daphne. How's everything going with the team?"

"That's really what I wanted to talk with you about. I really don't think I fit in here, and I'd appreciate it if you'd help me get a job on another team."

Possible Causes

The team is excluding Daphne for some reason.

Because the team isn't accepting her for some reason, she wants to leave. Perhaps they have become clannish and she's new and thus an "outsider." Perhaps they don't trust her. Perhaps the reason is based on her ethnic group. Whatever it is, she's reacting to exclusion from the team by wanting to leave it.

Daphne has a problem with the team and would rather leave than confront its members.

This may happen more often when an individual is relatively new to the team, but it can happen at any time. Daphne may feel the matter is too personal to bring up (perhaps someone on the team made an unwelcome pass at her and she's unwilling to raise the matter formally). Perhaps she feels that she's already brought the matter to the team and the team refused to deal with it satisfactorily.

Either Daphne or the team have unrealistic expectations for her performance.

The team may misunderstand Daphne's skills. She wants to leave because they expect a kind or level of performance from her she can't provide. Perhaps she'd been billed as an expert in an area that was particularly troubling the team, but she isn't able to help the team solve the problems it's facing as quickly as it wants, so the team is frustrated with her. Perhaps the team operates in a different way from the team she left, so she feels out of place. Perhaps she's just not accustomed to being on a team.

Daphne really would perform more effectively on another team.

Each team and each individual has a personality, a balance of skills, and interests unique to that team or person. Daphne may have the wrong balance for this particular team.

Cures

If the team is excluding Daphne:

Listen carefully to Daphne and try to draw her out. If this is the problem, the best solution is for Daphne and the rest of the team to discuss the situation and try to resolve it. Both Daphne and the team need to be mature for this to happen. If they are, everyone can get the real problem out on the table and deal with it together. (This is another point where, unless the team is experienced at conflict, having someone facilitate the session will be helpful.)

What if she and/or the team are unwilling to do this? You can meet with the rest of the team and help them surface the real issue as they see it. You may need to speak for her at points (another good reason for having listened closely to her), but that isn't really your role. If the team does bring up its basic concern with Daphne, try to get Daphne and the team to agree to meet and discuss the issue.

If Daphne has a problem with the team but doesn't want to confront the team:

If you believe Daphne is leaving because of an unresolved conflict, take whatever steps you can to bring the conflict to the surface. This kind of situation often requires more patience and skill than the one above, because Daphne has made a decision not to talk about what's bothering her. You need to talk with her, of course. More accurately, you need to listen to her and try to create a trusting atmosphere in which she'll share her concern with you. If she doesn't feel free to speak with you, is there someone on the team she might talk with? Ask him or her to talk with her. You might call the team together and see if anyone knows what the problem is.

If you can find the problem, then you and the team will probably know what to do. If you find it without her telling you, be particularly sensitive to the situation. Perhaps the best way to handle this is for you or someone she trusts to tell her that the team knows the situation and would like to discuss it with her. You'll hope she will choose to do so.

Note: Other cases in the chapter deal with discrimination based on prejudice and with overt sexual discrimination. What if you find out, or strongly suspect, that Daphne is leaving because she believes she is a victim of either? It becomes doubly important for you to find out the real situation and see that it surfaces in team discussion. Look at Cases 1–4 and 1–11 for suggestions.

If either Daphne or the team have unrealistic expectations for her performance:

This should be easier to resolve than either of the two situations above. As always, get the data, so you know just what the situation is. Then help the team as a whole, including her, deal with it, by putting what they expect and what she feels she can contribute on the table and reconciling the two.

If Daphne would perform more effectively on another team:

As always, don't reach this conclusion until you've explored the other ones. The best way to reach the conclusion, of course, is for Daphne and the team to discuss the alternatives and jointly agree that this is the right one.

If this happens, nothing more needs to be done except to help Daphne find an appropriate transfer. If it doesn't happen, you need to try to make it happen. Then both Daphne and the team need for her to leave without anger or resentment on either side. That way, everyone can close the book on the matter and get back to the tasks facing them in the present.

Team Strengthener

All of us carry around with us baggage from the past, in the form of painful memories and unresolved situations and emotions. None of us ever gets all of them worked through. In a traditional organization, we have little opportunity to do so. When the organization empowers teams, though, it creates a true opportunity for each team member to deal with each other member in the present. This happens only when each member is willing to put any issue on the table and accept each other member doing the same. The first few times this happens it will probably be awkward, and tempers may flare. (Here's another spot for a good facilitator.) When the team finds that it can not only handle but resolve these situations, it begins to develop tremendous self-confidence. It makes a quantum leap to a new level of effectiveness.

The Problem

A new team member won't relax and be "part of the gang"

The Scene

You've been watching Martha for several days. The other members of the team are doing everything they can to make her feel at home, but she keeps resisting. She keeps to herself, responds very stiffly to their overtures, and seldom says anything in team meetings unless someone asks her a question directly. You know this can't go on.

Possible Causes

Martha is accustomed to being an independent worker.

In traditional organizations, many individuals perform jobs that don't require them to work closely with others. They may prefer this way of working, or they may just have gotten used to it. When they suddenly find themselves part of a team, they don't know how to handle it. They may even be afraid of the team's advances.

Martha has come from an uptight organization.

It may be possible for a team to be stuffy and uptight and also effective, but it certainly isn't common (or, from my perspective, advisable). Traditional organizations, though, often encourage their members to keep at arm's length from one another and to treat one another formally. Martha may have come from that kind of organization, and she's simply behaving the way she's been taught is the correct way to behave on the job.

Martha distrusts the team's overtures for some reason.

Martha may be afraid one or more team members are coming on to her, or that they want to create friendships she's not ready for. She may even have heard bad things about the team and be afraid to respond to its approaches.

Cures

If Martha is accustomed to being an independent worker:

Remember that this is a new world for Martha. She literally may not know how to act as part of a close-knit team. You should talk with her, nonjudgmentally, about what the team expects. You should also encourage the team to explain their expectations to her, gently and without putting any pressure on her.

The two words, for both you and the team, are gentleness and patience. Unless Martha is a true loner, she'll begin to appreciate the advantages of working as part of a team. Encourage her, but don't push her. Let her find her own way.

If Martha has come from an uptight organization:

Since she's used to a formal supervisor, you're the natural one to talk with her in this situation. Explain to her how the team operates and how it's different from the workgroups she's known. Don't expect her to jump for joy at the prospect (though she may). Instead, give her time. The team needs to offer her the opportunity to be part of it, but without pressure or judgment. Look at the section just above and apply its principles.

If Martha distrusts the team's overtures for some reason:

You need to talk with Martha. Pick a time and place that's not threatening to her—perhaps the break room when the two of you are there alone. Feel her out very carefully; does she really distrust the team? Remember, she sees you as part of the team, so she'll probably distrust you, too. After both you and the team treat Martha with patience and gentleness, she will probably begin to open up. When she does, it becomes doubly important to respect her feelings and not assume that all of the problem has vanished.

Team Strengthener

Effective teams need skill at welcoming and integrating new members, since it's often an anxious time for both the team and the individual. Neither knows just what to expect. The team should take the lead and do its best to make its new member feel at home. This may be difficult, for either or both of two reasons. First, the new member may be replacing someone who was highly valued by the team, and the team "knows" this new person could never replace the one who left. Or the team may be very tightly knit and regard any new member as an intrusion. If you suspect either of these is the case, you should lead the team in a discussion of the situation *before* the new member arrives so that the team is ready to deal with the new situation the moment the new member shows up.

1–7

The Problem
A small clique within the team insists on always working together

The Scene

As you walk by, you see Saundra, Mack, and Tasha working away on the complicated procurement the team has agreed to make. They work very well together. The problem is that they don't work well with the rest of the team, and they don't want the rest of the team working with them.

Possible Causes

They like each other and enjoy working together.

If the team is lucky, the clique isn't really a clique. The individuals who want to work together just hit it off extremely well and want to work together because they like each other so much. They may, in fact, be surprised that the team sees them as a clique.

The rest of the team tends to exclude them, so they work together.

The group may be from a different ethnic group or a different function. They may be latecomers to an existing, highly cohesive team. They may have a reputation for poor work. But for some reason, they're not being fully accepted as part of the team.

They see themselves as the "elite" part of the team.

Perhaps when the team was formed it had several effective individual workers who began to stick together, and then the team never jelled as a whole.

Hint

No matter the reason, cliques within a team always pose problems. If nothing else, they always limit team flexibility by limiting the ways that the members of the team can work together on projects.

Cures

If they like each other and enjoy working together:

Present the problem, completely nonjudgmentally, in a team meeting. The team should *not* accuse them of being a clique; instead, individuals might explain how they feel about not being able to work with a group that has such obviously high morale and does such good work. The goal? You might try to get team consensus on letting the "clique" work together on some projects in return for its commitment that the individuals in it will work as parts of other groups on some projects.

If the rest of the team tends to exclude them, so they work together:

The clique is only part of the problem, and perhaps the smallest part. In this case, the rest of the team took the initiative; since they started it, they may not be motivated to change.

What happens next depends on what these causes were.

- If there may be racial, ethnic, or sexual discrimination, the situation demands immediate attention, to prevent the team from getting into serious trouble. See Case 1–4. (Some of the suggestions in the next paragraph may be useful here.)

- If they joined an already highly cohesive team, bring the matter up with the team, perhaps without the excluded "clique" there; if a facilitator is available, he or she will be helpful. With full discussion, the team will discover that it's handicapping itself whenever it excludes anyone. When this happens, have a meeting of the full team so that the others can explain to the "clique" what happened and how they want to correct it. Then the whole team can work out how to accomplish this.

- If the individuals in the clique have a reputation for poor work, the team has two problems to deal with: the exclusion of the group and the poor work. First, the team needs to begin including the individuals in the "clique" and seeing that they work with other members on the team. You'll hope that most of the poor performers will improve; but it will take patience on the part of the rest of the team. If one or more can't improve, then the team needs to find other work for them, as nonpunitively as possible.

If they see themselves as the "elite" part of the team:

Your approach needs to be just the reverse of the one used when the team excluded the clique. This time, you want to get together with the clique. Don't expect them to be particularly receptive. From their point of view, they're carrying the team. If they have to start working with others, the team's performance will go down. (This is the clique's version of the attitudes of outstanding individual workers in traditional organizations.)

There's no magic formula here. Once again, the best approach may be to get their agreement to work with other team members at times in return for being able to work together at other times. You may also consider using them as subteam leaders when a larger project must be broken into smaller parts. Your goal is to persuade them that they should use their skills to improve the performance of others on the team and thus of the team as a whole. It will be tough sledding, but keep at it. The payoff will be worth it.

Team Strengthener

The individuals who make up teams often have very different performance levels. In a traditional organization, high performers often go to great lengths to separate themselves from average or poor performers. Teams can't operate this way. Everyone has to support the performance of the team as a whole, which means that top performers have to be willing to work closely with other team members. This isn't an altruistic act. When high-performance team members work closely with other members, they often discover that these other members have skills and abilities that have been overlooked and that complement the skills of the high performers. Team members need to see themselves as a team and work to develop and use the abilities of every member of the team. When they do, both the level of individual performance and the level of team performance rises. When that happens, it's a great feeling for everyone.

1–8

The Problem

*Some members of the team won't work
with other members*

The Scene

The team just finished dividing up the different tasks for their latest project, and it was quite a scene to behold. Bonnie and Paul would have been naturals to take one of the projects, but they don't work well with each other. So Bonnie finally ended up doing a minor job and then became one of the three members responsible for writing the final report. She had to go because Holland and Bernie will work with her, but not with Ahad, who ended up where Bonnie should have been.

It made a simple task so complicated. There must be another way!

Possible Causes

The team received poor initial training.

Organizations often fail to see that individuals need effective training, particularly in "team building," to work together productively as a team. As you'll see in this book, though, working together productively in a cohesive team requires a high level of interpersonal competence. Most independent workers in traditional organizations have never had the opportunity to develop this competence.

Functional rivalries have carried over into the team.

The good news: Multifunctional teams often provide a real performance payoff for organizations. The not-so-good news: Multifunctional teams are difficult to organize and maintain so that they function effectively. Different functions often develop rivalries and even resentment toward one another in traditional organizations. Some of these negative relationships may be carrying over into the team.

Relationships from outside the team, both good and bad, have carried over into the team.

This may result from a fuzzy mission or one that team members aren't committed to. It may also result from a feeling on the part of some members of the team that other members aren't really necessary. Later chapters of the book deal specifically with these problems; you might want to look at them to help with this situation.

Cures

If the team received poor initial training:

If you can get good team-building training for the team, get it. Whether the team gets the training or not, have a skilled facilitator sit in on the next few meetings, to help the team become aware of what's happening and how they need to change it. Between the training and a good facilitator, the team should be able to turn the problem around.

Either of the next two situations may partially result from the lack of good initial training. Consider getting this training along with the other solutions suggested.

If functional rivalries have carried over into the team:

Is everyone focused on a clear mission that can be accomplished only if the team works together as a unit? Don't assume you know the answer to this; think about it and check it out carefully with the team. Individuals from one function may see no need at all to work with those from another function. Here it might be helpful to have someone from higher management talk with the team and make it clear why they need one anothers' skills (which is what should have happened when the team was formed).

If relationships from outside the team have carried over into the team:

If two specific individuals don't seem to be getting along, the team should bring up the matter very gently as a team concern. (If the team isn't mature enough, you could start the process by talking with the individuals concerned, then encouraging them to bring it up to the whole team.) It may take several attempts, but you or the team should be able to help the individuals see that their animosity is handicapping the team as a whole. More important, the team should try to facilitate the individuals getting the problem out in the open, where it can be dealt with.

Take care, though, that you don't just drive the animosities underground. When people feel pressured, they often go through all of the outward signs of getting along. If the basic problem hasn't been solved, though, the negative feelings will still be there. They may continue to poison the relationship and perhaps even the team as a whole. Now, though, they're more deeply hidden and even harder to deal with. Encourage, but don't attempt to force individuals to get along. It may take time, but it works, and the result is worthwhile.

Team Strengthener

Did your team have a facilitator available to help it start performing successfully? Does it have a facilitator available to help with the rough spots that occur throughout a team's existence? A good facilitator never tries to make a team do this or that or push it in a particular direction. Instead, he or she mirrors back to the team what's happening, helping it become aware of how it may be avoiding issues, ignoring specific members, and so forth. If your team doesn't have one available, you should start a campaign for the organization to either develop facilitators in-house or contract for their services. Yes, it's an expense, but the gain in team effectiveness will more than make up for it.

1–9

The Problem

Two team members are constantly fighting

The Scene

"Dammit, Charlie, I told you to leave my stuff alone!"

"I'd love to do just that, but you have the data from the survey, and I need it."

"I know you need it—so why don't you just ask me for it?"

"I tried to find you for an hour. I can't wait all day—this stuff is important."

And so it goes, for the hundredth time. Charlie and Pat have never come to blows, but their arguments have gotten heated enough to completely disrupt the rest of the team. And even when they're not yelling at each other, their arguments disrupt the team.

Something has to be done.

Possible Causes

Their relationship has carried over from their old organization.

Unless the immediate supervisor is skilled at helping individuals deal with each other, traditional organizations have few effective ways to resolve conflict. Charlie and Pat may have had a poor relationship for years. (Fighting with each other may also have been the only really interesting thing either of them did all day.)

They got off to a bad start with each other on the team.

This may be the result of failure in team organization. The team may not have had a skilled facilitator to help them work through the original incidents that continue to cause problems. The individuals were probably both new to teams, so they didn't understand how a team can openly resolve such conflict. And the team as a whole, being new, didn't understand it either.

The team shuts them out or eggs them on, which intensifies their poor relationship.

It may not be obvious, but the team may be encouraging the behavior. The team may be so irritated with them that it effectively shuts them out, forcing them to deal with each other constantly. Or the team, partly as a result of frustration, may be egging them on in hopes that one of them will leave. None of these situations is healthy, for the individuals or for the team.

Cures

If their relationship has carried over from their old organization:

Begin by dealing with the situation yourself. Talk to them together, explain how serious a problem they're causing, and offer to reassign either or both of them off the team. If the team is meaningful to both of them, this may make them pause and provide an opening for healing their relationship. You can help them with this, and at the later stages the team can get involved. The matter should end with the two of them specifically empowering the team as a whole to interrupt at any time they fall back into their old patterns.

What if one or both of them jump at the chance to be reassigned? Bring the matter before the team as a whole (including Charlie and Pat) and let it discuss and decide the matter. The team may feel that it needs both of them and decide to take a very active part in helping them get along (which they may or may not appreciate). Or the team may decide that the only recourse is to split them up and work out with them which one will be reassigned.

If they got off to a bad start with each other on the team:

Can you get a skillful facilitator? If so, do so—and let him or her help the individuals and the team as a whole face the relationship and deal with its causes. It doesn't matter what the causes are, and it's not up to the team to decide who was right and who was wrong. Instead, the function of everyone is to help the two of them get what's bothering them on the table, deal with it, and get it behind them. And it should end with the agreement that if the team sees their old patterns come back up it can intervene and help them look at what's happening.

If the team shuts them out or eggs them on:

If you believe anything like this is happening, get it before the team as quickly as possible. (Again, a good facilitator will help here.) *Warning:* This may be a stormy session or several stormy sessions. Be patient, because virtually everyone on the team may be irritated and resentful because of the situation. Let it all get out on the table, then deal with it. Let everyone take responsibility for his or her contribution, then get individual commitment to deal with the situation. After that, the team can decide what it needs to do to keep the old behaviors from coming back.

Team Strengthener

Conflict within a team arises from many sources: individual differences; perceived slights or put-downs; difference over how to handle a problem; gossip. The list is endless. Teams can learn to handle almost any kind of conflict, though it takes time. Part of the learning is the willingness to put conflict on the table. "I don't like the way you treated me yesterday." "Did you really mean it when you said I didn't know what I was doing this morning?" "I don't think any of you really listened to me yesterday, and I'm really mad about it" are hard comments for people to make who aren't used to open conflict. They are also hard for people to listen to without being defensive. But the saying and the listening must occur, and then the team must find solutions. And every time it finds a solution, it gets stronger and more competent.

1–10

The Problem

The team doesn't know what to do with a new team member who's weird

The Scene

"Do you have a moment?

"Sure. What's up?"

"That Jonathan guy we just picked up is weird! You ought to see the way he's dressed today."

"Norm, do you really think we ought to judge someone that quickly by what he's wearing?"

"No—but that's just a part of it. He said hello to everyone, including Jorge, in French, and he took off his jacket and put on a lab coat to start the day."

You say something about looking into it, primarily to satisfy Norm enough that he would leave. But Jonathan does sound weird. Exactly what has the team picked up?

Possible Causes

Jonathan is an effective worker who "does his own thing."

He may have been an independent worker in his former jobs and may not concern himself with how he looks to others.

Jonathan acts weird to cover up shortcomings in interpersonal abilities.

Jonathan may never have learned how really to relate to others. He may have been a "computer nerd" in high school or may have devoted all his time to mathematics or the sciences. His parent may have had very poor interpersonal skills, so that they were poor models for him. The reason doesn't matter; you're not in the business of analyzing him.

Jonathan wants to be the center of attention.

Who knows what the cause may have been; it doesn't matter. And in a traditional organization, his desire to be center stage may have caused few problems. On a team, though, it's a major problem.

Hint

Your immediate task is to get the team to withhold judgment on Jonathan until it's had time to work with him—several weeks, at least. With only a little bit of luck, they'll find that he's more like them than different, and the problem will go away. If it doesn't, start dealing with the causes above.

Cures

Jonathan is an effective worker who "does his own thing":

This, of course, is what you hope for. You may have to work with some other members of the team, particularly those who are very conventional. You don't want them to make "allowances" for Jonathan; you want them to accept him for what he is and make use of his talents. It may be difficult with one or two individuals; just keep working with them and keep them focused on his abilities.

If the team as a whole has been relatively conventional, this may be a marvelous growth opportunity for its members. Once they realize that Jonathan can be an effective contributor, their horizons may expand considerably. And their creativity may suddenly skyrocket because Jonathan may help them loosen some of their own inhibitions.

If Jonathan acts weird to cover up shortcomings in interpersonal abilities:

This may require a lot of patience on the part of the team, and your task is to persuade them to exercise this patience. After all, Jonathan may not be the only one on the team with less than marvelous interpersonal skills. You could send him to team training or "how to get along with people" training right away. It might be a better strategy to wait for several weeks or even a month or two, until he has started to function as part of the team. At that point, he should understand how important the skills he lacks are. That means he will want to get every bit of learning from the training he can.

In both this situation and the one above, Jonathan's weirdness may be a sign of high creativity. After all, most people who lack a high level of interpersonal skills just withdraw, or become terminally conventional. Jonathan didn't. He made a far more creative response. The team may be able to profit immensely from his creativity.

If Jonathan wants to be the center of attention:

Don't conclude that this is the situation until you've explored the first two alternatives and decided they don't apply. If Jonathan does want to hog the limelight, what do you do? You encourage the rest of the team neither to let him hog it nor reject him for trying. They need to appreciate him and at the same time absolutely refuse to make him the star.

How do they do this? Here are some ideas:

- Ignore his weirdness when he uses it to get attention. Treat him as an ordinary human being—a *worthwhile* ordinary human being.

- Openly appreciate his contributions to the team. If he begins to find that he can get attention more reliably by contributing to the team, he will probably begin to do more of it.

- Appreciate his weirdness when he uses it to generate new ideas, shake the team out of their daily rut, or otherwise spark the team to wake up and take a fresh look at things. Doesn't this contradict the first point above? Not really. You still reject the weirdness as a way of gaining center stage, but you support it as a way of relating to the team and adding a new dimension to it.

Team Strengthener

Wouldn't it be great if everyone on your team were at least a little weird? It really would, because you could then have an immensely creative team. The odds are you won't achieve this, though you should try. What you can do is encourage everyone on the team to look at things in new and productive ways. There are dozens of books and consultants that explain how to throw off mental shackles and solve problems in new and effective ways. Explore some of them.

1–11

The Problem

A new female team member files a sexual harassment charge against several team members

The Scene

When Cindy joined the team a month ago everything appeared to go smoothly. There were already several women on the team, but Cindy was slightly younger and more attractive than any of the others. The team welcomed her and made a point to include her in everything; it looked as if things were going well. Then you got the call five minutes ago telling you that she had filed a sexual harassment charge against several members of the team.

Wow—what a way to start Monday!

Possible Causes

She may have been sexually harassed.

The team members may have made inappropriate jokes, unwelcome suggestions, or another out-of-line comment or action, the point of which was all too clear.

She may have misunderstood the team's attempts to be friendly.

The team may be very casual. Their overtures, which felt like harassment to her, were just the team's way of trying to help her relax and feel a part of the team.

She may have personal standards that make some of the team's social practices unacceptable.

In today's environment, this happens more and more. Many organizations, teams, and individuals tend to withdraw into a formal, safe shell. This diminishes camaraderie, especially if it goes so far as to rule out hugs, pats on the back, and other everyday expressions of closeness. When this happens, the team and its members cannot help but suffer.

Cures

If she was sexually harassed:

This is the first alternative that you must investigate, and investigate quickly. Get the facts about her complaint: who was involved and what they did. Talk with the individuals. You probably won't find gross harassment, such as "copping a feel" or an outright proposition, though that does happen even today.

If this did happen, take action immediately. The best way to proceed, if it's possible, is to bring the matter up to the team. Let Cindy tell her story, then let the team hear from those she has accused. Let the team as a whole judge the situation. If it's mature and has its act together, it will give Cindy the necessary support and the offenders the necessary correction. If Cindy feels heard, and decides that her harassers really have "seen the light," she may drop her charge. But don't ever ask her to do this; avoid putting even the slightest pressure on her.

If the team isn't quite so mature, you'll have to start resolving the situation yourself. Make sure that the individuals whom Cindy has accused are aware of the seriousness of the situation. Don't expect them to agree with you right away. Give them time to think over their behavior; if necessary, talk with them several times. If you do get through to them, arrange a meeting between them and Cindy, to let them apologize and demonstrate that they realize they were out of line.

In this last situation, do you then bring the matter up with the team so that they know what happened? If possible. That will help clear the air completely. You have to make the judgment whether to do it or not, and you should never do it without Cindy's agreement up front.

If she misunderstood the team's attempts to be friendly:

This assumes that you or the team as a whole has looked at the situation as objectively as possible and concluded that nothing truly out of line happened. The next step, if Cindy will agree to it, is to air the matter in a team meeting. Cindy should have all the time she needs to explain what happened as she sees it. The team should take what she says seriously; perhaps things might have been done differently even though no harrassment was intended. If all of the discussion is open and frank, perhaps the matter can be laid completely to rest.

Again, don't make Cindy's withdrawing her complaint a condition of anything that you do or the team does. You're not trying to resolve a formal complaint; you're trying to restore trust and confidence within the team.

If Cindy isn't willing to let the team discuss the matter, let your organization's harassment procedures take their course, all the while trying to include Cindy fully in the team. The danger here is that the men will feel as if they're walking on eggshells. To a certain extent, that's normal. The goal of all this, however, is to gradually create a situation where Cindy and the rest of the team can communicate honestly with one another about the situation. No matter how the complaint comes out, if this communication doesn't happen both Cindy and the team have failed.

If she has personal standards that make some of the team's social practices unacceptable:

I cannot tell you what your firm's policy is or ought to be. I can tell you that I do believe that the standards of a new member ought not to be a mandate for the team (assuming, of course, that not even the semblance of generally recognized harassment is occurring). It may take some time, but if Cindy believes the team should change some of its practices she should bring it to the team as a whole and participate in honest discussion. Then the team as a whole can make the decision, taking full account of Cindy's feelings.

Team Strengthener

Every new member is edgy when he or she joins a team, and the team may be a little edgy as well. The presence of the new member will change the team, but it needs to happen by a natural process, not through formal proceedings outside the team. The new person may not have worked on a team before and may not understand how close the relationships within a team can become. Perhaps the team members should change some of their behaviors, but the matter can't really be raised until the new member is fully integrated into the team. The team might even formally voice this when the individual joins, asking all the members to put off making up their minds about anything until the individual is truly part of the team. If this is coupled with assurances to the new member that he or she is wanted and will become a full part of the team, it may give everyone the necessary breathing space. (However, there's no excuse for even the mildest forms of sexual harassment. Every team member should know that and the issue should never even come up.)

1-12

The Problem

Several members of your team tell you that they believe another member has AIDS and they won't work with him

The Scene

Tom, Al, and Carol catch up with you in the lunch room and corner you.

"We're concerned about Carl," begins Al. "Have you seen how thin and haggard he looks? He's out so much of the time—and he can't seem to concentrate even when he's here."

"Frankly," interjects Carol, "we think he has AIDS, and it's not fair to the rest of us on the team to have to work closely with him. You know that project the four of us volunteered for? Well, three of us just dropped out."

Possible Causes

Team members are concerned about the health risks to them.

With all of the publicity that AIDS has received, many people dread even the slightest contact with it. Your team apparently has several members who share this dread.

Team members are making a moral statement.

AIDS is most often associated with two groups in society: homosexuals and users of illegal drugs. Team members may be afraid that, by working with a person with AIDS, they're showing approval of a lifestyle they consider immoral. No matter what they think of Carl as a person, this prevents them from working with him any longer.

Team members feel betrayed.

Even if one or both of the causes above are part of the problem, this will almost certainly be part of it—at least for some team members. If the team is closely knit and sees itself as a true team, some members will feel that Carl has let them down by not telling them. They may feel strongly this way even if they don't fear AIDS or don't begrudge Carl his lifestyle.

Hints:

Regardless of the cause of the team's concern, AIDS is a delicate and emotion-laden subject. Above all, you and each team member must act with tact and sensitivity for everyone's feelings.

Remember, too, that because of the widespread concern about AIDS your organization probably has policies concerning it. And your city or state may have specific laws governing treatment of people with AIDS. The following sections concentrate on the immediate, human response to Carl's situation. But make sure you find out quickly what the policy and the legal requirements are, probably from your organization's Employee Assistance Office, and then follow them.

Cures

No matter what the cause is:

Because AIDS is such a terrible condition, fear of it is widespread. It's easy to understand how other team members may be concerned that they could get AIDS as a result of their contact with Carl or even that they could carry the disease home to their families or friends. But first find out what the facts are. Visit your Employee Assistance Office, Legal Office, or whatever office is responsible for knowing the laws and the organization's policies. Find out what limitations there are on the questions you can ask. (You may not be able to ask any.)

Then, if law and policy permit, try to find some answers. You tell Carl what the team's concern is. Then you ask him if he has AIDS.

If he doesn't and has a credible explanation for his physical condition, you and he need to take the situation to the team. Carl needs to be completely open with the team and the team with him. Then everyone needs to lay the matter to rest. This may require time and several sessions, because the situation may uncover strong feelings. In particular, the discussion may uncover some very hard and rejecting attitudes held by team members. Ensure that these are worked through. If necessary, get a skilled facilitator to help the team work through them.

Suppose, though, that Carl does have AIDS. If this doesn't violate any laws, you must convince him that he needs to level with the team. Since he hasn't told anyone, it may be hard for him to do so. No matter, he must be willing to open up to the team regardless of how much pain it causes him. Then you and the team can take whichever of the following steps are appropriate.

If team members are concerned about the health risks to them:

Locate someone with expert knowledge of AIDS to come talk with the team. (*Note:* you want the individual to *talk with* the team, not *lecture to* them.) With luck, your organization either has such a person or has a contract with one. No matter, get someone as quickly as possible.

When you've found a person to talk about AIDS, arrange for him or her to meet with the team. Call the team together about an hour before the individual arrives and let Carl present his situation. Anticipate an emotional backlash, particularly if team members have never dealt with a person with AIDS before. Your role is to be a calming influence and help everyone get over the initial shock. The person who will talk about AIDS shouldn't join the team until this part of the meeting is over. As soon as emotions calm down, however, he or she should meet with the team.

Don't let any individuals or the team as a whole make any hasty decisions, positive or negative. Help everyone talk with everyone else, but not with anyone off the team, because confidentiality is absolutely critical for everyone's sake. Over the next week or two, a consensus will probably form. You'll hope that the team will decide it can continue to work with Carl. Or, even though the team as a whole may decide it can't work with him, two or three members may be willing to do so. If not, you must honor the team's decision if possible and find individual work for Carl to do. As long as Carl is willing and able to work, do everything you can to find productive work for him to do.

The last paragraph mentioned the need for confidentiality. Everyone on the team must understand this and be willing to agree to it. This isn't just to protect Carl. The team will have endless explaining to do if confidentiality isn't maintained. At the same time, there may be legal requirements concerning who may or may not be informed of the situation. If there are, comply with them.

If team members are making a moral statement:

Carl must be honest with the team. If he contracted AIDS through a blood transfusion or a similar neutral source, that may solve the problem. But if he's gay or has abused drugs, he cannot avoid putting it on the table. Lying, no matter how strong the pressure to do so, has no place here.

If Carl is gay or bisexual, state laws and possibly organizational policy may protect him against job loss based on his lifestyle. But the team may be deeply offended and may need to find a way of dealing with the problem. Don't expect it to be easy. It may require a number of discussions by the whole team, and you may need to have even more one-on-one conversations. How long this will take and how hard it will be depends greatly on the culture of the area in which you work.

If Carl was a drug abuser but is now clean, the team should be able to "forgive and forget." If he's an active drug abuser, the team has a problem. While it may accept Carl and even the fact that he has AIDS, it cannot accept his continuing drug abuse. For his sake as well as the team's, the team must insist that he get treatment. If he gets it, fine. Support him. If he refuses, follow your organization's policy on the matter.

If team members feel betrayed:

Even if one or both of the previous causes are part of the problem, this will almost certainly be part of it, at least for some team members. If the team is closely knit and sees itself as a true team, some members will feel that Carl has let them down by not telling them. They may feel strongly this way even if they don't fear AIDS or don't begrudge Carl his lifestyle.

For everyone's sake, it's important that team members work through their feelings of betrayal. Unfortunately, the working through may begin with anger against Carl for hiding his condition from them. Support Carl and help him through the anger, but don't try to stop the anger. You'll almost certainly find that beneath the anger are deep feelings of concern for both Carl and the team.

As with every other aspect of this situation, it may take time to work through. Your role is to see that the team takes the time it needs and that it keeps dealing with the situation until it is resolved. If this happens the team will emerge much stronger and cohesive, no matter what happens with Carl.

Team Strengthener

We all enjoy sharing positive emotions—joy, happiness, enthusiasm, and so forth. We don't enjoy the negative ones—anger, fear, sorrow, and so forth. But both negative and positive emotions are important. Many cases in this book have stressed the need to confront these negative emotions. This case stresses it again. The stronger the team, the more capable it is in dealing with strong negative emotions. The reverse is also true: The more capable it becomes at dealing with strong negative emotions, the stronger it becomes. So when the emotional seas get choppy, help the team dive in, brave the surf, get to the issues, and resolve them.

CHAPTER 2

Interpersonal Problems That Affect Your Team as a Whole

Sometimes a team faces problems not with individual members but with relationships among the team as a whole. Traditional workgroups can often avoid or work around these problems. For instance, a traditional workgroup may be able to work effectively without ever having to solve serious disagreements among workers about how to get the workgroup's job done most effectively.

Not so with teams. They cannot work effectively when they're disrupted by underlying, unsolved interpersonal problems among team members. For instance, if team members keep fighting over trivial matters the team will never produce high-quality work. So a team must learn how to bring the uncomfortable relationships to the surface and work through them.

Many of the cases in this chapter deal with what's usually called "conflict management," a critical team skill. Effective conflict management requires the team to face its conflict and then work as a team to resolve it. This process can be painful, especially for new teams. You can use the cases to help your team; whether it's new or experienced, learn and practice effective conflict management.

The Problem

Team members compete with one another when they need to cooperate

The Scene

Your last team meeting ends with this dialogue:

Ramon: You know I can do better than anyone else on the team, so let me do it.

Cheryl: You and what three other people. Reports are my specialty, and I want to do it.

Bennie: I don't give a hoot who does the analysis for the report, but you all know I'm the best writer on the team. I want to do the report.

They keep wrangling until you call an end to the meeting to give everyone a chance to cool down and to give yourself some time to find a way to resolve the situation.

Possible Causes

The team is made up of highly motivated individuals.

Remember, they probably came from organizations where individual performance was valued and rewarded. They're just continuing to do what they've always done.

The team has never had training in team skills.

The organization may simply expect workers to perform effectively without training in teams.

Team members still get their rewards based on individual performance.

The organization's evaluation or merit pay plan concentrates on what the individual does, because that's how it's traditionally done it.

The team has too many big egos for one team to handle.

Again, traditional organizations usually valued and rewarded big egos.

Cures

If the team is made up of highly motivated individuals:

This is only a temporary problem. Their high level of motivation will strengthen the team tremendously.

How do you bring that about? Perhaps they need some team
training (see the next section). Perhaps all they need is the willingness and ability to negotiate with one another on how team
tasks should be passed out. Time, some gentle leadership from
you, and growing cohesion will accomplish this.

If the team has never had training in team skills:

Most teams will develop cohesion (the feeling of being a
team, not just a group of individuals) eventually. Without team
training, often called team-building, this may take a long and
painful time. Your task here is to speed the process.

If your organization presents or makes available team-building training, you and the team should arrange for it at your ear-
liest opportunity. If it doesn't, or if the training can't be scheduled soon, inquire whether there are experienced team facilitators available. If so, get the services of one for a few team sessions and explain to him or her—in front of the entire team—
what the team needs to accomplish. Then do it.

*If team members still get their rewards based on individual
performance:*

Suppose you can't change the reward system, at least not in
the short run. What do you do now? By far the best solution is
to get the team together and put the problem on the table: How
can we all be a team when each of us is getting our appraisal
and raise from our formal supervisor? If the team really wants
to be a team, it will deal with the problem. Perhaps members
will agree on the minimum they must do to get a good appraisal
and commit themselves to doing just this minimum, and
beyond that, to doing whatever is best for the team.

Suppose, for whatever reason, they refuse to do this? The team will have to do the best it can in the circumstances, but it will be handicapped until the reward system changes.

From reading this book, you will know that this problem shows up in a variety of situations. It's dealt with at length in the final chapter, so you'll want to look at the solutions suggested there.

If the team has too many big egos for one team to handle:

Toss this one directly to the team. Do they want to find ways to accommodate to one another, or do some of them prefer to transfer to another team? Try to get a good, honest (and probably heated) discussion. Many strong individuals prefer to deal with other strong individuals, so many or even all of them may prefer to remain on the same team. If one or more choose to transfer, though, the rest of the team should fully support the transfer and help find the best possible one.

For one reason or another, the team may not want to deal with the situation. You have no choice but to make some decisions as to who should stay and who should go. Then make the changes as quickly as possible. But use this alternative only as a last resort; it is by far the weakest solution.

No matter what the cause is:

Don't be scared, and don't let the team be scared by the presence of strong individuals. When the team becomes cohesive, they will add tremendous strength. However, while the team develops this cohesiveness, you may have to subdue these individuals, to ensure that the rest of the team gets a chance to develop.

Team Strengthener

When teams first form, one or more "strong" members usually assert themselves. The natural tendency of others is either to fight them or draw back and let them assume leadership roles. Neither response works very well. You may need to work with the assertive individuals and ask them to help you involve the other members of the team fully. Unless they are unexpectedly immature, most strong individuals will understand and help. Then, as all of the team members develop trust in one another, you can turn the problem over to the team as a whole. Most of the time the team will find ways to make each individual a full member with an important role to play.

2–2

The Problem
The team members don't appear to like each other

The Scene

You're walking through the team's break room, and this is what you hear:

Randy: I sure wish I know who made the selections for this team. Marie and Dave are unbearable. Who do they think they are, anyway?

Tina: And they're not the only ones. Sandy will hardly give me the time of day. And Lee just sits there without saying anything. I don't think either of the two of them like us.

Randy: Do you think we made somebody mad, and this is what they did to us?

You keep quiet, but wonder to yourself if they're ever going to like one another.

Possible Causes

The team is new and hasn't started to jell.

Several situations can cause this. The organization has simply mandated that people operate in teams, without proper orientation and training. Teams have been formed and told to operate effectively with no explanation of what it means to be on a team and how that's different from being an individual performer. There aren't enough facilitators, or they don't understand their roles. Whatever the cause, the team sees itself not as a team but as a number of individuals thrown together with nothing particular in common.

The team members were told they would be on the team, with no choice in the matter, and they resent it.

When organizations decree that everyone will be on a team, or even that lower organizations will form teams and start to operate that way, they make a basic mistake. Individual workers (and perhaps managers) end up on teams without a clear idea of what they ought to do and how to go about it. Some of them will make a valiant attempt to function, and if there are enough of them the team may succeed. Others may resent being forced into team membership and fight the situation from the beginning.

The team members are from different parts of the organization, and they don't understand one another.

Organizations often form teams made up of individuals with very different backgrounds. A manufacturing company, for instance, might form a team made up of a design engineer, a manufacturing engineer, someone from sales, someone from marketing, and someone from quality. These multifunctional teams can be very powerful, but they can also be very frustrating. Individuals in different functions look at work in very different ways, and without help they have tremendous difficulty communicating with one another.

Hint

When team members appear to dislike one another, it's normally a symptom of some deeper problem. It can happen that a team is made up of people who don't like one another, but this is relatively rare. Don't assume that you have a bunch of "personality conflicts." Look for the deeper causes.

Cures

If the team is new and hasn't started to jell:

Get training for yourself and the team. The best possible alternative is to find high quality training for the whole team and then get the services of a skilled facilitator until the team begins to feel and act as a team. Is the training not easily available? Raise hell until someone finds the training the team needs. (If you don't, the team will most likely disintegrate, with no hope of ever operating effectively.)

If the team members resent being on the team because they were told they would be on the team with no choice in the matter:

First, you and the team need to meet with higher management and work out the team's mission and charter so that everyone knows just what the team needs to accomplish. (Case 9–1 deals with this in depth.) Then you need to follow the team-building steps in the previous section; get effective training and a good facilitator.

One more point. Teams really do offer individuals the opportunity for more autonomy, and often the opportunity for more interesting and challenging jobs. In other words, for most workers teams are real progress. As the team's leader, you need to ensure that the team sees it that way and seizes the opportunity presented to it. Sure, it may be rocky and frustrating. Just remember that if the teams fail, the organization will go back to being as it was, and I doubt if you or the other team members want that.

If the team members are from different parts of the organization, and they don't understand one another:

This situation requires much harder work than the two above. It's not that you don't have to have a clear mission and effective team training; you must have both. But both together aren't enough. The individuals in different functions have to learn to value one another's functions and then work together in a way that makes their individual functions important but secondary.

Two points are critical here. First, the mission of the team has to be clear *and* it has to be important to everyone on the team. If this isn't the case, start there. (Look at the first four cases in

Chapter 9 for help.) You and the team work with higher management until you define a mission that meets these two criteria. Second, the members of the team must commit themselves both to the overall mission and to appreciating the perspective of other members. You may want to have several team meetings in which an individual explains his or her perspective, and each other member simply listens and asks clarifying questions. (A really good facilitator helps here, if one is available.) The team's key to success will be the ability of every member on it to understand and appreciate the perspective of each other member. When this happens, you won't believe how powerful the team will be.

Team Strengthener

Some individuals truly dislike other individuals. Most of the time, though, the reason is something other than their two personalities. I remember a friend telling me about two managers who couldn't get along, until they were given a task to do as part of a team that required them to work together. All of a sudden, they found that they could work effectively together. Did they like each other? I don't know, I don't care, and neither should you. When individuals need each other to accomplish a task, they don't really worry about whether they like one another. They simply do what the job requires.

2–3

The Problem
The team doesn't work together effectively

The Scene

Maxine, your manager, has called you into her office.

"I'm really concerned," she says, "because your team just doesn't seem to be working together very well. They're all very competent; I made sure of that when I made up the team. But I'm not seeing the synergy between them I expected. In fact, at

the moment, the team is producing less than most of them produced independently. If you can't do something about that, I'm
afraid we may have to disband your team."

You know the team has its faults, but think it's much too early
to decide to disband it. You wonder what you can do to
improve the current situation.

Possible Causes

As in the last case, the team hasn't jelled.

It hasn't had team-building training or proper facilitation.

The team has the wrong balance of skills.

Because teams are so popular, organizations may create a
team without looking closely enough to see that it has the right
balance of skills. Teams that lack skills in one or more critical
areas are seriously, perhaps fatally, handicapped. A team may
also have a different but related problem: It may have too many
individuals with the same skills. (For instance, an accounting
team responsible for serving a division may have several people
with accounts receivable skills, but no one who really understands cost accounting.) Since teams are normally under pressure to start showing results immediately, there's seldom time to
train individuals in the skills the team lacks.

The team's mission isn't clear, or no one cares about it.

The organization may not have thought through the mission
of the team in enough detail, or the team may not think that the
mission is a very important one.

*The team members are from different functions and don't
understand one another.*

Hint

Like the previous case, the inability of team members to
work together effectively is a symptom of something deeper.

Your job is to find and help the team overcome what's really troubling them.

Cures

If the team hasn't jelled:

All the comments in the previous case apply here. Turn back and review it for ideas on what to do.

If the team has the wrong balance of skills:

Make getting the skills balance changed your first priority. If you're lucky, there'll be at least one other team that has too many of the skills your team lacks. This is another case where you need to be as obnoxious as necessary to get the changes made.

And if management won't make the changes? First, make sure the team understands the problem. Then find someone to come in and train team members in the skills they lack. Try to find commercial courses that will develop the necessary skills. This won't make up for having properly trained individuals, but it may enable the team to get its mission done. It may also help the team members work more closely together, which will cure the initial problem.

What if you have too many individuals with the same skills? Try to find other teams that can use the individuals with surplus skills. If that doesn't solve the problem, find training for them in skills that the team does need. Never let there be individuals on a team who aren't really needed.

If the team's mission isn't clear, or no one cares about it:

You can hope that this happened because no one explained the team's mission properly. Have someone in higher management come in and clarify the mission. Have the manager explain why the mission is important. And assure the team that they'll be supported in what they do. If the mission really does matter, this last point is particularly important. Nothing kills a team's spirit more quickly than committing itself to a goal and then having higher management reject what it recommends.

And if higher management isn't willing (or perhaps even able) to clarify the mission and explain why it's important? Here's where your leadership becomes critical. You need to work with the team to redefine its mission so that it becomes both clear and worthwhile. In a few weeks or months, higher management may say, "Hey—this isn't what I intended you to do." That's OK, because when that happens you have an excellent opportunity to find out just what the team is supposed to do.

You will find more information on clarifying the team's mission in Chapter 9.

If the team members are from different functions and don't understand one another:

Multifunctional teams have become popular, but they also raise serious problems. Look back at the final case in the preceding chapter, which deals specifically with this problem, and at Case 11–10.

Team Strengthener

When a company seriously commits itself to teams, it creates the opportunity for much greater initiative than its workers have experienced before. No matter how clear or fuzzy the assigned mission is, a team always has the opportunity to redefine it and make it its own. This happens when—and only when—the team takes the responsibility for both its mission and its accomplishments. You'll hope it will do this with the full support of management. If necessary, though, it needs to just do it, using its best judgment. Remember, it's a great deal easier to ask for forgiveness than for permission.

The Problem
The team keeps fighting over trivial matters

The Scene

You sit there in disgust as Tommy, Edna, and Miguel fight heatedly over where to hold the Christmas party. Just when you think the battle is over, at least for now, Charles jumps in with a completely different idea. Four skilled team members, taking up their time and that of the rest of the team on a matter like this!

Possible Causes

This may be normal team behavior.

Does the team work together well on most projects? Or is it in the middle of an important, high-pressure project? If so, it may simply be "blowing off steam" from the strains of its more important work.

This is a symptom that the team hasn't become cohesive yet.

Once again, the problem may be occurring because the team sees itself as a group of individual workers, not a true team.

The team can't deal with its major issues, so it substitutes trivial issues.

There may be a major issue lurking in the background, such as team members getting to work on an exciting new project, or a team member who needs to be confronted by the rest of the team over her behavior. But the team is avoiding this issue and keeps itself focused on a minor issue.

There may be serious differences among team members about what to do for holidays.

In our increasingly diverse country, true differences can easily arise over a holiday as important as Christmas.

Hint

Spending time arguing over trivia may also be a sign that the team doesn't have enough to do (as in Case 5–1) or doesn't have a clear, doable mission (Cases 9–1, 9–3 and 9–4). If none of the causes discussed in this case seem right, read through those cases.

Cures

If this is normal team behavior:

If the team is simply blowing off steam, your main job is to ensure that it doesn't take up too much time. If the team isn't willing to put the matter to rest, suggest that two or three of the individuals most concerned meet as a subcommittee and try to come up with the main alternatives. At least this will keep any disagreement on target.

If the team insists on dealing with trivia at length, you need to help it face what's happening. It's a poor use of both the team's and the organization's time. The team should recognize this and be willing to limit its concern with trivial matters.

If this is a symptom that the team hasn't become cohesive yet:

Review the first three cases in this chapter, particularly the second case. They may provide you with workable suggestions.

You can take one very positive step to help a team develop cohesion, before or after it gets appropriate training. Identify the problems the team faces that it can most easily solve. When it's dealing with one of these problems, do whatever nudging and guiding you must to see that it finds and implements an effective solution. Then make sure the team understands and celebrates its success.

If the team can't deal with its major issues, and substitutes trivial issues:

This suggests that the team needs more experience functioning as an effective team. Once again, if a skilled facilitator is available have him or her work with the team.

The next three cases deal with this cause in depth; look at them for ideas.

If there are serious differences among team members about what to do for holidays:

It's easy to assume that when individuals argue over how to organize a party (or how to divide parking spaces, or what time to take lunch, and so forth) they are arguing over trivial matters. They may not be. One or more members of the team may not be Christians and may much prefer a New Year's party. Others may want to combine Christmas with Hanukkah, or may need to have the party at a particular time because of commitments to family members. None of these are really trivial reasons.

If the issues aren't trivial, the team needs to learn how to resolve them. In this case, you need to provide gentle guidance, but you also need to give them the time they need to get all their issues on the table. Dealing with intensely personal issues such as these is not only a test of the team's maturity but a means for the team to continue maturing.

Team Strengthener

As in all the cases, it's critically important to listen carefully and get all the facts before concluding what the real cause is. If you treat the situation as trivial when in fact it does impact the personal lives of several team members, you prevent team growth and hamper its ability to show concern for its members. Yes, things can get messy, and you can think they're terribly childish and trivial. That's a matter for the team as a whole to decide. Your job is to guide their decision-making process so that it produces an effective decision, one that takes into account the concerns of every member of the team. Easy? No. Necessary? Absolutely!

The Problem
The team can't handle serious disagreement

The Scene

Ethel: Well, I think it's a great idea.

Walt: Ethel, why do you keep on bringing that up? Don't we have enough to worry about?

Denise: I think Ethel's right—and I don't think so much of your idea, Walt!

Paulo: Can't I get anyone to listen to what I think we ought to do?!

And that's how it goes, until you end the meeting twenty minutes later, with everybody mad and nothing decided.

Possible Causes

The team hasn't functioned as a team long enough.

Everyone wants a new team to function effectively, and often the team feels tremendous pressure to do just this. But some things take time, and developing a competent, cohesive team is one of those things.

The team hasn't received effective team training.

This causes many problems, because the individuals on the team may want to act like a team, but may not understand how to do it. The organization just assumed they will learn how—and they may, but it will take a very long time.

The team has problems with mission, incentives, or other structural matters.

Is the team not clear about its mission, or is the mission too broad to tackle effectively? Are team members rewarded exclusively by functional supervisors? Are there any other structural problems that are frustrating the team?

There are deeper interpersonal issues that aren't surfacing.

If you've worked for a long time in traditional organizations, you know that many of them have a strong undercurrent of negativity running through them. It never really shows up for what it is, but it definitely shows up, as long-lasting resentments, personal feuds, the inability of two departments to get along. Often, there's no way to deal with the real issues, so these just continue to pollute the organizational environment. Teams offer the opportunity for their members to deal with these issues, but only if the team and the individuals on it are mature enough to face them honestly. If these underlying issues are interfering with the team's ability to be effective, they need to be dealt with.

Hint

This is actually more of a warning. When a team has serious problems functioning, particularly when they can't seem to agree or to find the right direction, it may try to find a "strong leader" who will tell it what to do. This is one of the most harmful things that can happen; it defeats the whole purpose of a team. Your role here is to refuse to be that kind of strong leader and to gently lead the whole team into accepting responsibility for its goals and actions.

Cures

If the team hasn't functioned as a team long enough:

If the team is relatively new, don't add to the pressure. Make sure that the team is getting the proper training and that it uses an experienced facilitator. In particular, watch for frustration and help the team deal with it. With patience, the team will succeed, and your job here is to keep the team believing in this until it happens.

Now if the arguing and disagreeing continue to drag on without improving, you need to take another look. There's probably more involved than just being a new team.

If the team hasn't received effective team training:

As you can see, this issue comes up again and again. But you may need to evaluate what "effective training" means in this context. Part of good training is training in how to handle conflict. Perhaps the training your organization offers doesn't include this, and/or the organization's facilitators have difficulty with conflict. If so, start looking for training and facilitators to help the team surface and resolve conflict.

If the team has problems with mission, incentives, or other structural matters:

It takes a certain amount of skill to look past the surface problem to these deeper issues, but you can learn the skill. So can the team. If you suspect that one of these issues is driving some of the disagreement, bring it up to the team. Work through it together. If the team finds the right issue, it will probably also reach a consensus on what to do about it.

If there are deeper interpersonal issues that aren't surfacing:

This isn't usually something that you can just "toss on the table" for the team to deal with. Watch your timing; a point may come in the discussion where you or someone else on the team can bring up what you believe is the underlying issue. If this happens, don't be judgmental or even consider accusing someone of something. Bring it up as an issue that concerns you because it matters to the team.

If it seems too touchy for the entire team to handle initially, you may be able to talk with the key individuals and persuade them to own the problem. Then they may be able to deal with it one-on-one with your help. If so, so much the better, with one caution. When they get it dealt with, they then need to "report back" to the whole team what has happened and give the team the chance to discuss it with them. Why is this so important? Two reasons. First, this is an important event for the team as a whole, so everyone needs to know about it. Second, the resolution of their issue may lead other members of the team with similar issues to open up to them. Just one or two people may start an avalanche that doesn't bury but uncovers a cache of hidden problems.

Team Strengthener

In many ways, the hardest problems for teams to solve are underlying ones that never quite surface as what they really are. Both deeper interpersonal issues and structural issues can be this kind of underlying problem. How do you tell when this is the case? When the team finds itself tracking over the same old ground, quarreling over the same old issues, going around in circles that never seem to end anywhere. This kind of stressful but boring repetition and sameness is an almost certain indication that the real problem is still hidden somewhere. When this happens, the time has come for the team to look beneath the surface and ask what's really going on. It may well be painful to do this, but the team will remain stuck until it's done successfully.

2–6

The Problem
Team members won't bring up their differences

The Scene

You run into Ahn in the snack bar. After a few casual remarks, you ask: "Don't you still think we should recommend that change in the report format?"

"Oh, yes. I think it would be much better."

"But you didn't bring it up in the meeting this morning."

"There just wasn't time. Besides, we were busy with other things...."

After the two of you finish talking, you sadly watch Ahn walk away. This is the third member of the team that had something to bring up in the morning's meeting, but didn't. What's going on?

Possible Causes

Team members are still reacting as they did when they were in a traditional workgroup.

We have all learned not to bring up painful issues, particularly those that might cause friction in the workgroup or cast doubt on the organization's current course of action. People don't change suddenly just because they're put on a team. They expect the same environment they've always known. Even when an instructor, facilitator or team leader tells them that it's all right to disagree, they take it with a grain of salt. It's not that they won't change; they'll just try out the water carefully and change if and when they believe it's safe to do so. (And, boy, can they change! But that's a different matter.)

This is the way the team is dealing with its inability to agree on solutions.

Look back at Case 2–5, where team members are constantly arguing with one another. If you've ever experienced this, even for a relatively short period of time, you know how painful it can be. The team may simply have given up, believing it will never be able to resolve serious problems. So, members tip-toe around painful issues and stay away from any area or solution that might be disturbing.

Cures

If team members are still reacting as they did when they were in a traditional workgroup:

If the team is relatively new, gently guide it toward greater openness, then demonstrate that disagreement is okay. Don't be confrontational, though. If Ann wasn't willing to disagree, don't make an issue of it. Keep presenting opportunities for honest disagreement, be open to it when it occurs, help the team be open to it, and then help the team find ways to resolve the disagreement.

This is another point at which to make haste slowly. Don't expect the team to suddenly engage in wild disagreement or suddenly develop the ability to resolve the disagreement. It takes time to break old habits. Whenever the team faces disagreement without trying to avoid it, note the fact. Then, when the team resolves the disagreement, note that too. Start with small steps; you'll find that they become giant strides if you and the team keep after it.

If this is the way the team is dealing with its inability to agree on solutions:

This situation is more serious than the one immediately above, because the team has already experienced conflict and has "learned" from it that conflict is too painful. In other words, the team has to unlearn before it can start growing.

What can you do in this circumstance? First, don't attempt to force the issue. That may push the team to hide any disagreements even further. As long as you can be even-handed about it and not appear to be short-circuiting the team as a whole, you might work with individual members to help them bring up issues. Do you know of another team that handles conflict openly and effectively? You might bring in someone from that team and have the person encourage your team. And, of course, a good facilitator can help.

Here, again, don't get impatient. Team members are afraid of what will happen if they start to disagree, and your fundamental task is to help them learn that they don't need to be afraid, that they can develop the skill to deal with conflict. Then, as some team members learn this, they can lend support for the rest of the team. It will work; it just takes time.

No matter what the cause is:

Remember that once people have learned one way to handle (or avoid) problems they change only when they see that the new way may be more effective and that they don't need to be afraid of trying it. How do they begin to see that the new way is effective? Partly because someone they trust emphasizes it or someone on a successful team says they can do it. But mostly they learn because their first, tentative steps at trying the new way are successful.

Team Strengthener

Effective team members have to unlearn a tremendous amount. We've all been taught not to make waves, to wait for a leader to tell us what to do and then do it with a smile—in short, not to cause problems by voicing our own opinions or disagreeing with others. New teams must spend significant amounts of time in the unlearning process before they can fully learn what it means to be a team. You, and probably most other team members, will get frustrated and want to hurry the process. Don't! Keep a clear picture of where you believe the team should go, share the picture with the team whenever it's appropriate, point out every step in the right direction, and keep going.

2–7

The Problem

The team compromises instead of working problems through

The Scene

Regina: Charlie, are you willing to leave the part about flimsy locks out of the report if I go ahead and put in a section on the poor training program?

Charlie: That's a bum trade; you know that both of them are important.

Regina: Maybe, but we need to quit arguing over this and get the report done.

Marsha: Regina's right, Charlie. I agreed to go ahead and put in the paragraph on the open desk drawer. I think it's silly, but we need to finish this thing.

Charlie: Well, okay. If we can't agree I guess I may as well give in so we can get on to something else.

You leave the meeting shaking your head. For the third time this week, the team has reached a poor conclusion because instead of really solving their problems the members compromised and came up with a lowest-common-denominator solution.

Possible Causes

The team hasn't learned how to deal with conflict.

The team has concluded that it must either fight, avoid difficult problems, or compromise as a way of avoiding this conflict. It has chosen the last alternative, perhaps because of attitudes the members brought with them from more traditional organizations. Since these organizations often couldn't deal with conflict, individuals and groups were encouraged to find quick compromises to "keep things from getting out of hand."

The team doesn't appear to care about some of its projects.

The team may have an informal standard for the projects it thinks are "important" and may simply try to get its other projects out of the way to get to these important ones. It may decide that some organizations are more important than others or that no one really cares about certain kinds of projects that they do. Or they may use another standard that produces the same result.

The team spends time only on projects that really interest it.

This is one of the worst work habits an individual or team can develop. If the team gets a reputation for doing good work only when something interests it, the organization will rapidly lose confidence in it (and, if you're the permanent leader, in you).

Cures

If the team hasn't learned how to deal with conflict:

Look at the suggested cures in Cases 2–5 and 2–6 for suggestions on how to improve the team's ability to handle conflict.

If the team doesn't appear to care about some of its projects:

Don't automatically assume that the team is goofing off or shirking its responsibility. It may feel, for instance, that it does-n't have time to do a good job on every project so it has to con-centrate on the ones that really count. You need to bring the matter up with the team and get their concerns on the table before you reach any conclusions about what's happening.

If the team is shorting some projects because it doesn't have enough time to do a good job on all of them, there may be a quick and relatively effective solution. Can some of the easier or less important projects be assigned to a two- or three-mem-ber subteam? Unless these subteams encounter problems that require help from the whole team, they simply complete the project for the team. With several subteams working projects at once, the team could do good work on each of them and still have time left to give larger or more important projects the attention they need.

Does the team believe that no one cares about some of the projects assigned to it or some of the products it produces? This problem needs to be resolved or it will begin to hurt morale (if it hasn't already). Discuss the problem in a meeting and help the team be as specific as possible about it. Are some projects or their products simply important to no one? Are others impor-tant but don't require your team's level of skills? Once you have the specifics, present them to your next-level manager and ask for his or her help in resolving the situation.

You might also want to look at the suggestions in Cases 9–2 and 9–6, which deal with this problem in depth.

If the team spends time only on projects that really interest it:

Bring the matter up with the team. This isn't the time to be subtle or indirect; the team needs to confront this one head-on. It may not even realize what it's doing; in that case, bringing the problem to their attention may be enough to get it solved.

It may also be that the team knows exactly what it's doing and has chosen to do it this way. Your best strategy is to point out to the team, calmly but clearly, what the consequences of its decision might be. It could even result in the team being disbanded. You'll hope that your reasoning will start to persuade some team members and that then more and more will fall in line. If this doesn't happen, and nothing changes, you will have to decide whether you want to remain with this team or not.

Team Strengthener

Often a team's preference for compromise is a symptom of its inability to deal effectively with conflict. The first step, of course, is for it to overcome this inability. Once it has learned not only to tolerate but sometimes to invite disagreement, it's time for it to take a further step. Situations often arise where everyone but one person agrees on a course of action. Even if the majority doesn't pressure that person, the temptation is strong for him or her to give in and go along with the majority. This is *not* a good practice for a mature team. Very often, the individual has spotted something the rest of the team missed. The team should insist that the individual stick with his or her point until the individual is confident that everyone on the team has heard it. At that point, the individual and the team may decide to go with the majority decision, but the decision should never be made before that point.

2–8

The Problem

The team makes decisions that members then won't support

The Scene

Mark: Teresa, you know we all agreed to change the way we go about mocking up the displays.

Teresa: I don't know what you're talking about. I'm doing what we agreed to.

> *Mark:* I don't know how you can say that. I think you're
> just trying to avoid doing it.
>
> *Teresa:* I thought it was a lousy idea, and I still think it is.
> But I'm still doing what we decided to do.

This has been happening all too much lately, you muse to your-self as you walk away. We've got to find a way to stop it.

Possible Causes

Once again, the team can't handle conflict effectively.

This is another symptom, like endless arguing, superficial compromises, and the rest, that the team hasn't learned to resolve effectively.

Some team members don't abide by team decisions because they don't understand them.

Several situations can bring this about. If the team has different functions on it (for example, manufacturing, sales, and marketing), some of the members may not really understand what they've agreed to. Or several members of the team may think very rapidly and leave others behind when they propose decisions. Or some members may just lack the background to really understand the problem.

The team appeared to agree, but each member interpreted the decision differently.

This can happen, of course, because some team members don't understand others. It can also happen because the team doesn't allocate enough time to decision making, so that the agreement reached is sketchy, superficial, and easily interpreted in different ways. Teams don't have a monopoly on this, by the way. It's all too common in traditional organizations. The basic difference is that it's easier to solve the problem when it happens on a team.

The team may also disagree on what to do because it didn't spend enough time making the decision. Even this, though, may be a symptom of a deeper cause. Perhaps the team doesn't have enough time to spend on its decisions. Perhaps it doesn't care about some of the decisions or doesn't believe that anyone else cares about them. Part of data gathering is to look beyond the obvious to see if a deeper cause is present.

Cures

If the team can't handle conflict effectively:

Look back at the previous cases in this chapter (especially 2–5, 2–6, 2–7) for suggestions. They all deal with handling conflict at length.

If some team members don't abide by team decisions because they don't understand them:

Quite possibly one or more team members don't want to expose their lack of understanding for fear the rest of the team will think they're dumb. If so, talk to one or more of the quicker and more outspoken members of the team individually and solicit their help. If they take the time to check for understanding—and to do it in a nonjudgmental way—they'll create an opening for the ones who don't understand to ask questions.

The problem won't be completely solved, though, until the team regularly checks with members to ensure that everyone understands the issue. This should become routine; when it does, the team may start to wonder why it ever had the problem.

If the team appeared to agree, but each member interpreted the decision differently:

As always, do the data gathering you need to make sure that this is the situation. Then bring it up before the team. Do it nonjudgmentally; it's just your observation on what's happening. The team should recognize the problem quickly. Then it can develop a plan for ensuring that its discussions are more complete. It may also want to rephrase the decision in two or three different ways to check that everyone understands it.

Team Strengthener

Toyota Motors contributed a very valuable tool to the Total Quality movement: "The five whys." When you look at a problem, you ask why it's occurring. When you find the cause, you ask why that's happening. And so on through five levels if necessary, of asking why. Let's take this case as an example:

Problem: Some team members don't carry out team decisions.

Why? Because the team doesn't spend enough time exploring the problem and formulating the solution.

Why? Because it doesn't think the problem is that important.

Why? Because it doesn't think anyone else believes the problem is important.

Why? Because no one thought the mission of the team through clearly when it was formed.

And so forth. It works.

2–9

The Problem
Team members keep blaming one another for mistakes

The Scene

"Don't gripe at me!" Marie says, not even looking up from her work. "I not only had the information to you on time, I had it to you a day early."

"Yeah, sure," Pat fumes, "and it took me two days to get it organized to the point where I could use it."

"Well, if you'd have clued me in on what you wanted . . ." Marie starts to respond.

Charlotte breaks in: "You guys argue some other time! Right now, you need to get the summaries to me—and quick. If it weren't for you, I'd have finished my project two days ago and . . ."

And so it goes, time after time. It seems that one of the most highly developed skills that each team member has is the ability to blame other members for every problem. If something isn't done, and done quickly, the team is simply going to fall apart.

Possible Causes

The team is new, and members are carrying over old behavior patterns.

What kind of environment did team members come from? What probably counted in their previous jobs was getting work done without getting into trouble, without "making waves." In that environment, it's important not to make mistakes that someone can blame you for.

Individuals expect to be rated on the basis of individual performance, not team results.

Almost all organizations have rating and merit pay plans based on individual performance. Many times, when they institute teams they leave the old performance plan in place. Even when they want to change, they often find it very difficult to do so. This catches everyone in a bind; a team succeeds only when it acts as a team, but individuals need to make themselves look good at the expense of the team.

The team is under pressure not to make mistakes.

Organizations that want teams to succeed have to give them latitude to experiment and make occasional mistakes. Particularly when a team is new, it has to try new ways; this lets it learn quickly and effectively. Unfortunately, not all organizations understand this. They may establish teams but then expect the teams to live by the traditional commandment: Do your job, keep out of trouble, and don't make waves. That doesn't work. In fact, it may result in teams that are less productive than the traditional workgroups they replaced.

Cures

If the team is new, and members are carrying over old behavior patterns.

Teams can't operate effectively when members are in a blaming mode—period. Your team needs to find a way out of this self-defeating behavior pattern as quickly as possible. Did the members of the team all participate in "team-building" exercises or training? If not, can you arrange for it now? Has the team ever had an experienced facilitator work with it, to help it understand what's happening? If not, can you arrange for a facilitator to sit in for several sessions and help the team understand what's happening and how to correct it?

Whether you can get help from training or from a facilitator, you need to take prompt action to help the team deal with the problem. Here is a three-step action plan you can use:

1. Meet with the team and encourage members to talk about the situation. Be prepared for strong feelings, because they'll come out. Individuals may feel anxious because they have to depend on others. They may want to loosen up but not really know how. Whatever the members' feelings, let them express them. Don't try to control them, with one exception: Blaming others is strictly out of bounds. (It's the basic problem, so it has no place in the attempt to find a solution.)

2. When the feelings are all "out on the table," help the team move to discussing solutions. Don't look for global solutions like "from now on, none of us will blame anyone else again ever." Start with simple steps, like "We will work with each other up front to be clear about what we expect." It doesn't really matter just what the beginning steps are, as long as they're clear and practical and everyone can agree on them.

3. Arrange specific times to follow up to see how the steps are working. If something isn't working, examine why and then either change or discard it. Where the team is having success, build on the success with more ambitious steps (such as, "I will never complain about what you do to anyone else until you and I have talked it over and tried to resolve it").

Keep up the momentum. If the team never takes anything but small steps, but takes these small steps consistently and builds on them, it will resolve the problem quickly and reliably.

If individuals expect to be rated on the basis of individual performance, not team results:

How does the team handle this? While it probably can't accomplish anything right away, it should make sure that higher management knows how individual ratings are affecting the team's performance. Make a presentation to management if possible. Don't get caught up in a lot of theory; give personal examples of how the individual rating process interferes with team performance. And if team members are being rated by managers back in their functional areas, be sure to point out how this affects the team.

In the meantime, what can the team do? Perhaps you can get authority for the team as a whole to suggest ratings for each individual member. This may cause some problems, but it will let the team as a whole have a voice. (One way of doing it is to let each member prepare a rating of himself or herself and then discuss it with the team as a whole.) Whatever else, get the team members together and help them discuss the problem that individual ratings cause. Get their suggestions on how to handle the situation. If you can, come up with specific steps, agree on them, and then review them regularly to see that they're working.

If the team is under pressure not to make mistakes:

If this is the situation, discuss it with your next-level manager. Make sure this person understands the impact that this environment has on the team. Enlist the manager's aid in giving the team more freedom. If need be, negotiate with him or her the kind of flexibility he or she will accept. (Is the manager willing to let the team occasionally miss a deadline by a day or so if the reason was the team's attempt to produce a more useful product?) Perhaps the manager is willing to meet with the team a time or two to discuss the situation and let the team as a whole try to work out a solution.

The team also needs to tackle the situation head on. You can use the three-step process in the first section. Let everyone discuss the situation and get his or her feelings out. Then start looking for solutions, and in this case a basic part of the solution is finding how the team can start acting as a team and present a united front when problems come up. (For instance, the team might agree that no member will blame another member to anyone outside the team.) Remember, take small, practical steps. Don't try to solve the problem overnight. Then follow up regularly, to modify or drop what isn't working and build on what is working.

Team Strengthener

An effective team maintains a delicate balance. On the one hand, it values each member's contribution and expects him or her to contribute fully as an individual. On the other hand, it thinks of itself as a team, not just a collection of individuals. In team meetings, members may be very critical of one another when they believe that they're letting each other down. But to the outside world, the team is a team. Did something go wrong? The team did it. Does someone want to know just who on the team made the mistake? That's not their business. Whoever did what, it was really the team that did it. Keep these boundaries clear. Within the team, members are honest in confronting other members and dealing with problems among them. To the outside world, though, the team as a whole takes responsibility for whatever it does. Insist on both.

2–10

The Problem
The team is very discouraged

The Scene

You walk away from the team meeting wondering what in the world you can do. Everyone—even José, whose enthusiasm has carried the team through tough times before—is discouraged. Several times, team members even said, "What's the use?" The team started off with enthusiasm and real commitment, but if something doesn't happen quickly it's going to fall completely apart. What can you do to prevent this?

Possible Causes

The team mission is unclear, not worthwhile, or uninteresting.

For whatever reason, the organization has created a poor match between the team and its mission.

The team's customers are never satisfied with its work.

Perhaps customers want changes the team is unwilling or unable to make. Perhaps the team isn't staffed to provide the service customers want.

The team is tackling an extremely difficult problem.

This happens. The team develops real competence at dealing with a certain range or level of problems. But then it confronts one it's never really faced before—a demanding customer, a job requiring skills the team doesn't have, a project that forces it to deal with a hostile organization. When this happens, and none of the team's customary methods work, it can get discouraged in a hurry.

Hint

Note that the three causes for this problem are very different. Once again, you need to do careful fact finding to ensure that you and the team solve the right problem.

Cures

If the team's mission is unclear, not worthwhile, or uninteresting:

Get the team together and identify exactly what the problem is, in as much detail as possible. You want to make the mismatch between the team's skills and interests and the mission as clear as possible. Then present your conclusions to your boss and ask her help to change the situation.

Suppose she's unwilling to help? Perhaps the team might be able to get a more fitting mission by swapping some duties with another team. Or there may be other solutions. Cases 9–1, 9–2, and 9–6 deal with situations where the mission isn't clear, worthwhile, or interesting. Look at them for suggestions on how to handle your situation.

If the team's customers are never satisfied with its work:

First, you need to ensure that this really is true. The team may be discouraged because of an offhand comment a customer made that it's taking too seriously. You and/or other members of the team should talk with your customers in depth. You may have to spend some time at this and ask some penetrating questions. Customers don't always level with you, so it's your responsibility to find out how they really feel.

Are customers really dissatisfied? Obviously the next task is to find out why. Perhaps your team doesn't understand their requirements (you're giving them apples when what they really want is pineapples). Or your team's work is sloppy, inconsistent, or undependable. You and the team need to get the most specific information you can. (People are seldom dissatisfied in general; instead, they get generally dissatisfied because of their dissatisfaction with specific products or actions.)

Your team should be committed to providing your customers with exactly what they want. Once the team finds out what the customer really wants, it should be a simple matter to get it working on the steps needed to provide exactly that.

What if your team doesn't care about what customers say they want? Then it has a serious problem, even more serious than its customers' dissatisfaction. You need to spend time finding out just why this is so. (Does the team believe it knows better than the customer what the customer needs? This happens all too often.) Then you and the team need to spend time discussing exactly what the team's mission really is. If necessary, the whole team should visit its customer(s) and hold a frank discussion on the matter. And you can help the team understand that any organization or team that isn't committed to its customers' satisfaction has a shaky future.

If the team is tackling an extremely difficult problem:

You and the team need to begin with an in-depth discussion of the situation. Why is it so difficult? What's not working? What's different about this project? Instead of beating itself on the head because it can't solve the problem, the team needs to understand exactly what's happening and why their usual approaches aren't working.

Once the team knows what's causing the problem, it can start taking the steps necessary to solve it. Are customers very demanding? The team needs to meet with these customers to understand what it needs to provide. And it should work on developing a trusting relationship with customers, one in which customers understand that the team is genuinely trying to meet their needs. Does the team lack some of the skills needed to solve the problem? Find an organization that has these skills and arrange to borrow the people you need. Once it identifies the problem, the team will almost certainly be capable of finding the right solution.

Team Strengthener

Discouragement, loss of self-confidence, the feeling that it doesn't really matter—any negative emotion such as these can begin to sap a team's vitality. Not that there shouldn't be any negativity; every one of us feels negative emotions at some time. But on an effective team, they need to be short-lived, passing episodes. This means that the team may need to develop specific ways of dealing with negativity. For instance, it may allocate fifteen minutes for unrestrained feeling sorry for itself, then turn around and get back to work. Or it may have a brief competition to see who can be the most negative—until the whole episode dissolves in laughter at its ridiculousness. Just be sure that you and the team stay aware of the dangers of negativity and are ready to deal with it whenever it shows up.

The Problem
The team spends too much time socializing

The Scene

As you walk through the team's work area, you see Angel, Sam, and Trisha talking around Angel's desk, Tonja talking with Ethel, and Bob and Kim relaxed in Kim's cubicle. They might all be talking about work, but if they are running true to form they're discussing, respectively, last night's TV movie, kids, and the local baseball team. Your team training never taught you what to do when the team becomes a personal discussion group.

Possible Causes

There are problems with the team's mission.

Perhaps the team's mission isn't clear, or team members don't believe the mission is worthwhile. Or perhaps they aren't committed to the mission.

The team hasn't enough to do.

In its own way, this is a mission problem, too; the mission isn't a full-time one. Or perhaps the team's workload comes in peaks and valleys, and the team is in a valley now.

The team is recovering from a particularly stressful project.

This is the natural letdown after several days or weeks of high stress. Team members are trying to "blow off" the stress.

The team is made up of very social individuals who need to keep themselves more focused.

Many kinds of work attract individuals who enjoy dealing with others, and working in a team can increase this motivation. But it needs to be directed primarily toward getting the team's work done, not just toward enjoying one another's company.

Hint

This chapter is about team interpersonal problems, but look how often one of the causes may be problems with the team's mission. No team functions well for long if it lacks a clear, worthwhile mission that team members are committed to.

Cures

If there are problems with the team's mission:

This creates a serious situation. Look back at Case 2–10; it has some specific suggestions on how to deal with the problem.

If the team hasn't enough to do:

Is the team has just finished the hard work of a peak period, they deserve some slack in the valleys. Give them some time to relax. If the relaxation continues to drag on, though, you may need to intervene. Look at the second paragraph in the next section.

But what if the team lacks enough work day in and day out? That's a real mission problem, because the team lacks a mission that fully occupies its time. Your best strategy is to bring the problem up with the team and ask for its suggestions on what else it might do. After all, it's going to look good to higher management if the team volunteers to pick up additional duties. And while all of us want occasional time to rest, most of us also want to be busy with challenging, worthwhile work most of the time.

If the team is recovering from a particularly stressful project:

Has the team just completed a project that challenged it and required everyone to work long, stressful hours? If no other project is pressing right now, it's all right for the team to take some recovery time. And you should relax yourself—after all, you probably need recovery time, too.

Of course, there's a limit to how much time you and the team reasonably need to recover. The team will probably know when it needs to get back to work seriously but clearly. Don't intervene unless you begin to feel that things are dragging on, then bring the matter up gently. One of your basic jobs is to support the team as it develops the ability to make good decisions on its own in areas such as this one.

If the team is made up of social individuals who need to keep themselves more focused:

The team must solve this one for itself. You can bring it up, but it's not your role to be the judgmental mother or father. Even a relatively immature team knows that it's there to get work done. Help the team focus on the problem; once focused, it will almost certainly develop its own rules or guidelines.

Before you conclude that lack of team discipline is the only problem, be sure you've looked at each of the other causes. Workers (and managers) in traditional organizations develop skills at looking busy even when there's no work that can be done. Don't let the team fall back into this, or into making up "busy work." Ensure that they have a full-time mission to perform, then deal with their socialness.

Team Strengthener

In the long run—and probably in the short run, too—teams perform effectively because they commit themselves to work that is challenging and worthwhile. If they don't have enough work and this causes them to invent work or simply to pretend to be busy, morale begins to suffer. After all, how satisfied can anyone feel going home at the end of the day having spent eight hours doing work that they know doesn't need to be done? You need to lead the team in ensuring that it has a real job to do. Anything else is fair to no one, neither the team nor the organization.

The Problem

Sometimes the team acts just plain silly and you don't know how to handle it

The Scene

Josie is walking across the room, nervously balancing a glass of water on her forehead, while Roberto walks behind her telling her she's going to lose it. Marshall is throwing spitballs at Roberto, telling him to stop. Reggie has just finished an off-color joke; Fred is laughing uproariously at it, while Paula in mock anger is banging him on the head with a paper. What in heavens' name has happened to this normally productive and sane team? And what in the world can you do about it?

Possible Causes

Maybe the team doesn't have a viable mission.

Because the mission isn't a full-time one, team members have too much time to cut up with one another.

You're part of a creative, productive team that's blowing off steam.

The team may have just finished a demanding project (see the case before this one). Or it may be in the middle of a demanding project and trying to relieve stress. Or, believe it or not, it may be actually working out a problem.

Hint

The more creative and hard working a team is, the more it will need to blow off steam. Socializing, as in the case just before this one, may not be enough. Besides, real creativity requires individuals and teams to get outside their everyday, serious behavior every so often.

Cures

If the team doesn't have a viable mission:

We're back to the same issue we've confronted in the last few cases. In this case, though, the situation may be more serious. If the team acts this silly, it's probably covering a strong need to do something useful. It's a direct, visible sign of wasted talent and motivation. Read the suggestions for the first cause in Case 2–10 and use them.

If you're part of a creative, productive team that's blowing off steam:

Teams that really produce, particularly if they have to do extensive and creative problem solving, need to relieve their tensions in a big way. The same may happen if the team is facing a major project that it knows will demand the best it can deliver; acting silly is its way of letting go so it can commit itself to the task ahead.

Are you accomplishing anything by not being in there with them? Don't forget, you may need to clear your mind and get your creative juices flowing again.

Team Strengthener

The people who developed traditional organizational theory seem to have been a rather uptight bunch. They believed deeply that work was never fun—in fact, if someone was having fun at work something was seriously wrong. Only in the last two decades have we begun to discover that having fun at work isn't blasphemous. Most of the time, it helps. Nowhere is this more true than on a team. Working hard and solving problems together always creates strains. Having fun, being silly, is an effective way to leave the strains behind for a few minutes and come together as a team. For heaven's sake, don't get uptight and try to break it up. You're the leader. You should be cheerleading the fun.

CHAPTER 3

Problems With the Behavior of an Individual Team Member

Workgroups often have problems with the behavior of individual workers, and these problems may handicap the workgroup. For instance, an individual who tries to hog the credit for what the workgroup does will present a problem for any workgroup.

Because team members must work closely together, though, the behavior of each individual team member becomes much more important. A team member who rejects everyone else's ideas or won't do what the team decides handicaps the team as a whole.

The cases in this chapter will help you and the team deal effectively with this kind of problem. Keep in mind that the way to resolve the problem isn't to force the individual to change but to find the underlying reasons for the problem and face them as a team. Every time the team works out a solution together, it strengthens itself and makes it easier for every member to be fully productive.

The Problem
A team member tries to hog the credit

The Scene

You walk up to Elaine and Roger just in time to hear Elaine exclaim, "We've got to do something about Gordon!"

"What's up?" you ask.

"He's done it again—he's taking credit for something we did as a team. Tomas heard him telling Miriam that he was the one who came up with the idea for the check-off form. I know he's good, and I really do like him, but if he keeps this up nobody's going to want him on the team!"

"Amen!" Roger exclaims. "He's just about used up all his credit with me, too."

Possible Causes

Gordon may not understand what's expected of him as a team member.

Gordon may be relatively new to teams or to this team. If no one has made it clear to him how he's expected to act as a team member, and how this is different from how he acted as an independent worker—well, he'll just keep on acting as he did when he worked independently.

He may not be comfortable working on a team.

While today's work requires more and more cooperation to be done successfully, there are still individuals who aren't comfortable in close working relationships. This doesn't make them poor workers, just poor team members.

Gordon's chances for advancement may depend more on the impression he makes with his formal supervisor than on his contributions to the team.

One of the most basic mistakes an organization can make is to put individuals on permanent or project teams but continue to make their salaries and chances for advancement dependent solely on supervisors outside the team. This happens a lot, for instance, with multi-functional teams where each member of the team still reports to a manager back in his or her functional area. No matter how much an individual may want to be loyal to the team, the situation may make it difficult if not impossible.

Hint

It's a real change for many individuals to switch from being individual workers to members of close-knit teams (perhaps even you are one of them). And it takes time to make the adjustment, even for many people that will become highly effective team members.

Cures

If Gordon doesn't understand what's expected of him as a team member:

The best way to handle this is aboveboard and openly in a full team meeting. Let Elaine or Roger bring up what they heard and saw and explain their disappointment with Gordon's behavior. It's important that the team be mature enough to do this without criticizing Gordon or blaming him for what he did. Instead, the other team member should explain what they expect and need from him, and why his behavior is interfering with this.

Things may get a little touchy, and the situation may not get resolved then and there. The team needs to be patient, to accept that Gordon may be upset and even defensive. But if the team is patient and continues to make it clear what it needs from Gordon, he will probably come around. (If he doesn't, look at the next two cases.)

What if the team isn't mature enough to hold the discussion with Gordon? In that case, someone on the team—either you or someone who's a good friend—needs to have the same discussion. That may be enough, or it may serve as an opening to bring the matter to the entire team.

If Gordon isn't comfortable working on a team:

The team ought not assume that Gordon doesn't want to be on a team until it's tried the alternative above. If Gordon truly isn't a team player, though, there's no payoff from irritating both him and the team by trying to make him one. If your organization has implemented teams thoughtfully, there are meaningful jobs around that individuals can do. (For instance, your team and several others may need someone to handle administrative matters, manage supplies, or do independent research.) The sooner the team can help Gordon find one of these jobs, the happier everyone is going to be.

If Gordon's chances for advancement depend more on the impression he makes with his formal supervisor than on his contributions to the team:

If this is the case with Gordon, and if there's nothing you can do to change it, it presents a real challenge to everyone's maturity and trust in one another. Why? Because the situation has to be put on the table and discussed honestly and openly if the team is ever to get beyond it. The team has to understand the pressures that Gordon—and quite possibly other members of the team—are under. And Gordon and anyone else in his situation has to understand the need for loyalty to the team. With a little luck, everyone can negotiate reasonable expectations for each other, and the team can reach a higher level of effectiveness.

If the team isn't mature enough to deal with the issue openly, it will continue to poison the interactions on the team. What do you do then? A poor second choice is for you or someone else he trusts to talk with Gordon and try to persuade him to loosen his ties back to his department as much as he can. Don't expect much from this, though. At best, you'll probably get some sort of uneasy truce.

There's one more possibility. Gordon may be perfectly happy giving his primary loyalty to his functional manager. In that case, the only satisfactory solution is to move him back to his department and find a replacement for him who can give more loyalty to the team.

Team Strengthener

Mature teams function in many ways as a single entity, with everyone committed to the goals of the team as a whole. But mature teams also accept the need of each member to be an individual. Individuals like Gordon may never function effectively as a team member, or they may be extremely effective if the team respects their individuality and uses their talents wisely. The relationship between the needs of team loyalty and the needs of the individual is a constantly changing one. Every team needs to remain sensitive to it and do a periodic check to ensure that members aren't feeling crowded by the team.

3–2

The Problem

A team member is extremely dogmatic and won't compromise

The Scene

"Aw, c'mon, Louise, give it up. Why can't you just fall in with the rest of us so we can get on with things?"

"I told you, I just don't think we should do that."

"And we just don't think your arguments are that good. Besides, you know the rest of us agree."

"Yeah—do you think we're all dumb?!"

"Dumb, no. Wrong, yes. I just don't want to do that!"

And that's where the meeting ends, with everyone—including Louise and you—walking off in disgust.

Possible Causes

Louise doesn't think that the team has really listened to her ideas.

Very often, particularly when teams are just getting started, individuals' ideas get overlooked, particularly if there is a strong agreement around other ideas. Teams can easily feel that if just one or two members disagree with the rest of the team, they should give in and go along with the others.

Louise doesn't feel that she's fully a part of the team.

Her refusal to agree may be her way of expressing the feeling that the rest of the team doesn't value her and her ideas. "If they're not really going to let me be one of them," she may think to herself, "I'll see that I get my points made this way."

Louise believes that an important principle is involved.

Most of us share the same general moral principles, and most of the decisions a team makes don't involve specifically moral situations. But, there are exceptions. What if Louise is a conservative Christian and the rest of the team wants to hold a dance? What if she genuinely believes that a decision is against the best interests of the firm? Or is unintentionally discriminatory against some ethnic group? These are all matters of conscience and must be dealt with as such.

Cures

If Louise doesn't think that the team has really listened her ideas:

Unless the issue is extremely time-critical, trying to overrule a team member doesn't work very well. Over time, it creates teams where members are less willing to voice their own ideas, particularly if someone else has just voiced a different idea. It also tends to create teams where one or two or three individuals dominate both the discussion and the agreements.

The solution is relatively simple, though not necessarily easy. The team must commit itself to hearing everyone out, even when the individual is a minority of one. Most of the time, there will be one of two results. The individual, realizing that he or she has truly been heard, will agree with the overall consensus. Or the group will realize that the individual has been saying something it needed to hear and change its decision. The practice may be time consuming at first, but in the long run it will produce a more flexible team that generates better decisions.

If Louise doesn't feel that she's fully a part of the team:

The whole team needs to take up this matter, preferably with Louise there. (You may have to prime the situation by talking with Louise and with a few other members of the team.) The team can explain how they see Louise's actions, then give her all the time she wants—and this is very important—to tell them how she sees the situation. If she and the team begin to level with one another, they can get beneath her immediate behavior to the real issues.

This may not be a one-time affair. The first time it comes up, either she or the team may be unwilling to put it fully on the table. Let it be, then help the team bring it up the next time it occurs. As long as it's not done judgmentally and confrontationally, the team and Louise will eventually deal with it. (If the situation is really sticky, this is another good place for an effective facilitator.)

If Louise believes that an important principle is involved:

What if Louise believes a clear moral principle is involved, and the rest of the team disagrees with her? What would be the best outcomes?

- Out of deference to Louise, the team might change its decision, to incorporate, or at least not violate, her principles. If so, this should be done openly and cleanly, with everyone reconciled to the decision. (By the way, this is not normally a good situation for the team to tell Louise she "owes them one." The matter is a little too serious for that.)

- The team might ask Louise to suggest alternatives that would not violate her principles but that would achieve the goals of the team. This enables her to maintain her principles, but puts a reasonable burden on her to be responsible to the team and its needs.

- If others on the team feel that their principles are equally involved, the team might decide to respect Louise's problem but go ahead with its decision. This requires great maturity both on the part of the team and on Louise's part; otherwise, she'll feel that they're ignoring her situation. And certainly this situation ought not arise often. (If it does, Louise and the other team members need to have some serious discussions about their differences and whether they should help her join another team.)

Team Strengthener

Teams generally function most effectively when their decisions are based on consensus, but only if a variety of ideas are brought into the discussion and considered. We often think of democracy in terms of voting and compromise. Formal democratic politics require these. But the root meaning of democracy is that each individual gets a full and fair chance to influence the decisions that affect him or her. On a team, this means that everyone's ideas get heard and genuinely considered. This is seldom easy at first and may sometimes get messy. But it is the heart of high-level team performance.

3–3

The Problem
A team member quickly backs off from her ideas if anyone disagrees

The Scene

Rachel: Say, what do you think would happen if we started fifteen minutes earlier in the morning?

Ron: Get up fifteen minutes earlier? You've got to be kidding!

Roger: Nah. There's got to be some other way to solve the problem.

Rachel: I'm sure you're right. What do you think we ought to do?

"She's done it again," you think to yourself as the discussion goes on. That's the second time in this meeting that Rachel has come up with an idea, then let it drop when someone disagreed. What can you and the team do to get her to stand up more strongly for her ideas?

Possible Causes

Rachel has been taught not to argue.

Many children, and particularly girls, are brought up in conservative homes and taught never to argue with their parents or fight with their siblings or other children. And rigid organizations can strengthen their programming not to argue. Rachel may believe that it's wrong to argue, no matter what the consequences may be.

She doesn't like conflict.

This situation resembles the one above, but there's a major difference. If this is the case, Rachel's aversion to arguing is much more emotional. Perhaps her home environment was filled with unresolved conflict; if so, she may find almost all conflict painful. And if she has worked in organizations that can't resolve conflict, that may have convinced her even more to avoid it.

She's unsure of herself.

Rachel may be willing to face some conflict, but she may not be sure that her ideas are any good. She may be depending on others on the team to support them as a way of proving to herself that the ideas are worthwhile.

Hint

In almost all cultures, including ours until recently, most women have been taught to be agreeable and modest. So this problem is more apt to occur with women. But men can fear argument, avoid conflict, or be unsure of themselves as well. In other words, don't think of this as just a gender issue. Depending on background, anyone on a team could have these characteristics.

Cures

If Rachel has been taught not to argue:

This is one of the few places where a little plotting behind the scene may be justified. Meet informally with two or three of the more assertive members of the team and solicit their support. There are several courses they might take to help Rachel and the team. For instance, whenever Rachel makes a suggestion, instead of stating their own opinion they could ask her to expand on her ideas and help her draw them out. Or after she's stated her ideas someone has disagreed, and the discussion has moved away from her, they could go back to her suggestion and ask her to elaborate on it. In other words, they can gently and supportively prevent her from disowning her ideas too quickly.

With luck, this will help her become more assertive. When she does, the team should notice it and respond positively to it. And if someone disagrees and she lets the idea drop, another team member can gently call her on it and ask if she really believes the idea should be dropped. With a consistent, positive approach you'll enable her to participate fully in the give and take of the team.

If Rachel doesn't like conflict:

Rachel doesn't need to be analyzed; no one needs to ask probing questions about her life history or otherwise get involved in pseudo-psychology. That's almost always a dead end trail, and almost none of us have any of the skills we need to help in this way. Instead, she needs to learn that when conflict is honestly confronted it can be resolved. She will learn this not by being told so but by seeing it actually happen on the team.

You can hope that the team develops conflict resolution skills quickly and that the early conflicts aren't too dramatic. (A facilitator helps greatly with this.) With luck, Rachel will carefully, hesitantly begin to support her ideas even when they conflict with those of others on the team. Once she gets over her early reluctance, you and the team can use some of the tactics described in the section above.

Remember, if Rachel has a strong dislike of conflict you and the team must be careful not to push her into conflict before she begins to learn that it can be resolved. If the team pushes too hard too soon it may make her even more fearful of conflict, and that may push her to leave the team.

If Rachel is unsure of herself:

You and the team want to draw Rachel out. When she puts forth an idea, ask her to elaborate on it instead of rejecting it or presenting another idea. Ask her to return to an idea after the discussion has moved away from it. Agree with her basic ideas, even if they may need significant change to be workable.

Your primary purpose is to demonstrate to Rachel that she has worthwhile ideas that others can agree with. But that's not the final purpose. The ultimate goal is to demonstrate that, like the others on the team, her ideas are worthwhile but may not be the ones accepted, and that this is all right. She needs to develop both the confidence to express her ideas and the realism to know that some of them won't be used.

Team Strengthener

Teams need to learn that individuals are different and that all of them can make significant contributions to the team. The fact that individuals are shy or boisterous, forceful or reserved, doesn't have much to do with the quality of their ideas. Their manner may sometimes get in the way, as Rachel's unwillingness to support her ideas does. The team's job is neither to reject nor try to change people. It is to respond to them, find their strengths, and let them contribute fully. As the team grows more mature, members can begin to provide feedback to one another on habits and mannerisms that may interfere with open communication. This gives individuals the opportunity to change, not because they are forced to, but because it will make them more effective members of the team.

3–4

The Problem
A team member rejects everyone else's ideas

The Scene

"Nah, I just don't think that will work," Randy says.

"Why not?" Edith responds.

"It just doesn't sound right. I like my idea of delaying the whole thing better."

Edith is beginning to sound exasperated. "I know you like your idea, but I wish you'd listen to what Nina and I are trying to say."

"It's happened again!" you think to yourself. "Once Randy expresses an opinion, it's almost impossible to get him to change it, or even to listen to anyone else." And you wonder what you can do to change the situation.

Possible Causes

Randy is new to the team and trying to establish his place in it.

When individuals join teams, they often act in ways that aren't necessarily characteristic of them. This is their way of reacting to a new and strange situation. Randy may be trying to "muscle his way in," by showing how effective he is.

He is accustomed to working on his own.

Most individuals who come to teams when the organization first begins to use them are in this situation. All of their experience to that point has been as an individual worker. That's what they know how to do. And since they used their ideas as individual workers, they expect the team to use them.

He came from a position where his boss relied heavily on him.

This is similar to the section just above, but with a major difference. In that case, Randy used his own ideas. In this case, he not only used them but his boss used them, and his boss clearly depended on him to have them. That was a powerful role, one most of us would be happy to fill.

Cures

If Randy is new to the team and trying to establish his place in it:

The team should not only accept his ideas but invite them. Team members should agree with them when that's appropriate. If the ideas aren't adequate, but have the beginnings of something usable, the others should attempt to build on them, making clear that they recognize his initial contribution.

If the team maintains this positive approach, neither caving in to nor rejecting Randy's ideas, he will probably change his behavior quickly. He will see the advantages of give and take and will see that even when his ideas aren't workable in their initial form they can still form the basis of something workable. And he will probably start to build on the ideas of others.

If Randy is accustomed to working on his own:

The approach in the section above will work here too. Here, too, he needs to learn that his ideas are good and valuable, and that the ideas of others are also good and valuable. If he persists in defending his ideas too far, the team can raise the issue with him and even suggest that it may be a carryover from his previous job. As always, though, it needs to avoid sounding judgmental.

If Randy came from a position where his boss relied heavily on him:

When he finds himself having to compete with others on the team, Randy may feel devalued. He will certainly feel his loss of power. To help him change, the team needs to demonstrate that being a member of an effective team is also a powerful position—that he can now influence the entire team. With this, of course, he needs to learn to listen to the other team members. He will learn if they are competent and work together well.

The team may want to raise the issue with him directly, especially if he is clearly refusing to consider other ideas. And it may have to do this more than once. (But remember that pushing him to change his ideas just because he disagrees with others is a poor strategy.)

Team Strengthener

Strong individual workers may feel disempowered when they become a member of a team. The scope of their authority seems to diminish sharply, and they suddenly have to compete with others to get their points across. The team helps individuals solve this problem by helping them see that membership in an effective team is also a very powerful position. The moral: The team never attempts to disempower a member, no matter how much of a problem his or her behavior may seem. Instead, it keeps working to include the individual, to demonstrate the value of membership on the team. It helps the person redirect his or her power to make an important individual contribution to the team.

3–5

The Problem
A team member won't bring his problems up openly

The Scene

You have waited all through the meeting for Kevin to bring up the problem that Steg was causing him. And he had two or three good opportunities. But he never said a word. You'd never know he had a problem if you hadn't heard him griping to Vi earlier in the day. What can you and the team do to get him to speak out on what's bothering him?

Possible Causes

Kevin is still caught in "if you can't say something nice, don't say anything."

In many homes, children are still brought up not to say negative things. They carry the idea with them to work, where they're often told to do their job and keep their mouth shut. They learn to keep their complaints to themselves, though they often voice them to people other than those the complaint is with.

The bosses he's worked for before haven't tolerated controversy.

Kevin may or may not have learned not to complain at home but he certainly learned that lesson at work. Some organizations don't like controversy; others go even further, expecting everyone to have a positive attitude all the time. All these train individuals to hide their complaints.

He believes whoever caused the problem should take the initiative, not him.

Kevin may not raise the problem because he's waiting for the individual who offended him to raise it and apologize to him. All too often, an individual believes he or she has been wronged and is due an explanation or apology, when the individual committing the "wrong" has no idea anything has happened.

Cures

If Kevin is still caught in "if you can't say something nice, don't say anything":

Kevin needs to learn not only that it's okay for him to raise issues with others but that issues get resolved when this happens. The most straightforward way is for someone who believes Kevin has a gripe against him or her to raise it with Kevin, probably one-on-one. If the individual raises the issue in a nonjudgmental, nonangry way, Kevin may begin to open up.

This might also happen in a team meeting, though it's somewhat chancier there. If the individual does get the problem with Kevin resolved one-on-one, though, one of them should bring the matter up with the whole team. The individual can explain what happened and how it was resolved, and the team can make it clear that the incident was important. It may take a while for the breakthrough to occur, but when it does Kevin will begin to change noticeably.

If the bosses he's worked for before haven't tolerated controversy:

The good news is that when "don't make waves" starts not at home but on the job, it's easier to change. Kevin may very much want to make his complaints known. Unlike the situation above, the best strategy is often to bring the matter up with the full team. Someone who believes Kevin is unhappy with him or her can simply describe the situation and then ask Kevin if that's correct. Kevin may be surprised, but he will probably respond honestly.

If Kevin believes whoever caused the problem should take the initiative, not he:

This situation involves a different factor from the two above: Kevin may be resentful because the other party hasn't understood what the problem was and apologized for it. So the team needs to deal not only with the problem but the resentment as well.

In this case, it's probably best for the individual who "wronged" Kevin to talk with him one-on-one. The person can bring the matter up and check to see if that is the situation. If it is, he or she and Kevin can deal openly with Kevin's expectation that the other should apologize. The other individual can try to help Kevin see that he or she didn't realize the situation, and how helpful it would have been if Kevin had said something immediately. If the conversation goes well, the matter can then be brought up with the team as a whole, which may want to make a ground rule or two about how individual complaints should be handled.

Team Strengthener

Just as it's difficult for many of us to disagree sharply with others' ideas, so it's hard to seem critical of them or complain about them face-to-face. One of the major hurdles a team must jump is the tendency for team members to be "nicey-nice" with one another and swallow potential controversy or complaints. Many a promising team gets stuck here, and the quality of their performance drops sharply. The first three chapters are full of tips on how to overcome the phoney niceness. Use them.

3–6

The Problem
A team member refuses to do what the team has decided

The Scene

"Roberto, we all decided to split the telephone calls up among us. Now, which organizations do you want?"

"I think it was a bad idea, and I don't intend to do it. The rest of you go ahead and do what you want, but count me out."

"Roberto, I don't understand how you can go against the team like this...."

You walk away, also wondering how Roberto could reject the team's decision this way and what you and the team can do about it.

Possible Causes

The team refused to listen to Roberto's ideas.

When a team won't listen carefully to all of its members, it runs the risk that it will alienate them. Roberto may feel alienated.

Roberto is angry with the team for another reason.

This situation is more difficult than the one above, because the real problem is hidden beneath the apparent one.

The team intentionally made a decision the others knew Roberto didn't like.

The team may be trying to teach Roberto a lesson for some reason, or to get him to change some behavior the rest of the team doesn't like. Whatever the reason, this kind of crooked dealing is extremely harmful to the team.

Cures

If the team refused to listen to Roberto's ideas:

This qualifies as a priority topic for the next team meeting. The great danger is that the team will attack Roberto, or at the least be very judgmental. This approach won't do anyone much good. Someone speaking for the team needs to bring the situation up, clearly but nonjudgmentally. If Roberto didn't feel heard, the team needs to deal with that problem head on, particularly since other members may feel the same way. Hurt feelings may get expressed; if they do, they need to be worked through.

The team may currently be so angry that the others want to punish Roberto. If this appears to be the case, you may want to delay the next meeting for a day or so to give everyone a chance to cool down. The situation is already a problem; it doesn't require an extra jolt of intense anger and resentment.

If Roberto is angry with the team for another reason:

You and the team need to deal with the surface problem in the way that the section above described. But you need to do it even more sensitively, because everyone needs to work through the surface problem to the real one. If nothing else seems to be accomplishing that, another team member may take his or her best guess and ask if such-and-such a behavior was what both-ered Roberto.

Whatever means it uses, the team needs to keep after the sit-uation until the real problem surfaces and is dealt with. When individuals on teams develop "hidden agendas" that aren't worked through and resolved, the team's effectiveness begins to drop sharply. In fact, such hidden agendas are cancerous when they appear in an otherwise healthy team.

If the team intentionally made a decision the others knew Roberto didn't like:

If you suspect that this is the case, you need to bring it up to the full team. The team may be honest and talk about what's going on; at least you can hope that will happen. On the other hand, the situation may be serious enough that no one wants to talk about it. Here, though, you really have no choice but to force the real issue out on the table. This is one of those situa-tions in which you're justified in using every bit of authority and persuasiveness you have as a leader.

If you have trouble getting the team to discuss the matter, you should seriously consider that the team is trying to force Roberto to leave. (Case 1-3 deals with this situation; you may want to look at it for help.)

Team Strengthener

Nothing is more destructive to a team than members with "hidden agendas." If you're not familiar with the term, a hid-den agenda is a goal that one or more members have that they're unwilling to talk about. If asked, individuals with hid-den agendas will deny them or disguise them. For instance, there's nothing wrong with an individual hoping team member-ship will get him or her a promotion, as long as the individual is open with the team about the goal. When the individual denies and attempts to hide this motivation, it becomes a hid-den agenda. One of the most important functions you can per-form as a team leader is to keep an eagle eye out for possible hidden agendas, and then see that they are dealt with and resolved.

The Problem

A team member criticizes fellow members to other teams

The Scene

Rene: Chandra, are you sure Talita was telling you the truth?

Chandra: I have no doubt at all. Talita and I are good friends, and she'd never lie to me about something like that.

Lorena: I thought Mona liked being on the team. Why in the world would she say that about us?

"Why, indeed?" you ask yourself. "And how do we stop it?"

Possible Causes

Mona resents something the team has done.

What happened? Perhaps they excluded her from a decision or from a party. They didn't like one of her pet ideas. Or any of dozens of other events. The precise cause isn't important here; the fact that she resents what other team members have done is.

This is how she's always been.

Some people grow up habitually "bad-mouthing" others behind their backs. In fact, all too many people grow up this way. (And almost all of us grow up at least partly this way.)

Mona is setting things up to leave the team.

She may be trying to get another team to want her, or may be building up a case in her own mind to support her decision to leave.

Cures

If Mona resents something the team has done:

Once again, we have a situation that's in danger of becoming a hidden agenda. This one is dangerous because it's going to be very difficult to confront Mona with her behavior without a great deal of anger.

But that's exactly what has to happen. The team must confront Mona with her behavior, as calmly as possible. She may try to deny it, but if the team is sure of the facts it needs to hold its ground and keep pushing. Be warned: The situation may get explosive. Maintaining openness and trust is so important, though, that it's worth using every reasonable means to get at the real problem.

If the team can get the real problem on the table, it must deal with it openly and honestly, no matter how upset individual team members may be. The ability to do this is a true test of the team's maturity.

If this is how Mona has always been:

Again, the team must confront Mona with her behavior. In this case, it's not looking for a problem but trying to make it clear that what she's done is completely out of bounds. The team needs to do this nonjudgmentally but firmly. In this situation it cannot take "no" for an answer from her. And you need to exercise leadership by ensuring that the matter is confronted as long and as painfully as necessary to get it resolved.

Prepare yourself and help the team prepare itself. This situation may take a long time to resolve. Mona may agree in the meeting, but then go back to her old, comfortable behaviors. Or she may genuinely try to change but slip every so often. The team needs to get a firm commitment from her, then do whatever it must to see that she keeps this commitment.

If Mona is setting things up to leave the team:

The team needs to get the issue on the table. If she truly wants to leave, there are other, less stressful ways to arrange it.

Or it may be that her wanting to leave has a hidden agenda and that getting it on the table enables the team to deal with it. She then may leave much happier, or may want to remain a member of the team.

The team needs to be as calm and objective as possible; you've heard that over and over. Here, it's particularly necessary because it wants to make Mona's leaving as painless as possible for everyone. And, of course, it doesn't want to close the door if she decides to stay. If she does decide that she wants to stay, the team needs a firm commitment that she will change her behavior—permanently.

Team Strengthener

Teams need to be understanding of their members and the problems they may have with the team. At the same time, teams need to be firm that they will not accept an individual expressing these problems in crooked, unacceptable behavior. (Bad-mouthing the team is crooked because it doesn't deal openly with the problem; it's obvious why it's unacceptable.) Combining genuine concern for the individual with insistence on straightforward behavior isn't easy. It is, however, a skill that every team must master and use.

3–8

The Problem
A member of the team has stolen several dollars from the team coffee fund

The Scene

As you're walking toward the break area, you notice Paul in there, acting somewhat suspiciously. You feel a little silly doing it, because Paul has been on the team for a long time, but you draw back behind a post and watch. Paul walks over to the coffee pot, looks quickly around, then reaches in and pulls out the bills in the change cup. He sticks them into his pocket, then walks quickly away.

Now you know what's been happening to the team's coffee fund. The question is what to do about it.

Possible Causes

Paul is a thief.

How do you tell? You don't have to; the fact that he took the money is proof that he's a thief. If there are extenuating circumstances, it's up to Paul to convince the team of them. He may be able to. Until he does, the fact is that he took money that didn't belong to him, and that makes him a thief.

Paul is temporarily short on money and is just "borrowing" the cash.

If this is Paul's excuse, you have a problem. How do you know that what he's saying is true? Has money been missing before? If so, someone—presumably he—has been taking it and not returning it. Does he claim this is the first time? How do you tell? Paul may be telling the truth, but he has raised a significant trust issue. If nothing else, why did he "borrow" the money from the coffee fund instead of another member of the team?

Paul has a real economic crisis.

Paul may be in such dire straits that a couple of dollars from the coffee fund might make a significant difference to him, perhaps the difference between eating today or not. But does this matter? Why keep stealing from the fund when someone would probably have been happy to lend or give him the money?

Cures

If Paul is a thief:

Confront Paul. In this case, it's better initially to do so alone rather than have it happen in a team meeting. Of course you listen to his reasons. If he has a reason that might make a difference (such as one of the two below), it's time for the two of you to take it to the full team. Paul should present it; if he's not willing to, he probably isn't worth keeping on the team. Then the team decides.

What if he doesn't have a mitigating reason for his behavior? Offer him the opportunity to resign quickly. Promise him nothing more than that the incident won't show on his formal personnel records. (He may want to bargain for more, but the difference between resigning and being fired for theft is quite enough of a benefit for him. So don't bargain. This is a "take it or leave it" situation.) If he opts to resign, give him the option of explaining what has happened to the team or of simply leaving. If he doesn't admit what he's done to the team, call a meeting and tell the rest of the team yourself.

He may not want to resign, but to take the matter up with the full team. Arrange for him to do so immediately, preferably within a few minutes or hours. Let him make whatever plea he wants. Then propose that the team see he is either fired immediately or the situation is reported to higher management with the request that he be taken off the team. Hold out for that solution, no matter what. Paul has broken his trust with the team. Because trust is so essential, there's no way back. He has to go.

If Paul is temporarily short on money and is just "borrowing" the cash:

The solution is probably the same as the one in the previous section: Paul has to leave. He will surely want to talk with the team, and he has every right to do so. But unless he comes up with a reason that clearly explains his action, you should propose that the team see that he's fired or removed.

Suppose most other team members don't want to be so harsh. What then? Paul might want to do something to demonstrate his desire to remain on the team. For instance, he might volunteer to keep the coffee area clean for a period of time (particularly if that's a chore others dislike) or to buy the coffee for a month. Be careful here, though. The team can offer Paul a chance to make up for what he's done, but it must completely avoid anything that looks like punishment. If the team is determined to punish him, and he's determined that he doesn't deserve it, it's better for everyone if he leaves.

If Paul has a real economic crisis:

If Paul offers this as a reason, the team has every right to ask for the details. Paul may not want to give them, but he's asking the team to forgive him for stealing from it. That entitles the team to know about his situation. If he's not willing to talk about, the team has no choice but to assume he's lying and proceed on that basis.

Suppose, though, that he has serious economic problems? He still has to answer some hard questions, like why he couldn't get a loan or why he didn't ask the team to help him. If his reasons ring true to most of the team, the team then needs to make a decision. It may seem unfairly harsh to recommend that he be fired or removed from the team, but as long as he remains in this serious financial condition he'll be suspected of every shortage that occurs.

The team might explore one other avenue. If Paul is a valuable team member, the team might agree to overlook the entire matter on the condition that he get continuing counseling and assistance until his finances are cleared up. And it's not at all out of bounds for the team to ask him to give it regular reports on how he's doing. (After all, if he does seriously look for and use assistance, he will want to tell the team how he's improving, which will give others a chance to recognize him for his accomplishment.) If the team takes this route, it needs to be clear to Paul that if anything resembling the incident happens again he's gone.

Team Strengthener

Several important characteristics divide teams from traditional workgroups, and trust is at the top of the list. Teams cannot be effectively self-managing unless members' trust in one another remains high. What happens when someone on the team violates this trust? The team is crippled, and no matter how the situation is handled it will take time for it to recover from being crippled. Offering someone who violates this trust the option of resigning or being fired seems harsh. In some rare circumstances, it may be. When something as clear as theft is involved, though, firing the team member, removing him from the team, or permitting him to resign is usually better for everyone. If the thief remains, he'll be suspected of any irregularity that occurs for months. And removing the person will help the team concentrate on its mission and may ultimately be kinder even to the individual. If the team resolves the situation in any way short of this, it needs to be sure that it has thought the situation through very carefully.

3–9

The Problem

The team suspects that one of its members has been going through others' desks and personal belongings

The Scene

"I hate to accuse anyone of anything," Fred says, "but Janine was bending over Elaine's desk when I walked in. I couldn't see what she was doing, but when she heard me she jumped and backed away from the desk as if she'd been shocked. When I asked her what she was doing, she said it was none of my business and walked out. Several of us think someone has been going through our stuff, and it looks as if we've found out who that someone is."

Is this good news or bad news? Several members of the team have suspected that someone has been going through their desks. They've even complained that someone has been taking their cigarettes and one said that his good fountain pen was missing. Now you have a "suspect," and you know Fred is going to tell everyone on the team before quitting time. What do you and the team do?

Possible Causes

Janine denies that she was looking through the desk.

Because Fred didn't actually see Janine do anything, no one really knows what happened. There's no formal action to be taken. But the team still has a painful situation on its hands.

Janine says someone took something from her and she was looking for it.

Now the situation is more serious, because other members of the team are involved. The team has the right to know what is missing and why Janine believes that Elaine may have it. Her answers may raise other questions, and there may be questions that Elaine needs to answer.

Janine claims that Fred made the whole thing up to embarrass her.

She claims not only that Fred didn't see her looking through the desk but that he made up the story to harm her.

Hint

Remember that you will never know what Janine was doing except as she tells you. The basic issues are her credibility, Tom's credibility, and the damage that the situation can cause to the team. And every explanation calls the credibility of at least one team member into question.

Cures

If Janine denies that she was looking through the desk:

Perhaps Janine has high credibility and can give a good reason for being at Elaine's desk. If she deals openly with the rest of the team, everyone may be able to lay the matter to rest.

But what if her credibility is doubtful and/or she can't provide a good reason for being there? She may not be formally guilty of anything, but the team needs to confront her with its anger and suspicions. She must understand the consequences of her actions, no matter how innocent she may think the actions to be. She has seriously disrupted the trust that the teams needs to have in her and that she needs to have in them. She has to understand the kind of suspicion she will be under for weeks or months and its consequences for both her and the team. She may understand this and respond to it, so that she and the team can begin to get past the incident. She may not, which will leave the situation too much on the team's mind for a long time.

If Janine says someone took something from her and she was looking for it:

For everyone's sake, the team needs to get every answer it can, and everyone needs to cooperate with giving and getting them.

Unless the situation gets resolved, it will remain like an open sore on the body of the team, especially if different members take sides with different people involved in the problem. You can plead for everyone to get everything out in the open. You can even, if it seems appropriate, talk with the individuals involved and see if they will talk with you. If they will, then you and they can decide what the next step should be.

If the team can't get everything on the table, it needs to brace itself for hard times. The distrust generated by the incident will poison relationships in the team for a significant period of time. What can you do to help? Perhaps the most useful task you can set yourself is to make sure that all team members continue to communicate with one another.

If Janine claims that Fred made the whole thing up to embarrass her:

This is the most serious explanation of all. It demands that the rest of the team distrust either Janine or Fred. It must be dealt with as rapidly and strongly as possible.

While you could talk with the two principals, the best solution will likely be to bring the matter up as soon as possible at a full team meeting. While all the members need to hold their emotions in check as much as possible, this is not a time for a quiet, refined discussion. These issues must be gotten onto the table and resolved. That may produce a stormy session, or several stormy sessions. No matter how mature the team is, you may want a competent facilitator to help the process.

As disruptive as it may be, the team needs to stick with this one until it gets resolved. The costs in emotion and in lost productivity if it continues to hang over the team are too high.

No matter what the explanation:

No matter what the explanation, this case and the one before it can create situations in which the team gets divided into two (or even more) cliques. In this case, some members may strongly back Janine, while another group backs Tom. Hidden feelings on race and/or sex may emerge as part of the division. That makes it doubly important to get the situation on the table and find a resolution for it.

Team Strengthener

As the Team Strengthener at the end of the last chapter pointed out, teams require a continuing high level of trust to operate effectively. Incidents such as the one with Janine disrupt this trust and tear the fabric of the team. Sometimes these incidents can be resolved, and sometimes they can't. One test of the strength and cohesion of a team is its ability to continue operating in the presence of these painful unresolved situations. This means not ostracizing an individual such as Janine who is suspected of wrong deeds of one kind or another. If the team continues to value all its members, without denying the underlying problem, it creates the possibility for a solution. The problem may go away. Or the individual involved may decide to level with the team. Whatever happens, the team needs to fight however it must to retain its inner cohesion.

3–10

The Problem

A team member has lied to another member about completing a task

The Scene

"Charlotte, you told me you'd done that. Dammit, I need it—and I need it now."

"I know I told you that, Lee, and I thought I'd have it done soon enough that I could give it to you. But something came up and . . ."

"Something came up, nothing! Charlotte, you lied to me! Now how am I going to believe you the next time you tell me you've done something?"

"It was just this once, Lee, I promise. It won't ever happen again."

You watch Lee walk away angrily as Charlotte stands there looking after him. They might think the incident was over, but you know that can't be the end of it. What Charlotte did could poison her relationship with Lee for a long time, and his resentment might well spread to other members of the team. You have to do something—but what?

Possible Causes

Charlotte is performing poorly.

The fact that a team member performs poorly doesn't justify her lying to another team member (or to anyone). But Charlotte may have felt that she needed to cover for her poor performance.

Charlotte felt pressured and tried to lie her way out of the situation.

Individuals tend to make promises they can't keep and even to lie about what they have done when they feel pressured to deliver something they don't believe they can deliver. Charlotte may have felt this way. Lee may have pressured her very hard to have what he needed. Finally, to get him off her back, she simply promised what she knew she couldn't deliver and then tried to lie her way out when she didn't deliver.

Charlotte doesn't understand what it means to be part of a team.

Once again we have a problem because a team member doesn't understand what it means to be part of a team. There may be two reasons for this. She may still be reacting as she did in the traditional organizations she worked in, particularly if those organizations handled truth carelessly. Or she may not feel part of this particular team, even though she wants to be.

Hints

The three causes don't exclude one another. In fact, all three could be true.

No matter which cause, or combination of causes applies, you have definite preferences for how the situation gets resolved. At the top of the list is for Charlotte to take the situation to the entire team, tell them what happened, apologize to Lee, and then resolve the problem with the team. She may refuse to do this, from embarrassment or from trying to hide the situation. That puts the ball in Lee's court. He needs to bring it to the team, not judgmentally but objectively, so that the team can deal with it. Your taking it to the team is a poor last choice, not to be used unless forced on you.

Cures

If Charlotte is performing poorly:

When the team considers her situation, it needs to deal first with the fact that she lied and resolve that. Poor performance is no reason for lying, and lying is her major offense. The team needs to take that up with her. It should give her every opportunity to state her side, and it should listen. But no resolution is acceptable except her commitment not ever to lie again.

Now that the lying is dealt with, it's time to take up her poor performance. It's a problem on its own, a problem that must also be dealt with. How does her performance fail to meet standards? Does she understand what's expected of her and where she falls short? The team needs to get the whole issue of her performance on the table and be as specific about it as possible. Then she and the rest of the team need to work out a plan for improvement. She commits herself to improve; the rest of the team commits to support her, but without taking responsibility themselves for the improvement. Chapter 4 contains several cases containing suggestions that will help here, as does Case 5–8.

If things have gone as they should, Charlotte has made a double commitment to the team: She will not lie again, and she will improve her performance. But what if they haven't gone as they should? What if Charlotte remains defensive and refuses to accept responsibility? The team shouldn't give up, but it should convey to Charlotte that she has seriously jeopardized her membership in the team.

Charlotte felt pressured and tried to lie her way out of the situation:

Of course, this doesn't justify the lying either, and the team needs to begin with that problem. (Use the suggestions from the section just before this one.)

When that's resolved, the team turns its attention to the problem between Charlotte and Lee and helps them work through it and resolve it. The team needs to deal with Charlotte's belief that Lee put too much pressure on her. Is Lee routinely too high pressure? Is the team routinely that way? Or does Charlotte not deal well with everyday amounts of pressure? Do team members not trust some or all other members to deliver unless they're pressured? These important questions require answers, for everyone's sake.

Once the team gets the answers it needs, it starts to work on the situation. If the problem belongs mainly to Charlotte, it helps her work out a program to handle pressure more effectively. She might want to go to some stress-management training or be mentored by someone on the team who's particularly good at handling stress (or both). If some or all of the team is too quick to pressure other team members, the team needs to find a fix for that. Team members have every right to expect high levels of performance from one another. If they don't get them, there's a problem, but not a problem that can be solved by pressuring one another to meet unrealistic deadlines.

If Charlotte doesn't understand what it means to be part of a team:

After the team discusses the problem with Charlotte's lying and lays it to rest, it needs to move to this problem. Does Charlotte act as she does because she doesn't understand how to be part of a team or because she doesn't feel part of this team? Or perhaps both? The team needs to spend whatever time it takes to understand where Charlotte is coming from and why.

Then the team works with Charlotte to resolve the problem. If the problem is understanding, some training and/or mentoring may solve it. If the team hasn't made her feel a part of it, she and the team need to talk about what must happen for this to change. Then she and the team need to make the change happen.

Team Strengthener

Nothing except the most extreme circumstances ever justifies one member of a team lying to another. And both the individual and the team need to deal with the lying, openly and cleanly. But that's almost never enough, as the sections in this case point out. Lying always has causes. Occasionally, an individual is a pathological liar. In that case there's seldom a way to resolve the situation except to get the person off the team. Most individuals who lie, though, do so because they're accustomed to lie in certain circumstances. The team needs to help the individual and itself determine these circumstances. The team may need to change so that the circumstances don't occur so frequently. And the individual needs to change so that lying never becomes a way of dealing with the ordinary problems of work. All this isn't easy, but it is crucially important.

CHAPTER 4

Problems With the Performance of an Individual Team Member

No team is ever made up of members who perform alike, or even at the same level. One individual may be relatively slow but good at details. Another may be creative but poor at following through. Effective teams find ways to balance the skills and interests of their members to emphasize their strengths and minimize their weaknesses.

At times, though, the performance of an individual is simply a problem for the team. A member may perform well individually but won't work with the rest of the team. Or may do well only on tasks that he or she enjoys. Whenever a problem such as these arises, it begins to limit the performance of the team as a whole.

Teams can easily fall into the trap of "working around" a problem performer. This approach causes problems of its own, and often these new problems are worse than the original one. The team should not only expect but insist that every member perform effectively.

This chapter presents eight cases illustrating individual performance problems. It explains how the team as a whole can work with its members to resolve these problems. And it provides specific ways that you can work with the team to accomplish this goal.

The Problem

A team member has an excellent attitude but doesn't produce much work

The Scene

"Edmond, just don't let yourself be discouraged."

"I know you're right, Marty, but we're getting so much flack these days."

"We are, but it'll come to an end. You know we're going to lick this."

"I suppose so, Marty. And whenever I forget I come talk with you and that makes it easier. Thanks."

You smile a wry smile to yourself. Marty is the true spark plug for the team, and everyone values him for it. The problem is that he's not a very productive worker.

Possible Causes

The team has forced Marty into a mold that ignores his real talents.

Sometimes our obvious talents get us into trouble. Marty may have been so obviously helpful to the team because of his positive outlook and willingness to support others that the team hasn't looked for his other talents. He may be aware of this but his positive approach to things may be preventing him from bringing it up.

Before he joined the team he was valued primarily for his positive outlook.

Because traditional organizations both value positive attitudes and lack methods of resolving conflict to generate these positive attitudes, they are prone to cynicism and negativism. If Marty was able to maintain his positive attitude in this environment, his managers may well have depended on him for it

and accepted his lower production in the process. So his experience on the team is nothing new.

*He leans on his positive outlook because he knows he's not a
good producer.*

Some individuals conclude early on that they don't have the
ability to compete with others. It's an easy jump from there to
developing an attribute like a positive attitude that others will
value. This can lead to a self-fulfilling prophecy: Because the
individual gets good at his or her "attitude," everyone expects
it, so that other skills aren't developed, so that the individual
has to identify even more with the attitude, and on and on.

Cures

*If the team has forced Marty into a mold that ignores his real
talents:*

You probably can't count on Marty to bring up the matter,
so you need to take the initiative. This is one of the cases where
talking with him or raising the matter in a team meeting could
both be first steps. The one you take depends on your sense of
Marty and of the team. Your goal is to have an open discussion
in the team, in which the team concludes that they want to offer
Marty the chance to use his other skills. This requires a commitment to actively do so.

Both you and the team need to be careful: Don't communicate this as a rejection of the real contribution his positive and
supportive outlook makes. You are offering him the opportunity to contribute more broadly, as well as asking him to do so.
Everyone can still value his attitude.

Something to watch: If Marty has other skills, and the team
begins to use them, do other members begin to display a more
positive attitude? In a group, an individual may be unconsciously assigned the responsibility for a group function, such
as keeping up morale. Once the group recognizes the individual's fuller contribution, others may begin to exercise part of the
initial function. Stay aware of this possibility. If it occurs, it's an
excellent sign.

If Marty was valued primarily for his positive outlook before he joined the team:

What do you do? Your course is similar to the one in the section above, but you might want to start by talking with Marty. You need to get an insight into his experience before he joined the team. Did his managers ask him to do difficult work? Did they ever test his abilities? Would he like to contribute more fully?

If the answer to the last question is "yes," it's time to bring up the matter before the whole team. You might pave the way, but Marty should speak for himself. He and the team need to explore other skills that he might contribute to the team. Then both he and the team need to make the appropriate commitments and follow them through.

Look at the last two paragraphs in the next section for guidance from here on.

If Marty leans on his positive outlook because he knows he's not a good producer:

Don't conclude this until you've carefully explored the two alternatives above. Even then, if it seems to be true, don't yet take it at face value.

Either you or the team can suggest to Marty that the team needs to make wider use of his skills. This requires sensitivity. If the team pushes Marty too hard, he may become so uncomfortable he leaves the team. But it does need to begin asking him to make a broader contribution and then seeing that he does so. Either Marty will begin to develop other skills or the situation will become more frustrating for him and the team. If the first, you're home free. But what if the second?

If the second, the team has a decision to make. Does it profit sufficiently from Marty's positive attitude, and whatever other skills he has, to make up for his poor productivity? If possible, this discussion should be held with Marty as part of it. If the team concludes that Marty cannot make a sufficient contribution, then as gently as possible it needs to find him another job.

Team Strengthener

Individuals with honest, deeply rooted positive attitudes are not a dime a dozen. When a team has such an individual for a member, it has a powerful resource. It can also hope that the positive attitude is catching, that the entire team can absorb it. (This is a great advantage of teams; they offer the best prospect that good characteristics will spread among the team.) The team should regularly communicate its appreciation for the attitude and make the individual's contribution to team success clear. In short, the team must ensure that the individual's positive attitude triumphs over any negativity that may be present in the team.

4–2

The Problem

A team member doesn't keep her commitments to the team

The Scene

"Dammit, Cheryl, you promised you'd have our recommendations coordinated with both other teams by this afternoon!"

"I know, Art, and I really tried to. But I kept having trouble getting hold of them. And you know the pressure we've been under because of the new inventory project."

"Yeah, all of us know about those. But right now we're working on this, and we need the coordination you don't have."

It happened once again: Cheryl didn't deliver what she promised. If this happens many more times, she's going to kill herself with the team.

Possible Causes

The team is sloppy about keeping its commitments.

Cheryl may have learned from the team's behavior that it's not important to keep commitments, regardless of what the team says. If she's questioned about her failure to keep commitments, this may be her defense.

Cheryl doesn't understand how important it is to keep commitments.

Sad to say, many individuals and organizations make commitments and then regularly fail to keep them. Cheryl may have come from this kind of organization. She's simply continuing the way she worked there.

Cheryl makes commitments without thinking them through.

Individuals have all kinds of reasons for making commitments without thinking through whether they can keep them. They may do it because of pressure from a customer or supervisor, or simply to get someone "off their backs." They may make a commitment with every intention of changing it later or even of forgetting it unless the other person or organization calls them on it. The list goes on and on.

Cures

If the team is sloppy about keeping its commitments:

Before it considers how well an individual keeps commitments, the team needs to consider its own performance. If there's any question, if the team excuses its failures, that's the place to begin. Don't hesitate to bring this up. If you need a strong rationale, just look at the Team Strengthener in this chapter.

To be effective, the team must pledge itself to keep its commitments. It cannot settle for less, and as its leader (even if only for this matter) you cannot permit it to settle for less. Keeping commitments doesn't require unusual skills or iron willpower. It simply requires the active intent to do it.

If Cheryl doesn't understand how important it is to keep commitments:

Do you talk with Cheryl or does the team as a whole talk with her? Either will do, but the best solution is for an individual whose work was held up because she didn't keep her commitment to bring it up to her privately or at a meeting. It needs to be done nonjudgmentally; if it sounds as though someone is accusing her of something she'll probably get defensive. (She may anyway, but why make it more probable?)

The goal is a team discussion, with Cheryl participating. There are some conditions under which a commitment may have to be changed or delayed. Cheryl and the team can negotiate these. Then the team should expect Cheryl to keep her commitments from that point on and should enforce this if necessary.

What if Cheryl doesn't get the message? That's not an acceptable outcome, any more than it is for the team as a whole. If she doesn't respond, the team pushes harder. Again, it should be as nonjudgmental as possible, but the message needs to be clear and consistent. And the team may want to ask whether the next cause, making commitments without thinking them through, isn't part of the problem.

If Cheryl makes commitments without thinking them through:

If the team believes this is the case with Cheryl, it should explore the matter with her. Did she feel pressured to make a commitment? Did she think through what the commitment would require from her before she made it? Did she make assumptions without asking whether they were realistic? Questions like these need to be raised and answered. But the result of the discussion must be that she understands that commitments are made to be kept and begins to do just that.

This may also apply to the first cause, the team not keeping the commitments it makes. The team may not fulfill its commitments because it makes them without thinking them through carefully. Even when it faces extreme pressure, the team should never make a commitment it does not believe it can deliver. Yes, this is hard, both for individuals and for teams. But the alternative is harder and more painful.

Team Strengthener

Keeping commitments is not a trivial issue. Quite the reverse—keeping commitments is the single most important factor in developing trust. Everyone on the team needs to understand that commitments are to be made carefully and kept completely. The basic rule is simple: Make a reasonable commitment and then keep it. What if you can't? First, the only reason for not keeping it should be unforeseen circumstances. Second, if something does happen that it can't be kept as made, everyone concerned should be made aware of it immediately and a new commitment negotiated. Every individual and team can learn to do this, and they must do so if they intend to be effective.

4–3

The Problem

A team member who is a good performer keeps disrupting the team

The Scene

"Hey, let's go over to the snack bar and grab a cup of coffee."

"Bennie, you know we're in the middle of the calculations for next year's budget."

"Yeah, I know—but I need a break, and I don't want to take it all by myself."

"Bennie, bug off. We're going to finish this before we do anything else."

"A fine set of teammates you are! Just wait 'till the next time you want me to do something."

Bennie's at it again. He's an excellent worker by himself and reasonably good working with the team. But he has no sensitivity at all for what others need to do; he must disrupt others on the team at least three or four times a day. How can you get him to stop?

Possible Causes

Bennie isn't used to working as part of a team.

As this book points out, many undesirable behaviors occur simply because individuals are new to teams and don't understand how they need to change their behavior.

Bennie is immature.

Certainly this is a possibility. Perhaps Bennie has never learned to curb his impulsiveness. If he wants to do something, he assumes that others ought to go along with him. Perhaps he came from a work area where several individuals could drop what they were doing and go with him, further encouraging his immaturity.

The team generally shuts Bennie out.

Even if Bennie's behavior is due to one or the other of the causes above, this may also be part of the problem. The team may be put off by Bennie's disruptive behavior and simply ignore him in any but clear business situations. The result? Bennie becomes more disruptive, trying to overcome his isolation, which drives the team to ignore him more, causing Bennie to become more disruptive, and so forth.

Cures

If Bennie isn't used to working as part of a team:

Has anyone on the team ever taken Bennie aside and explained to him how his behavior disrupts the team? In situations like the example above, has anyone ever told Bennie that if he would wait for a few minutes they would get a cup of coffee with him? If the problem is simply that Bennie hasn't learned how to act as part of a team, simple actions like these by team members should help him change quickly.

As always, when Bennie starts changing in the desired direction the team should show that they notice the change and are happy with it.

If Bennie is immature:

Why Bennie is immature is far less important than what needs to be done about it. If Bennie is immature, he will probably react defensively to direct confrontation. Team members need to encourage him to join them on their schedule, while as gently as possible discouraging him from interrupting them. They need to be consistent in this and make it clear to him why they're doing it and that he is still an important member of the team. The one thing the team doesn't want to do is accuse him directly of being immature.

If he doesn't begin to change? Then the rest of the team needs to confront him, explain the situation as they see it, and give him a chance to respond as he wants. Then they can make it clear to him that if he doesn't change they will get him reassigned to a position somewhere else. Perhaps the thought of leaving the team will bring Bennie to change. Perhaps it won't. But either alternative is better than letting him continue as he is.

If the team generally shuts Bennie out:

If this may be the case, start with the team. If Bennie can participate without becoming defensive, include him. Otherwise, meet with the rest of the team. Put the issue on the table and lead the members to recognize their part in the problem. If Bennie is part of the meeting, he and the others can work on the situation together. If not, the rest of the team can work on it and then ask Bennie to join them. However it's done, Bennie needs to be included in the resolution.

Team Strengthener

The relationship between team members and between a member and the rest of the team is always a two-way affair. One side of the relationship may be more visible than the other; in this case, Bennie's disruptive behavior was obvious. But the other part may be just as important. The team's treatment of

Bennie may be a critical part of why he behaves as he does. Or suppose a team member begins to get the reputation for poor work. If the rest of the team responds by putting more pressure on him to perform, the stress may degrade his performance even further. And so it goes. No matter where a problem appears, always look for both (or all) sides of the relationship before concluding what the "real" cause is.

4–4

The Problem

A team member is an excellent individual performer but won't work with the team

The Scene

"Hey, Carmine—can you believe how disruptive that guy on the finance team was?"

"That was really something. You know, though, I'd almost rather have him than Elaine."

"Yeah, maybe so. At least he interacts with the rest of the team. Once Elaine leaves a meeting, we don't see her until the next meeting. I guess she does pretty good work, but trying to get her to work with anyone else is like pulling teeth!"

Like pulling teeth indeed! Elaine isn't just good, she's an excellent worker. But if ever there was someone who shouldn't be on a team, it's her. You've already talked with your next-level manager, though, and he says you've got to give her a fair chance. Is there anything you can do?

Possible Causes

Elaine was an excellent individual worker who hasn't changed to fit the team.

Once again, an individual on a team is causing a problem because she's carrying over behavior that was appropriate as an individual worker but doesn't fit a team.

Elaine didn't want to be on a team, and this is how she shows it.

Organizations often don't ask individuals whether they want to be on a team. They just put them on one. For a good worker, particularly one used to working with great independence, this may be a serious insult. And it may be just as insulting not to be asked *which* team the individual would like to join.

Elaine doesn't think the other members of the team are up to her standards of performance.

We know Elaine is good, but how good are the rest of the individuals on the team? Are any of them up to her standards, really? Is everyone an average performer? Or are some of them mediocre?

Cures

Elaine was an excellent individual worker who hasn't changed to fit the team:

The team needs to ask Elaine why she doesn't want to work with others. Her answer may very well be that she has her job to do and she does it. She may even ask if they're dissatisfied with her work. Then the team needs to explain to her how talented they believe she is and how much other members of the team would like to work with her. Perhaps a member could ask her specifically to work with him or her on a project. She may not change quickly. Remember, she's been an effective individual worker for some time (perhaps years). But if the team continues to make clear what it needs from her and how it values her, she will probably change.

If the team isn't mature enough to deal with the situation as a group, you or someone Elaine clearly respects might take the team's part initially. As the leader, you may have more influence with her than other team members. If so, use it. Remember, though—you're not blaming her for something. You want her to share her skills with the rest of the team.

Elaine didn't want to be on a team, and this is how she shows it:

In this case, Elaine is demonstrating her resentment. No, the team didn't cause her problem, but it must try to resolve it with her. Again, if the team is fairly mature the whole team should take the matter up with her. Someone should observe that she appears not to want to be on the team. They'll hope that this will lead to a discussion about her real feelings and reasons. And it may help her get over some of her resentment.

What then? The team might offer a deal. For her part, she will attempt to work with the rest of the team for, say, three months. If she decides she likes it, fine. If she would rather be an independent worker again, or on another team, the team will do its best to help her get what she wants. If the team presents this as an honest alternative, Elaine may decide it's worth a try. If not, she and the team may need to part company as gracefully as possible now.

If Elaine doesn't think the other members of the team are up to her standards of performance:

If Elaine really is better than most other members of the team, your best move is to have a frank conversation with her. She may not be willing to have her performance "dragged down" by the other members of the team. If she believes you see the performance difference she sees, however, she may be willing to work with at least some of the team. She may be willing to work with them as an informal leader or as an informal tutor. If the rest of the team recognizes her skills, she may be willing to train some of them. In other words, if you offer her a relevant leadership position her whole attitude toward the team may change.

But what if none of this happens? In the interest of the team overall, you may want to work with her to get her transferred to another team or to an individual position where she'll be happier. But don't even think of doing this if the performance of the rest of the team is mediocre or thereabouts. The job then isn't to get rid of her but to get the rest of the team performing closer to her level. If she won't help, the job is on your shoulders.

Team Strengthener

Team members get comfortable with each other. If the team is effective, this comfort helps, as long as it doesn't lead to complacency. But if the team is mediocre, comfort is the last thing it needs. What it needs is to be challenged constantly. Having someone like Elaine on the team can be an excellent way to accomplish this, if she's willing to do it. If you don't have someone like Elaine, or if the person isn't willing to help, you have to initiate the process yourself. Perhaps the team needs more training, or friendly competition with another, similar, effective team, or some stretch goals. Whatever it takes, do it.

4–5

The Problem

A team member goes around the team to the next level of management when the team makes a decision she doesn't like

The Scene

You come out of the office of Marie, your next-level manager, breathing fire. Eileen has gone around you and the team again, the third time in the last two weeks. Every time the team comes up with a decision that Eileen doesn't like, she goes straight to Marie. Then Marie calls you in, and you have to defend the decision, even though the team had the authority to make it. This has got to stop!

Possible Causes

Marie and Eileen are friends.

This doesn't explain anything. It's not just that they're friends, but that Eileen or perhaps both of them are using the friendship to subvert the team. Marie may not feel she can refuse to listen to Eileen. She may have positive reasons for wanting Eileen to bring problems to her (see the next section). Whatever the other reasons, Marie is permitting Eileen to use the friendship in a way that's harmful to the team.

Marie encourages Eileen so she can "keep tabs" on what the team does.

Many managers resist giving teams the freedom and authority that organizations want them to have. They hold on to whatever control they can maintain. Marie may be encouraging Eileen so she'll have some voice in team decisions. In fact, she may even be suggesting to Eileen the kinds of decisions that she wants brought to her. ("If they decide to ask for the videoconferencing setup again, you be sure and let me know."?

Eileen believes the team doesn't listen to her.

This is probably a "chicken-and-egg" problem. Eileen may have used her friendship with Marie to go around the team. Then, because of this, the team began to shut Eileen out. So Eileen went to Marie more often, so the team shut her out more completely . . . You get the picture.

Hint

As you'll see, Marie is at least as much of the cause as Eileen is.

Cures

If Marie and Eileen are friends:

Where do you start? With Marie, of course. If she's not willing to change, you and the team will have great difficulty changing Eileen. How you bring the matter up with Marie depends on your relationship with her, but you must bring it up. If possible, begin by asking Marie if you can talk with her about her relationship with Eileen. Then point out how the relationship is harming the team. (See the last section in this case.) Ask her to listen to Eileen if she wants, but then to tell Eileen to go back to the team and solve her problem as part of it.

What if Marie won't help? If Marie is unwilling to make the hard decision to stop listening to Eileen because she's a friend, just keep working the problem patiently and consistently. Marie may be comfortable listening to Eileen, calling you in and talking with you, but then letting the team decision stand. This isn't the best solution, but it's a workable one. If you can't create this situation, the next section may describe the real cause.

Marie encourages Eileen so she can "keep tabs" on what the team does:

If you think this is the case, the place to start is again with Marie. But your approach is different. Is the issue Marie's need for control or that she doesn't really trust you and the team? Perhaps she got chewed out by the next level of management for a decision the team made. What do you and the team need to do to gain her full confidence and trust? Because you don't know Eileen's role in the situation, this is one of the few places where you need to talk with team members individually or in small groups. Do you see ways that Marie is uncomfortable with what the team does? What kinds of decisions does she seem to be most uncomfortable with? Where is she most likely to support Eileen?

When you and the rest of the team answer these questions, you can develop a strategy for dealing with the situation. The strategy must be designed to demonstrate that you care about what Marie cares about and that you want to help make her successful. For instance, does she get uncomfortable when the team makes decisions to change their work processes? Work out a way to get Marie's input, perhaps in person, while the team is still working the problem. If she wants her finger in the pie, try to create a situation where she gets it there before the decision is made. If she approves or at least accepts the decision, she has no reason to talk with Eileen, except perhaps to suggest that Eileen deal as part of the team and leave her alone.

If Eileen believes the team doesn't listen to her:

No matter the cause, the team acted wrongly in shutting Eileen out and not listening to her. If it felt that her complaining to Marie was wrong—and it certainly must have—it should have brought it up to her. It doesn't matter; both Eileen and the team are carrying around resentment that needs to be worked through. This can happen only in the full team.

Perhaps the feeling that Marie would support Eileen kept the team from confronting Eileen. In this case, work with Marie at the same time you work with Eileen. Just remember that the team isn't fighting either of them. It wants to get Marie's full confidence at the same time that it restores Eileen as a full member.

No matter what the cause is:

Whatever the cause and whatever the rest of the solution, the problem isn't solved until the entire team discusses it with Eileen. As long as she had a direct route to Marie, she may have avoided this; once that route is shut down, she can't, and the team needs to see that she doesn't.

Team Strengthener

Until someone abolishes all hierarchy in an organization—don't hold your breath—a basic responsibility of a team is to make its next-level manager successful. Teams, particularly when they're new or when they begin reporting to a new manager, can fall into the trap of protecting their independence at all costs. No matter the structure of an organization, freedom must be earned, and it can only be earned by gaining the confidence of the next level (or preferably two levels) of management. That means you and the team need to understand the goals of these managers and then act to help them achieve their goals. (What if this gets in the way of the team achieving its goals? Look at the cases in Chapter 10 for suggestions.)

The Problem

A team member performs well only when the rest of the team "gets on his case"

The Scene

"Oscar, you still haven't cleaned up the backlog of purchase orders—and there are two of them in there I have to have."

"You know how busy we've all been."

"Yeah—all of us but you. You promised to have that done day before yesterday—so when are you going to get it done?"

"Well, maybe I can get it by Friday."

"Is there any reason why you can't get it done by tomorrow afternoon?

"Well ..."

You slip quietly away, though you doubt that either of them noticed you. Why is it that Oscar can't get anything done as it ought to be without the rest of team jumping on him? Isn't there something you and the team could do?

Possible Causes

Oscar is accustomed to being closely supervised.

There are some supervisors in traditional organizations who want to know exactly what their workers are doing and to tell them exactly what to do. What does a worker do in this environment? Nothing, until he's told to. Oscar may have had just this kind of supervisor in his previous jobs and carried his habits with him from that situation.

Oscar believes the team doesn't appreciate him.

This may be another of those circular situations. Oscar failed to deliver a time or two, so individuals, or perhaps the whole team, responded by griping at him. So, he got angry at them and expressed the anger by failing to deliver more and more times. You recognize the pattern.

Oscar is lazy.

Don't reach this conclusion unless you're sure neither of the causes above is the right one. And don't jump to conclusions about what "lazy" means. Oscar may simply be uninterested in the job, or may not want to work that hard, or may not see any real payoff for putting forth effort. But it doesn't matter.

Cures

If Oscar is accustomed to being closely supervised:

Has the team discussed the matter with Oscar? If not, it needs to do so—clearly. While it shouldn't accuse Oscar of anything, the members who are frustrated with him should express their frustration. Most important, though, the team needs to communicate exactly what Oscar is doing that frustrates them. (Remember, if he was oversupervised before, when his boss was angry with him it was most likely because he took initiative, not because he avoided it.)

As always, Oscar deserves to be heard. But he does not deserve to continue his way of working. The team's goal is a program of progress for Oscar. Other members might agree to work or check in with him at times while he's working on his tasks, to provide him support. (But *no one* complains to him or offers to do part of the work.) When he gets the task done as promised, the rest of the team should notice that and recognize him for it. When he doesn't, the rest of the team needs to bring the matter up. (He may complain that he has too much to do; the team will have to negotiate that with him.) Just keep it between the team and him, not individual members and him. You'll be much more apt to succeed this way.

If Oscar believes the team doesn't appreciate him:

The team needs to bring up the matter, as in the section above. But it needs to be particularly careful to encourage Oscar to express his feelings and for them to accept them. If he truly does feel he's not appreciated, one good response is to ask him how the team would act if it appreciated him. Get this clear. Then negotiate an agreement that gives him this in return for his performing his work right and on time.

When he keeps his side of the agreement, make sure that the rest of the team recognizes and appreciates him for doing so. If he fails to do so, the matter needs to come up in a meeting and be resolved. And if others on the team fail to keep their side of the agreement, this needs to be discussed—with plenty of input from Oscar—and resolved. It may be tough sledding at first, but the results will turn out to be worth it.

If Oscar is lazy:

The team cannot put up with this kind of behavior from a member. Period. It must bring up the matter to Oscar, giving him every chance to speak up for himself. Then it must make clear it needs more from him and must have it. If not, he will have to leave the team.

In that circumstance, Oscar may begin to change. Or he may pretend to change for a while, to get the pressure off. (After all, if he's really lazy it's more convenient for him to stay on the team than to have to find a new and unfamiliar job.) The team needs to keep the pressure on—no yelling, no griping, but clear communication of what it needs and how he's going against that need. Either he changes or finds a new job. And this is one of the few situations in which the team doesn't necessarily help him find the job.

Team Strengthener

An effective team learns the difference between griping at someone constantly, keeping up constant pressure and insisting that an individual live up to his agreements. If I complain that you're not doing what I want, I make it easy for you to avoid the situation by getting angry with me. If the team keeps pressure on you, listening to you but insisting on what it needs from you, it's much harder for you to keep blaming the team. But if the team negotiates an agreement with you that both you and the team are satisfied with, and then keeps its part while insisting that you keep yours—you have hard decisions to make that you can't blame on others. The moral: Surface the problems, listen to everyone, work out an agreement that includes everyone's interests, and then insist that everyone either fulfills or renegotiates his or her part of the agreement.

4–7

The Problem
A team member performs well only on tasks she enjoys

The Scene

You're looking over the interim reports on two of the team's projects, and you can't help but notice the difference in Celia's part of each one. On the first, where she's suggesting alternatives, her work is excellent. She's identified almost half a dozen possibilities and described them objectively. On the second, where she agreed (under a bit of pressure) to do the data collection, her results are so-so at best. You're quite sure the team will ask her to redo them. You wish you were as sure what you and the team can do about the problem.

Possible Causes

Celia prefers to spend her time on familiar tasks.

During our school and work careers, all of us become skilled in certain activities and not in others. A star athlete may be so-so at math and completely unskilled musically. An accountant may be able to make very complex estimates of the expenditures for the next quarter, but have no idea how to evaluate the candidates for his new clerical position. Once we develop these skills at certain tasks, we prefer to spend time on them rather than on activities we are less familiar with (and thus less skilled at). This may be Celia's basic reason for doing better at some tasks than at others.

Celia has never had to use a range of skills before.

This situation closely resembles the one above, but with an additional factor. Traditional organizations hire individuals for specific jobs with specific duties and tasks. Promotion usually depends on doing these tasks, and only these tasks, well. So Celia's previous jobs may all have encouraged her to concentrate on one set of tasks and develop one set of skills.

If this is Celia's situation, she may never have thought in terms of developing and using other skills. She may do the tasks at which she lacks skills to be a loyal member of the team, but she may not think of them as opportunities to learn new skills. She may be surprised if other team members suggest that she develop these extra skills.

Celia isn't good at certain kinds of tasks.

While we can all expand our range of skills, it's also true that there are real differences in the kinds of work we can do well. Some individuals are extremely good at detail work but have great difficulty in seeing "the big picture." Others are just the reverse. Some people can deal only with carefully defined problems, while others excel at tackling vague and ill-defined ones. And so it goes.

Should individuals spend time dealing with situations they're not good at when so fundamental a difference is involved? There's no cut-and-dried answer.

Hint

Keep in mind that, no matter what the cause or cure, every individual is better at some tasks than at others. Teams offer the opportunity for individuals both to work at the tasks that best use their skills and to learn new skills by performing different tasks. (See the Team Strengthener for this case, for more on this.)

Cures

If Celia prefers to spend her time on familiar tasks:

The team needs to bring up to Celia that there are real differences in her performance depending on the kind of work she does. She probably already knows this even better than the team does, so if the team avoids being judgmental she can provide more information on the problem.

If the problem is simply one of Celia's preference, she and the team should be able to negotiate an agreement to help her perform better at unfamiliar work. Perhaps she needs somewhat more time at these tasks. Perhaps she would agree, with the team's help, to do most of her work in an unfamiliar area; then she could pick up additional skills and be comfortable doing new kinds of tasks.

If Celia has never had to use a range of skills before:

The solution is almost like that in the section above, except that the team may have to work with Celia somewhat longer. It has to help her understand that putting time into developing new skills is not only okay but important. And then it must support her as she develops these skills. Remember, though, that when Celia is learning new skills she will often feel incompetent at first. The team's job is to help her through this period, until she begins to develop confidence in the new skills.

If Celia just isn't good at certain kinds of tasks:

Here is where the confidence that team members have in one another becomes critical. The team may start with the idea that Celia can learn to do these new tasks well, but she responds that she's tried and just can't. This requires honest, responsive dialogue on everyone's part. The team and Celia may decide that she will do mostly work she's good at, but will agree at times to try other work. But this or any other solution will work only if everyone participates openly and the decision represents a genuine consensus.

Team Strengthener

Teams offer a unique opportunity for individuals both to do work they enjoy *and* to learn the skills to do other work. This permits them to build their overall competence. It also permits them to perform a variety of work and remain challenged by their job. The attitude of the team is crucial. If it's easily critical of mistakes, particularly when made by someone who's trying a new skill, it will lock its members into very narrow skills. But if it supports them as they learn these new skills, encouraging them and helping them whenever necessary, everyone will build a wide range of skills. This makes the job much more interesting for everyone. It also gives the team an overall flexibility that translates directly into higher performance.

4–8

The Problem
A team member will perform only tasks he enjoys

The Scene

> *Dale:* Warren, we need you to contact the other three teams that are working on this project and work out how we'll coordinate with them.
>
> *Warren:* Oh, no—not me. That's not my kind of work.
>
> *Esther:* Yes, we know. But someone has to do it, and everyone else already has plenty to do. You have to do it.
>
> *Warren:* I don't have to do anything. I thought we were a team. Doesn't anyone care what I want to do?
>
> *Cindy:* It's not a case of us not caring. It's a case of a job that has to get done and your being the only one who can do it.

Someone else finally agreed to trade tasks with Warren, but everyone—including Warren—ended up resentful. What can you and the team do to keep this from happening again?

Hint

As you'll see, many of the causes are the same as in the case before this one. Warren's response is different from Celia's, though, and that makes a real difference in how to cure the problem.

Possible Causes

Warren has never had to use a range of skills before.

Because of this, Celia may not have been good at certain tasks. But she did them anyway. Warren refuses to do them. In other words, he closes the door on learning new skills. Does he get so uncomfortable when he tries to perform unfamiliar tasks that he backs off from them? Is he perhaps even afraid at the thought? It doesn't matter. For whatever reason, he's decided not to expand his skills.

Warren isn't good at certain kinds of tasks.

Like Celia in the case before this one, Warren may have tried to do certain kinds of work and decided that he lacks the ability to do them. Perhaps he's tried to be persuasive and consistently failed at it. In this case, the team needs to take the same approach that it would take with Celia.

The team doesn't take account of Warren's preferences and skills.

This may have been a part of the problem with Celia. Because Warren has reacted so much more strongly, though, it's more apt to be a problem here. Warren may have tried to make it clear that he didn't do certain tasks well, but found that the team insisted on asking him to perform these tasks when (to him) there were other options. So he decided that the only way he could get the team to take account of his preferences was to refuse to do certain things.

Cures

If Warren has never had to use a range of skills before:

The team has to bring this up to Warren, and it may need to do so forcefully. It has two goals. First, it wants Warren to understand what he is doing and how it limits the team (and, probably, how it irritates the other team members). Second, it wants to work with him to start expanding his skills. The team needs to reach an agreement with Warren that he will begin to accept some unfamiliar tasks. In return, members of the team will work closely with him to get him through his initial discomfort and help him develop the skills he needs.

If he refuses to agree to this? Go to the next section.

If Warren isn't good at certain kinds of tasks:

In the last case, the team could be confident that Celia had tried to develop her skills at new tasks, because she was willing to do the tasks even when she didn't like them. Not so with Warren. He may have refused even to try. The team may need to do some serious negotiation with him to learn new skills before it concludes there's a real difference in ability.

Does it sound as if the team is being rough on Warren? Perhaps he's very likeable and a valuable member of the team. The team needs to make clear that it appreciates his contributions. But if he confines himself to a narrow range of tasks and skills, he handicaps the team's flexibility and its effectiveness. He needs to understand this and to make a genuine effort to expand his skills. When the team sees him do this, it can begin to back off.

If the team doesn't take account of Warren's preferences and skills:

This situation requires airing out by everyone in an open meeting. You can bet that Warren and many other team members are resentful about the situation. Each may want to blame the other; that often happens in a situation where each "side" is pushing the other side farther and farther away. The team needs to work through the resentment and get past the blaming. Warren needs to hear what the rest of the team is saying; they need to hear why he's resentful.

When everyone's issues are out on the table, Warren and the rest of the team can look at them from a new perspective and start to agree on what they need to do. What will that be? It's almost impossible to say. When an issue is bound up with strong feelings, it gets tremendously distorted. When everyone comes to terms with his or her feelings and is willing to address the issue on its merits, the situation always looks different. Once Warren and the team cross this divide, many of the suggestions in the case before this one will be applicable.

Team Strengthener

When individuals perform new tasks that require them to learn new skills, they move from competence into incompetence. This doesn't just apply when someone is learning a new skill. Consider what seems an almost trivial issue: The team decides to start work half an hour early. If one team member is a single mother who must prepare her children for school, she may literally not know how to do so half an hour early. After a few weeks, though, she develops a new routine that gets everything done and lets her leave on time. She has moved from incompetence to competence. And so it is with every change. When the team is supportive, the challenge of the new tasks overwhelms the feeling of incompetence. The individual becomes excited about the experience. If the team is judgmental? Why not think back to a time when you were trying to learn something new and others were very critical of you. What happened?

CHAPTER 5

Problems With the Performance of the Team as a Whole

Sometimes the problem isn't the performance of individual team members but the performance of the team as a whole. Nothing guarantees that a team will be effective. It may make all kinds of mistakes in trying to do its job, such as refusing to get or use feedback from its customers.

The cases in this chapter describe ways that a team may fail to perform effectively as a whole. The reasons vary, from team members not helping one another to the team as a whole making poor decisions. The net result, though, is the same: The team fails to perform as effectively as it should.

In these cases, the team is at least partly the cause of the problem it must solve. That makes the situation particularly difficult, because the team must first admit it has a problem and face what the problem is. (After all, it's easiest to blame the problem on someone else.) Getting the problem into the open is at least half the battle.

The chapter will help you and the team face the problems honestly and then solve them. While this may be painful and unsettling at first, you and the team will experience a tremendous sense of power whenever you do it successfully. And the team will get stronger and stronger.

The Problem

The team doesn't have enough to do to keep it busy

The Scene

So far this week:

Three arguments have broken out between Beth and Howard;

Tom has scored over 5 million on Space Aliens;

Ginnie has rewritten the request for new computers six times;

Millie has worked through every exercise in her word-processing manual;

And Pat and Ollie have rehashed Sunday's football game a hundred times.

You've never seen so many people with so much time on their hands. And this is supposed to be a high-performance team?

Possible Causes

The team has plenty to do but is avoiding it.

Why are they avoiding the tasks? Do they believe they lack proper training or skills? Are they afraid that what they do will be shot down? Are they used to easy projects and this is a difficult one?

The team's mission isn't a full-time mission.

This, of course, is a very different situation. On the surface, it might look desirable. Performing a less-than-full-time mission lets you spend time on quality and still have time to relax. Unfortunately, it doesn't make you very competitive. If the organization decides to cut back on the number of teams, it may decide it can combine your mission with that of another team and cut or redeploy team members. Besides, not having a full-time job can get awfully tedious.

This is an unusually productive team.

The team may be made up of very capable individuals who work extremely well together. When this happens, the team's productivity can be mind-boggling. What seemed a full-time mission becomes much less than that.

Cures

If the team has plenty to do but is avoiding it:

It's critically important that you find out why they're avoiding work before you take any action.

Talk with team members, bring the matter up in a team meeting, do whatever you need to find the root cause.

Now you and the team are ready to proceed. Discuss the matter in a meeting until there's consensus on the real problem. Then use whatever problem-solving method you normally use to solve this one.

If the team truly lacks training and/or skills, it may have to get help. Go find the training. Find individuals on other teams who have the skills you lack and "borrow" them. But don't put off doing your work any longer.

If the team's mission isn't a full-time mission:

What do you do? You and the team go looking for work. If the organization permits it, start looking outside the team for work that needs to be done and start doing it. If the organization exercises more control, look outside the team for work that needs to be done and then propose to management that your team do it.

This strategy has two great advantages. First, you look good to higher management. Second, you get to pick the work to do.

If this is an unusually productive team:

If this is the case, you and the team go looking for work. But it needs to be more aggressive than in the section above. It needs to look for the really hard, challenging tasks, particularly those that other teams may want to get rid of.

When the team gets known as the one that can tackle any problem, perhaps even as the organization's most effective trouble-shooters, lots of good things can happen. Members may get the chance to start new teams or serve on higher-level teams. They may get higher raises or promotions. The team will certainly get respect. And talk about job security!

Team Strengthener

Every team, like every individual, has a certain balance between capabilities and workload where it is most effective. If it has less work than this balance, boredom and sloppiness set in. If it has more, it rushes through tasks and compromises quality. Thus every team has two tasks. First, to find the balance. Second, to keep adjusting its workload as the balance changes, perhaps down if it has several new members, up as it acquires more skill and confidence. But if a team allows its workload to overwhelm its capabilities for long, or if its workload doesn't make full use of its capabilities for long, it will get into serious trouble.

5–2

The Problem
The team has more work than it can accomplish effectively

The Scene

"Hey, got a moment?"

You look around to see Marion, the unofficial leader of a team that's one of your team's main customers. "Sure. What's up?"

"Have you been keeping tabs on what you've been giving us lately?"

"Sort of. I know we've been late once or twice."

"I'm afraid it's worse than that. You've been late three or four times in the last two weeks, and one of those times made us miss an important deadline of our own. And we had to give you back what you gave us yesterday so you could redo it. You know I like you guys, but this is getting sticky for us."

"I'll get the folks together and see what we can do. You know that's not the way we want to treat you."

And it isn't—but you're not quite sure how to solve the problem.

Possible Causes

The team lacks sufficient training and/or skills for its mission.

This problem pops up in a variety of forms. Teams that lack proper training or the right skills balance for their mission can easily become demoralized and lose their self-confidence. In some cases, this feeds on itself, so that the team begins to believe that it can't even do the work effectively for which it has skills and training.

This creates a serious vicious cycle that must be stopped or else.

Several members of the team aren't performing effectively.

If a team has a demanding job, everyone on the team has to contribute to its success. In this circumstance two or three members whose performance is substandard can drag the entire team down. The rest of the team may then react to the situation with resentment and make a bad circumstance worse.

The team has an unreasonable amount of work.

When a team is set up, it's often difficult to estimate the correct workload for it. And even if it begins with a balanced workload, conditions change. Whatever the cause, your team has more work assigned than it can complete effectively.

Cures

If the team lacks sufficient training and/or skills for its mission:

You hope your team is at the start of the cycle, when training and/or a new member or two with the necessary skills will bring the team back up to full performance. Go find the training, even if you have to contract with a local community college to provide it. If necessary, ask for the additional skilled members the team needs. This is one of the cases when you need to press hard, before the situation spirals downward any more.

If you can't get any new members for the team, one or two current members might volunteer to pick up the skills in one way or another. In the short run, you may be able to find a team that will lend you someone with the skills you need. Or you might combine the two and borrow someone who can do the work but also show the members of your team how to do it.

If several members of the team aren't performing effectively:

Don't waste time. If this is the case with your team, you and the team need to act quickly.

The rest of the team needs to be frank with the underperforming members. Do they lack the skills and training they need? If so, follow the suggestions in the section above. If one of them lacks the skills you need but has skills that might be useful to another team, perhaps you can arrange a swap to get the skills you need. If lack of skills or training is the problem, don't punish or blame the individuals. Just take the steps necessary to get them up to speed.

Suppose it's motivation. Perhaps the individuals don't want to be on a team or don't feel they're accepted by the team. Chapters 1 and 3 deal with this kind of problem; you'll probably find suggestions there that will help you solve the problem.

If none of these are the case, the problem may be individual capability. One or more of the individuals not only can't do the work but don't have the capacity to learn it. Clearly, being angry with them won't help. Help them find other positions in the organization more suited to their abilities, so both you and they can begin to perform effectively.

If the team has an unreasonable amount of work:

You want to consider this alternative last, because the team can't control it by themselves. If the team has too much work, it may have to go to higher management and ask to be relieved of some of its responsibilities. Such a task is never pleasant, and it can create a negative impression of the team with management. That doesn't mean you don't do it.

It does mean that you do it only after you've genuinely explored the other alternatives.

First, the team needs to carefully analyze its workload. Has the entire team been performing some tasks that a subteam can perform effectively? Are there some tasks that would fit easily in with the mission of another team? You may be able to negotiate with that team to take them over. (Perhaps, like the team in the case before this one, they need additional work.) You might even solve the problem by swapping some tasks that your team does only fairly well for others that it performs very effectively. Just make sure you look at a wide range of possibilities.

If you can't solve the problem by working with other teams, you've no alternative but to go to higher management. Identify the tasks you want to get rid of, with clear reasons why you need to get rid of them. Try to suggest other ways that the tasks might get done. Stress the team's desire to do effective, on-time, high-quality work. Then, if it gets relieved of some tasks, it needs to make sure that it does in fact begin producing this effective, on-time, high-quality work.

Team Strengthener

There are times when a team has too great a workload on a continuing (rather than just a peak) basis. When this happens, the team must deal with the situation head on. Otherwise, it risks entering a vicious spiral where it becomes less and less effective. The team always begins by looking at its performance, its processes, its motivation—everything it can control.

It turns to someone outside, such as higher management, only when it is convinced that the cure lies beyond its control. Like the team in the case just above, it continuously looks for the right balance in workload—one that will challenge it but still enable it to produce high-quality, on-time work.

5–3

The Problem
The team isn't performing its mission effectively

The Scene

Max, your next-level manager, has called you into your office.

"Your team just isn't cutting it."

You sigh. "I wouldn't put it quite that badly—but we aren't doing as well as I wish we were."

"Well, I would put it that badly. You have a reputation for missing deadlines, every day someone tells me about a job of yours they had to send back for you to rework, and you probably get out less work than any other team I know."

"I know we have problems, but . . ."

"No buts. I'll give you sixty days. If the team isn't up to snuff by then, I'm probably going to abolish it and scatter all of you among other teams."

Well, that's clear. Now what can you and the team do?

Possible Causes

The team lacks training and/or skills.

If you've read many other cases, such as the one before this one, you know that lack of training and/or the wrong skills balance is a real barrier to effective team performance. While this doesn't always produce as severe a result as real mission failure, it may. When team performance falls short, this is the first place to look.

The team is poorly organized.

There's no magic in being a team. For any number of reasons, the team may have simply taken off without developing the internal organization it needs. When a new project comes up, the team may not know how to parcel it out effectively. For instance, it may not know how to separate different responsibilities clearly or set realistic milestones.

The team just doesn't care about its mission.

Hint

You might want to look at the case before this one. Some of the material there may help explain what's happening in this situation.

When organizations create teams, they sometimes create teams just to have teams everywhere in the organization. It may have happened that your team doesn't have a significant mission. The team members understand the mission, but they don't think it's important. So they don't commit themselves to it.

Cures

If the team lacks training and/or skills:

How do you tell if this is the problem? Get the team together and present the situation as you see it. Let everyone else describe it as he or she sees it. One thing to watch: the tendency to say "It's not really that bad," or "It's just a bad time." It is that bad, and there's no reason to think it will improve. The team needs to face the circumstance it's in without denying its seriousness. Then it needs to look honestly at the reasons it can't perform.

If the reason is lack of training or lack of needed skills, look at the first two cases in this chapter, which suggest how to deal with these situations. The important point is this: Act quickly and positively. You don't have a great deal of time.

If the team is poorly organized:

This is first of all a training problem. Does your organization offer training for teams in how to organize and operate effectively? It may not, because everyone tends to assume that teams can figure this out for themselves. If the organization doesn't offer this training, see if you can get the entire team some basic supervisory or managerial training. This will expose everyone to the concepts of work planning and organization. Then the team will have to translate these concepts into the team situation. A good facilitator can help throughout this process.

Once you and the team learn how to organize effectively, do it! Just knowing how doesn't change the way things are. Make plans and review them individually and as a team. See that team members help one another whenever necessary.

If the team doesn't care about its mission:

When the team thinks its mission isn't important there are only two alternatives if it wants to remain a team. First, you, higher management, or someone has to convince the team that the mission does matter. Or the team must find a new mission.

If you believe that the mission is important, even though you may not fully understand why, ask someone from higher management to come in and explain it to the team. Make sure it happens in an environment where the team can ask questions and show their concerns. A quick "sell" won't solve the problem. If nothing can convince you and the team that it is important, you need to talk with higher management about that issue. At worst, perhaps your team can switch missions with another team who might find this mission worthwhile. Case 9–2 deals with this problem in more detail.

Team Strengthener

There is no magic to teams. Just because individuals are organized into teams doesn't mean that all the problems of a traditional organization get solved. Planning, organizing, and executing tasks are just as important for teams as for any other organization. Many times, teams will discover how to do this for themselves. At other times, they won't, and they'll try to operate without these planning, organizing, and executing skills, or without the internal structure required to use them successfully. If this is happening to your team, put the problem on the table and start working it. An effective team is more than the sum of the abilities of the individuals on it. If it cannot effectively organize itself, it accomplishes much less than the individuals on it could accomplish by themselves.

5–4

The Problem
The team doesn't want to do administrative work

The Scene

"Okay," Marcella says, "who's going to work out the budget for next quarter?"

There's a deafening silence.

"Come on, now—you know we have to do it. Tomas, don't you have some time that you could work on it?"

"Whoa—not me! I did it two quarters ago. Let someone else have the pleasure."

"Lisa, what about you?"

"I'll never get my regular work done if I have to do that too . . . ."

And so it goes. Every time some administrative work comes up, everyone has an excuse not to do it. The team is great at its primary job, but getting worse and worse at the administrative tasks it has to perform to keep itself going.

Possible Causes

The team hasn't been trained to do administrative work efficiently.

This is most apt to happen if the team members are from a blue-collar background, where they handled "things" and other people took care of the paperwork. It's not that team members aren't smart enough to do it, but compared to things, paper is both strange and difficult. So, as most of us would in the same circumstance, team members prefer to avoid it.

Team members think the administrative work is "beneath" them.

Perhaps the team is composed of "knowledge workers," such as engineers, programmers, instructors, or inventory managers. Before they joined the team, most or all of them had administrative units that did the administrative work. They personally never had to bother with it. And they look on it as clerical or administrative work that someone like them shouldn't have to deal with.

Team members don't think the administrative work is "real" work.

Either cause above may be part of the problem, but this cause will almost certainly be involved as well. Every job requires administrative support, but most of us would rather concentrate on the job than on the administration. It's only natural: The job is what we came there to do. But it creates a problem.

Hint

Don't feel like the Lone Stranger if you encounter this problem. It's very common.

Cures

If the team hasn't been trained to do administrative work efficiently:

The cure is straightforward: Get the training. You may have to do something of a selling job at first, because some members may feel that taking the training means they're "dumb." If you're not comfortable with the paper work (after all, you may be one of the ones avoiding it), lead the way by volunteering for the training first. The best alternative is a group decision to take the training together, coupled with agreement *before the training* that each individual will perform a share of the administrative work after the training.

With only a little bit of luck, you and the team will get past this hurdle quickly. Paperwork is seldom fun, but neither is it overly bothersome when you know how to do it. However, no matter how good the team becomes with paperwork, you'll want to explore getting computer support to help with the chore. See the next section.

If team members think the administrative work is "beneath" them:

The first and best alternative is this: Get a computer with the right software. The team may already have a computer. If not, powerful machines are becoming cheaper and easier to use every day. And it's simple to find off-the-shelf programs to help do budgeting, planning, personnel administration, and other administrative chores. More and more of these programs have excellent "advisory" modules that ask helpful questions and guide the individuals who use them through the process. It won't make administrative work painless, but it can make it easy enough that team members will be willing to do it.

If you can't get a computer or the right software? If the team has enough work to support a full-time administrative person, that may be the next best alternative. Or perhaps the team could join with another team to hire someone for administrative support. If the team can't do this and can't find another practical solution, the only alternative left is to bite the bullet and agree to share the pain equally. (And your team has advanced far enough that it would never even *think* of imposing the administrative work exclusively on its female members, hasn't it?)

Watch out for one danger. Administrative work can never be separated completely from the mission work of the team. Making up a budget, for instance, is never just routine work; decisions have to be made that will influence how the team can operate. For all substantive work such as this, even if you have an administrative specialist or one team member who is a whiz with the computer, the team as a whole needs to be the decision maker, whether anyone likes it or not.

If team members don't think the administrative work is "real" work:

Again, as in the section above, try to solve the problem with an appropriate computer system.

If you can't do that, try to hire an individual to do the administrative work for the team. If you do, pay attention to the danger the section describes. But there's another aspect—not really a danger but a potential irritation. If you do have one individual specifically responsible for administration, then administration becomes this person's *mission*. That means the individual will take it seriously and may start pestering the team with suspenses, follow-ups, and the other necessary administrivia. The solution? Include the person fully on the team, so that he or she understands both the team mission and how the administrative job fits into it.

Team Strengthener

Teams need effective technology to function effectively. This doesn't mean having the latest and glitziest gadgets or the fastest computer in the city. It does mean having what you need to help get the job done and to let the people on the team concentrate on what they do best. For most teams, this means having effective computer and communication support. Chapter 12 has several cases dealing with poor computer support. Don't let those examples fool you, though; most teams can't operate effectively without computers, e-mail, local area networks, and the like. You should always be on the lookout for ways that the team can make greater use of computers and communications to relieve it of the burden of administrative work and to help it perform its mission effectively.

The Problem
The team's decisions often aren't very good

The Scene

John, Marie, and you walk away from the team meeting dejectedly. Though all three of you went along with the team's decision, each of you believes that it was another mediocre decision. No one will yell at you for it, but none of you can take much pride in it. The team has to find some way to make better decisions.

Possible Causes

The team isn't committed to its mission.

This comes up again and again as a cause of poor performance. If the team doesn't believe that what it does matters, or that it doesn't even need to be done, it won't spend the effort required to do a good job. For instance, suppose the team has been charged to develop a new procedure that no one cares about. Even worse, suppose it's been given a project where it's sure that higher management has already decided what should be done. All these situations are fatal to team success.

The team is burned out.

This in turn can have several causes. Perhaps the team's decisions are being consistently overruled by higher management so that the team feels it has lost in a guessing game it can't win. Perhaps it's seen its decisions ignored, or even given to another team to evaluate. Or it's consistently sent back to redo its decisions. Any of these situations, and others besides, can burn out a team in a hurry.

The team isn't up to its assigned mission.

Don't entertain this as the cause unless nothing else works. But it may be the cause, and you and the team need to think long and hard about how to solve the problem.

Hint

You will also find relevant information about causes of poor team decisions in the first eight cases in Chapter 2, particularly Cases 2–7 and 2–8.

Cures

If the team isn't committed to its mission:

What do you and the team do? If the situation is temporary, with the prospect of worthwhile work before long, just hunker down and do what you have to do well. If the team's mission as a whole appears unimportant, it's time to talk with the next level of management about the mission. Don't talk in general or dump the problem in management's lap. Do some careful research, identify other work the team might do that members believe is worthwhile and explain how it can be assigned to the team. (Cases 9–2 and 9–4 provide some additional suggestions.)

Do neither of these alternatives seem realistic for you and your team? Then look for other alternatives. Don't let the team stagnate! Very little can be as harmful to the team and its members as letting this happen.

If the team is burned out:

You can't let the situation continue. The team needs to find out why it consistently fails to produce what higher management expects. If the organization encourages open communication, perhaps a delegation from the team can ask. (If you do, listen carefully and *don't* be defensive. If you fall into the trap of rejecting what's said and just defending yourself, you make the situation worse than it was.) If higher management won't communicate its intentions openly, it's time to do intelligence work. Talk to a team that's more successful to find out why it is. If another team evaluates your decisions, ask them. But go in search of the answers. When you believe you've found an answer try it out and watch the results. Keep trying, until you discover what management wants from you.

What if the team feels lost in a guessing game? It can't find what management wants? If nothing else seems to work, you've no alternative (short of transferring or a similar drastic solution) but to go to higher management, paint the situation as you see it, and ask for help. Then see what happens. If there's any improvement, build on it and make sure that higher management knows you recognize the improvement and are taking advantage of it. With luck, you can begin with a little progress and then nurture it into real change.

If the team simply isn't up to its assigned mission:

Perhaps the team lacks one or two skills it needs and you could trade with another team to get individuals with these skills. Perhaps you can get training, either formally or from another team, in the skills. Perhaps only one or two members are holding the team back. If that's the case, see the second section of Case 2 in this chapter. If you can remedy the problem by moving one or two people around, by all means try to do it.

But suppose it's deeper than that and the team has been assigned work that's beyond its capabilities? Can you find another team that has assigned work your team could do but is bored with it? Perhaps you could trade responsibilities. Explore avenues such as this one first. If all this fails, though, go to higher management and explain the situation to them. And, as always, have alternatives to offer them, preferably some important work the team has identified that it's confident it could do.

Team Strengthener

How does a team tell when it does a really good job? Easy—when it can take pride in what it does. But there's one qualification on this, an important one. A team can know when it has done a good job only when its customer says "good job." Everything else may be great, technically it may even be superb, but if the customer isn't satisfied with it, it isn't a good job. So the team should always listen to its customers and listen to them carefully. Then it should produce work it can be proud of. When that happens, it will have done a good job.

The Problem

The team doesn't have enough time to do quality work

The Scene

"Well, we got it done on schedule."

"Yeah, and just barely in good enough shape to be usable."

"I understand how you feel, but no one's complained yet."

"I don't care whether anyone complains. I'm not satisfied with it."

That's your team. Another job done on time with mediocre quality. Will the team ever have enough time to do quality work?

Possible Causes

The team doesn't practice continuous process improvement.

Many organizations began a Total Quality Management (TQM) program, but most of them then let it drop before it was fully implemented. And many other organizations didn't adopt TQM. If your team is in either situation, it may be a victim of poor processes and not know how to improve them. (What's a poor process? It might be an order-approval system that takes two weeks to approve an order, but one in which the order spends all but two hours of the time in transit or sitting somewhere waiting for someone to take action on it.) The team doesn't have time enough to do quality work because the way it has to do the work is wasting its time.

The team wants to build "Cadillacs," but all the organization needs are "Fords."

More than anything else, quality means giving the customer a product (or service) that meets the customer's needs as delivered. Your team may want to spend more time and effort on what it does than the customer needs. For instance, it may want to spend time dressing up a report that the customer takes information from and then discards. In this case, quality means to the customer that the report is well organized and readable. How fancy it looks has nothing to do with real quality.

Higher management forces unrealistic deadlines on teams.

In the first few chapters, we saw how workers who had not made the adjustment to working on a team could cause problems for a team. Managers who haven't made the adjustment can also cause problems. In traditional organizations, managers often try to control workers by imposing very short deadlines on them. This has no place in an organization based on autonomous teams.

Hint

This situation seems similar to that in the case just before this one, and it is. But there are some significant differences. If your circumstances sound a little like both, you might want to look at both of them before deciding what to do.

Cures

If the team doesn't practice continuous process improvement:

Does your organization have a TQM coordinator or director? Get hold of this individual and have him or her come talk with the team. Learn what continuous process improvement is. Learn how to do it. Then practice it. It may push the team at first as it takes extra time. That won't last long. If you practice it, you'll soon find that as you simplify processes you get work done both faster and in higher quality. It wouldn't hurt to use the services of a TQM facilitator, if one is available, until the team becomes proficient at process improvement.

If there's no internal TQM staff? Get a videotape or a book. Take a course at a local college, junior college, or technical school. Visit another organization with teams that use TQM methods. Do whatever you have to do to learn about continuous process improvement. Then do it, however you can. It takes time at first, but then you'll find that it saves more time.

If the team wants to build "Cadillacs," but all the organization needs are "Fords":

If this is the problem, the solution is simple: Set priorities based on your customers' needs. Always meet these needs, but don't waste time on extras that don't have value for the customer. Then spend the extra time and effort on the jobs where extra effort will matter to the customer.

Any of us can get frustrated if we believe we are producing low-quality results. But everyone needs to focus on what quality means to the customer. If the team produces products (or services) that meet customer needs, it has produced quality. Everyone needs to understand this and take pride in this kind of quality.

If higher management forces unrealistic deadlines on teams:

The problem, of course, is how you help higher management to realize this. You might suggest that for a two- or three-month trial period, the manager let the team set its own deadlines and see how that works out. If this won't work, you could suggest that the manager at least listen carefully to the team before imposing a deadline. And, of course, the team needs to demonstrate that it will set (or suggest) deadlines that the manager will recognize as both realistic and challenging. The worst thing the team can do is to pad the deadlines because that locks everyone back into the low trust/high control pattern of traditional organizations.

When the team gets a voice in setting its deadlines, it needs to keep aware of the genuine business pressures that cause tight deadlines. Even if higher management fully understands the problems a tight deadline will cause, competitive pressures may force it to go with the deadline. Don't fight it. Learn to work smarter and use creative shortcuts. Learn to improve processes. In short, the team needs to get better at its job.

Team Strengthener

You're not familiar with the quality movement and TQM? Its basic idea is simple and powerful: When an organization constantly improves its processes, it improves its quality but also lowers its costs and the time it takes to accomplish its tasks. That sounds too good to be true, perhaps, but it really does happen. Your team, the organization, and your customers all win when your team learns how to identify and get rid of wasteful actions, procedures, and steps. It's not that hard to do, so if you're not doing it now, find out how to do it and start doing it.

5–7

The Problem
Team members won't help one another

The Scene

Teresa is obviously having a problem with a spreadsheet. Roger, Wilma, and Lois all walk by and stop to chat for a moment with her. None of them offers to help, though both Wilma and Lois are whizzes at spreadsheets. And Teresa doesn't ask anyone for help. That's the team; everyone is a good individual performer but none of them will work together unless they're absolutely required to do so. This is a team?

Possible Causes

The team members haven't made the transition from being individual performers.

If you've read some of the cases in the chapters before this one, you know that many problems can be caused because individuals haven't made this transition. They don't understand what it means to be on a team. In this case, though, that's apparently true of most or all of the team. *No one* understands how he or she expected to act as a team member.

The mission doesn't require them to work closely together.

Unfortunately, many organizations that decide to use teams don't stop to analyze where teams can best be used. Instead, they expect everyone to be on a team, whether the team's mission requires them to work together or not. Many times, the mission can get done by individuals working as individuals.

Members of the team are from different functions or have different statuses.

Teams are often put together to combine different functions (such as sales, credit, and fulfillment). And teams may have individuals with different statuses in the organization (such as one composed of an engineer, a technician, an administrative assistant, and a draftsman). In both cases, individuals may not work together because they are not used to working with jobs so different from their own.

Hint

The following cures presume that the team is successfully accomplishing its mission. If it isn't, you may still want to look at these cures, but you'll also want to look at other cases in this chapter that deal with less-than-satisfactory team performance.

Cures

If the team members haven't made the transition from being individual performers:

Did the team members receive any team training, particularly training in "team building"? If not, it's time to return to square one and see that everyone (yourself included) gets this training. It may also help to have a facilitator sit with the team for several sessions, to help members understand how they're reacting to one another and to learn new ways of cooperating.

If the team did get good training but still won't work together, look at one of the next two causes.

If the mission doesn't require them to work closely together:

What do you do? Is the mission getting done satisfactorily? If so, perhaps you don't need to do much. You probably want to encourage the team to help one another. Don't expect too much though, because they don't need to do this consistently to be successful.

Keep your eyes and ears open. Are other members of the team beginning to feel uncomfortable because they don't need and help one another? Then the team as a whole needs to confront the situation and explore options. Perhaps there is a mission the team could perform that requires the team to work together. Perhaps some kind of trade could be worked out with another team to get such a mission.

If members of the team are from different functions or have different statuses:

A team functions at peak effectiveness only when it needs every member to accomplish its mission. Begin to attack this problem by ensuring that this is the case with your team. If it's not, you have a sticky situation on your hands.

Do you discuss it with the whole team? If the team is mature, yes. See if the team is willing to be candid enough to discuss the problem openly. Perhaps it can reach a consensus on what member(s) could be reassigned to another team. Even better, perhaps it could reach a consensus on reassigning duties within the team so that everyone becomes an essential part of the action.

Suppose the team isn't ready to discuss the matter openly, or you find that individual team members don't believe the mission requires them to work with "those other people." If you believe that the team does need every member, do your best to help them understand why they need each other. You can help each individual explain to the team what he or she has to contribute, or have someone from higher management explain why each individual is necessary. Perhaps these individuals can give examples of decisions that were made without their input and the problems these caused. Whatever you do, your goal is to help everyone on the team value everyone else, no matter their background or pay level. It may take a while, but it can be done.

Team Strengthener

A team is a group of individuals who need one another to succeed. Think about that for a minute. In a true team, everyone needs everyone else. The job can't get done unless they work together. That's how you tell a team from a collection of individuals. And this is the critical point: If individuals can get the job done without working closely together, there's no advantage to their being on a team. Have you stopped to ask yourself how much members on your team need each other to get the team's job done? If not, perhaps you should.

5–8

The Problem
The team refuses to do anything about a nonperformer

The Scene

You've done your best to prime key members of the team, but every time the same thing happens. The team meets, goes through other business, and then you indirectly bring up the problem of Victor's performance. That's the cue for Tom or Frieda or Adele to confront Victor with how he let them down. But they never take the cue. Even when you ask, they duck the question. How in the world are you ever going to get the team to deal with Victor's poor performance?

Possible Causes

Team members like Victor and don't want to hurt him.

When other team members like someone, they often hesitate to be critical of him or her. They'd rather put up with the inconvenience of the individual's performance than run the risk of hurting his or her feelings. This is a carryover from traditional organizations, where criticism was almost always judgmental and painful and where only supervisors were supposed to criticize. And there's no way to force a team to confront a member.

The team doesn't know how to confront Victor.

This may lie at the root of the problem in the section above. The team is afraid it will hurt Victor's feelings because it doesn't understand how to confront him without judging or blaming him. It may have this fear no matter how it feels about Victor. Confronting a poor performer effectively is a real skill, similar to the skill of dealing with conflict. Some individuals develop these skills as they grow up; the rest of us have to learn them later.

The team is afraid it will lose control if it confronts Victor.

If a situation looks as if it may involve conflict, any team but a very mature one will fear losing control. What does this mean? It may mean the team is afraid that everyone will start shouting at everyone else and the meeting will break up with hard feelings and resentment. It may mean that people will pull back, making it hard for the team to work together in the future. Or it may mean any other outcome where the team can't keep itself from splitting apart and harming itself as a team.

Hint

We don't know anything about *why* Victor is performing so poorly. But that's not the issue. If the team had dealt with Victor's performance, it might have found out the why. But it is refusing to deal with his performance, and that—not the performance—is the problem.

Cures

If team members like Victor and don't want to hurt him:

Teams that haven't fully matured often act this way. Only taking the time and patience required to help a team mature will resolve problems like this one successfully.

What can you do in the short run? You're going to have to talk with Victor yourself. Do it as nonjudgmentally as possible, but don't duck the issue. If he hasn't been performing, he hasn't been performing. Give him every chance to explain his situation. Be constructive and offer to help wherever it's appropriate. Various cases in Chapter 4 may provide you with more ideas on how to deal with him.

If the team doesn't know how to confront Victor:

Perhaps the team is mature enough that with the help of a good facilitator it can deal with Victor's performance. If so, take this alternative. If this isn't a possibility, you may need to confront him (see the section above). Whatever means you choose, his performance must be made an issue and be resolved.

This deals with the immediate problem, but the deeper problem is the team's lack of skills at confrontation. If the team can do it with a facilitator, it's already on its way. If you had to do the confronting, the team needs development. Get appropriate training, have a facilitator work with the team to help it develop the skills, do whatever is necessary to see that the team doesn't shy away from unpleasant circumstances because it doesn't know how to deal with them.

If the team is afraid it will lose control if it confronts Victor:

What can you do about this? In the short run, not much. Once again, you may have to be the one who talks with Victor and takes responsibility for resolving the situation. But you also have to look for a longer-range solution. How can you help the team develop the confidence in itself that will help it risk losing control to confront and resolve a problem? The best answer, of course, is to encourage the team to confront simple disagreements or performance problems and then move to progressively more difficult situations. At the same time, you need to ensure that they are developing the cohesion that makes it possible for them to let go and deal with any situation constructively. If a good facilitator is available, he or she can help speed the process along.

Traditional organizations are built on control. Managers are expected to be in control at all times, and workers are expected to control themselves no matter what. Effective teams don't operate this way. Such teams don't attempt to control themselves or their members. Instead, they develop strong cohesion and become proficient at dealing with conflict. Instead of avoiding problems, they tackle them head on and work through them. Good training and a good facilitator can shorten the time it takes to reach this level of maturity. But only working together, actually tackling problems and solving them, will enable a team to reach this level.

Team Strengthener

No team should take responsibility for carrying nonperformers. The team may encourage them, help them, show them how to perform effectively, take any other steps to make sure they understand the situation and that the team supports their efforts to change. But the team must also insist that they change (if motivation, not capability, is the problem). It does this by ensuring that they understand what's expected of them, but not by hassling them, nagging them, or otherwise taking responsibility for their performance. Then if they don't (or can't) improve, the team needs to work with them to find another job for them—not to turn its collective head and ignore their performance. The basis of any effective team is the agreement that everyone will contribute, and every team needs to make and enforce this agreement.

5–9

The Problem
The team refuses to get feedback from its customers

The Scene

You begin this section of the meeting with: "Okay, last time, we talked about having a couple of meetings with our customers to see what they think of what we give them. Shall we do it?"

"Correction," Magdelena says. "Last time, *you* talked about meeting with them. As I recall, nobody else was very excited about it. I know I don't have the time to spend on more meetings."

"Me, too," Arnold chimes in. "I think we all have enough to do, don't we?" He looks around, and most of the rest of the team nods. "Besides, it's up to them to tell us if they don't like what we do." Again, most of the rest of the team nods.

That ends that, at least for now. You're convinced that the team would do a better job if it got feedback from its customers, but you certainly haven't convinced anyone else. Now what do you do?

Possible Causes

> *The team thinks it knows what its customers want.*

Traditional organizations seldom spend time worrying about direct feedback from customers, whether the customers are internal or external. (If this language isn't familiar, an internal customer is a unit in the organization that uses your work, while external customers are those to whom the organization provides products or services.) Everyone assumes that everyone else is happy unless someone gripes.

This can be worse in some occupations, particularly the professions. Engineers, systems analysts, training designers, and individuals in a host of other, similar occupations believe that they know what the customer "needs." So, they give it to the customer, without checking to see whether the customer agrees.

> *The team is convinced it doesn't have the time to spend meeting with customers.*

In today's highly competitive world, few teams have surplus time. In fact, workers and managers are lucky if they get to go home somewhere close to quitting time and then don't have to work once they get home. For most of us, there's always more work waiting to be done, just in case we catch up with what we're doing now.

The team doesn't understand how important customer feed-back is.

Perhaps the organization doesn't practice Total Quality Management (TQM) or have another program that emphasizes how important both internal and external customers are to the firm's success. Or perhaps it has a program but doesn't practice it.

Or perhaps, worst of all, it has an effective program but the team ignores it.

Cures

If the team thinks it knows what its customers want:

First, unless it's asked its customers, it's almost certainly wrong about what they want. That's true even if it asked them once but hasn't asked recently. The only organization that understands what its customers want is the one that stays close to them and keeps asking them.

So the problem is this: How do you change the team's mind? The most direct way is to have a customer representative meet with the team and explain what they need and how the team falls short of giving it to them. It's less effective, but having a customer put it in writing will accomplish the same basic goal.

Look at the third section of this case for more ideas.

If the team is convinced it doesn't have the time to spend meeting with customers:

This is one of the facts of life: All of us always have time for the important tasks. Time is a matter of priorities. If the team doesn't have time to talk with customers, it's because talking with customers isn't a priority.

Is the problem with the organization as a whole, because it doesn't have time to focus on customer needs? Is the problem the organizational unit the team works in? Or is it the team itself? What's the source of the belief that there's not time to listen to customers? Find that out first.

Then meet with the team and present the problem. You may want to have a customer representative explain how important it is to his or her organization for you to spend time with it. The how isn't that important; choose the most effective way to present the problem available to you. At this point you lead, push, and if necessary coerce the team to reevaluate its position and commit itself to getting customer feedback. It doesn't need to commit large blocks of time; it just needs to commit itself to start. Once it finds out how productive talking with customers is, the momentum will carry it from there.

Look at the next section for more ideas.

If the team doesn't understand how important customer feedback is:

Pardon me while I preach for a moment—and this is based on years of personal experience. You can't read books or articles about Total Quality Management (TQM) without learning how important customer feedback is. And your organization may have a formal TQM program. But until the good ideas get put into practice, they remain good intentions, and we know what road to what warm place is paved with those intentions. This is the simple fact: Nothing an organization does is more important than getting clear, honest, frequent feedback from its customers.

Why? If nothing else, high-quality feedback tells an organization, and a team, what it needs to concentrate on. The sixth case in this chapter explained how important continuous process improvement is and how it can enable a team to produce both higher quantity *and* higher quality. Customer feedback is the other part of this equation. If your team isn't getting constant customer feedback, it's probably wasting at least some of its time on aspects of the goods or services it produces that aren't important to the customer.

Don't count on customers to tell you when you're not satisfying them. If you don't make the effort to ask, they'll take what you give them. If it's not what they want, they'll complain about it all right, but not to you. They'll complain to friends, other organizations, and higher management. What do you think that does for your reputation in the organization? In short, if the team doesn't see how important customer feedback is, it's because it's never seen its results.

Now, what do you do? What's your standing with the team? The best alternative is this: Ask them to trust you enough to do one set of customer visits. The entire team doesn't need to go; two or three members (one of whom can be you) is enough. You can probably find another member or two who will squeeze in the time to go with you. (If you're not willing to go, by the way, that's the first problem you need to face and solve.) All it takes is one visit. If you ask the right questions, you'll come back with enough information and enthusiasm that the next visit will be a snap.

What if you can't get the support of the rest of the team? Find time and go by yourself. This is less effective than having other team members go with you, but if you have to do it, do it. Again, you'll probably come back with enough information to persuade at least part of the team to go on future visits. Then hope that the effect snowballs.

Team Strengthener

There is only one way to know if you're providing a product or service that satisfies your customers: Ask them. And don't ask them just once. Keep asking them. Use survey forms if that helps. But always use personal visits to them. You'll find out far more from customer visits than from even the best survey form. And, to anticipate the next case, pay attention to what your customers say. Adopt it if it makes sense. If you decide not to adopt it, call or write the customer who suggested it and explain why. Do this a few times and you'll find that it becomes the way you do business. And you'll wonder how you ever managed to do business any other way.

The Problem

The team refuses to accept feedback from its customers

The Scene

"I don't care what those turkeys think," Emile almost shouts. "We're giving them exactly what we're supposed to!"

"I agree," Saundra chimes in (she almost always agrees with Emile). "I don't know what in the world they're complaining about."

"Ah, don't pay attention to them," Vera adds. "They complain about everything. We couldn't satisfy them in a million years."

Well, so much for your idea of visiting customers. You talked two other members of the team into it, and the three of you got an earful. But the team won't listen. Now what do you do?

Possible Causes

The team "knows better" than its customers what they need.

If you've read the previous case, this should sound familiar (especially see the first cause in that case). For various reasons, individuals, teams, and organizations come to believe that they know exactly what their customers want, or should want, or need. That's what they give them. If customers complain about this, it's because they don't understand, or don't "appreciate" what the team has done.

The team doesn't want to change.

Teams, just like individuals, can get set in their ways. They find ways of working that are comfortable and successful, so they stick with them. Paying attention to customer feedback may conflict with these ways so they ignore it.

The team doesn't have a motive for using customer feedback.

People don't do something because they lack a reason for doing so or have positive reasons for not doing it. Knowing what's best for customers without asking them and not wanting to change are two reasons for not using customer feedback. Behind them, though, is an even more fundamental reason: There's no payoff to the team from seeking and using the feedback. Team members get their paychecks, get recognition (or not), and go home at night satisfied without the feedback. Why bother getting and using it?

Hint

It's a problem if the team doesn't want to get feedback, but it's a far more serious problem if they get feedback and refuse to use it. If a customer tells you why he or she isn't satisfied, you'd better do something about it or else.

Cures

If the team "knows better" than its customers what they need:

You may not be able to solve this one quickly. At least get the team to respond to the customer(s) and explain why it won't use the feedback. It may not want to do this—after all, it knows best—but this is the point where you put your foot down. Try to make it a response from the full team. If you can't, at least make the response yourself.

Part of the cure for this cause is in the next section of this case, so look at it. And if you can't get the team to change, look at the third section because that's probably the reason.

If the team simply doesn't want to change:

As important as it is to listen to customer feedback, not getting into a rut—or getting out of it—is just as important. Think of some new ways that the team can try (including using customer feedback). Then bring up one or two of the ways in a team meeting and try to get support for it. Lay out the situation as you see it before the team; you're advocating this not because you want it, but because the team needs it.

This won't work? Then consider a completely confrontational approach. Tell the team that unless it's willing to explore new alternatives you're going to recommend to higher management that it make switches among teams so that your team will end up with two or three new members. That may shake up the team enough to try something new. If it doesn't? Do exactly what you said you'd do.

No matter what, though, remember that the next section probably describes the core reason why you have the problem.

If the team doesn't have a motive for using customer feedback:

Part of the answer is in the previous case: Getting and using feedback makes the team's job easier in the long run. But what if you can't persuade the team of this? The ultimate answer belongs to the organization. As long as it ignores the need for feedback, it makes it easy for your team and others to ignore it. The organization itself needs a positive program that insists on *everyone* getting and using feedback; it needs to provide leadership by soliciting relevant feedback at every level; and it needs to insist that the policy is followed. So, if you can't persuade the team, start on higher management. If it isn't currently doing this, you need to agitate whenever and wherever you can to get the situation changed.

The bottom line is this: Your team will be far more successful if it constantly gets and uses feedback from its customers. Do whatever you have to do to persuade the team to do so.

Team Strengthener

You can suffer from too much data—inches and inches of computer printouts, for instance—but no one ever suffered from relevant feedback. The reverse is generally true: Most of us suffer from the lack of good feedback. (When was the last time a boss gave you really good information on just where your performance fell short and how you needed to improve it?) The problem is that most individuals, teams, and organizations don't realize this unless (1) their customers go somewhere else or (2) they actually get and use feedback. If nothing else works, try to find someone from another team or organization that regularly uses feedback and have this individual talk with your team.

5–11

The Problem
The turnover on the team is too high

The Scene

"I really like working on this team, but I just can't turn this opportunity down."

"Sure, none of us want to stand in your way. When do you have to leave?"

And so the conversation goes. Laurie is the third person to leave in the last three months, and Cara's replacement still hasn't been hired. The team is going to be spending more and more time training new members and integrating them into the team. This is disruptive.

Possible Causes

The team isn't such a good place to work.

When turnover goes up, especially if there's no clear reason, dissatisfaction with the team is the first place to look. Does the team have problems (such as those described in the last four chapters) that it hasn't dealt with? Is its mission unclear or unsatisfying? Does it have consistent problems with higher management?

(By the way, don't count on members who are leaving to give honest answers to the Human Resources Department about why they're leaving. Few of us want to burn bridges behind us; after all, we might have to return someday. If the team is close and effective, someone leaving may level with it, but if the team were close and effective, the individual probably wouldn't be leaving because it isn't a good place to work.)

The team has a great reputation.

This is the best reason in the world for high turnover. The team is so good that other parts of the organization, or even other organizations, can't wait to get their hands on its members.

This is part of the organization's high turnover rate.

For some reason the organization has a high turnover rate as a whole. Perhaps pay or working conditions aren't up to par; workers have to put in long and/or strange hours; the organization has a poor reputation in the community or a poor reputation for quality. Whatever, no matter how good your team is, the overall opinion of the organization rubs off on it.

Hint

When an individual leaves the team, the team should always ask him or her to recommend a replacement. If the person was a productive member of the team, the recommendation is normally the best place to start recruiting.

Cures

If the team isn't a good place to work:

Whenever anyone leaves, the team should ask why and listen carefully to the answer. It should take the answer seriously, but it also needs to evaluate its performance and look for reasons why someone would leave. This may be painful, and it may open up conflicts the team has been trying to keep covered. That's good. Remember, a team either stagnates or grows. This is an opportunity to seek growth. As you look for problems, you might scan the contents page of this book to see if anything sounds familiar. Then you can put that on the table to see if anyone else shares your view.

If the team has a great reputation:

You never try to stop this. Why? Because if individuals know that being an effective member of your team identifies them as an outstanding worker, they'll want to be part of the team. You'll get your pick of the cream of the crop whenever a vacancy occurs.

The team does need to get expert at training new team members and integrating them into the team. If the team hasn't worked on this, now is the time to begin. You already have one point in your favor: You're getting in talented, motivated people who positively want to be part of the team. That's half the training and integration solution right there. See the Team Strengthener at the end of this case for some further suggestions.

If this is part of the organization's high turnover rate:

You can't directly control any of this, but you can affect it. If the team develops a great reputation, it may both cut its turnover and draw talented individuals from less satisfying parts of the organization. It may be good enough that the next level of management can brag about it, which may influence how other parts of the organization work. And if the team is very good it may enhance its bargaining position to the point that it can get a better deal for itself.

Another reason for becoming as effective as possible: As you probably know, working in an unsatisfactory organization is frustrating. ("Well, what's the latest dumb idea from the front office?") The best antidote for this is a close, effective team where members support one another and go home at the end of the day with pride in their performance.

Team Strengthener

Training new members and integrating them quickly into the team is a key factor in maintaining a successful team. This is true even if turnover is relatively rare. The team should work out a clear process to bring in new members. Perhaps one member can be a mentor to the new person, explaining the ropes, what's expected, all the other "tips" that members need to know to succeed. The team might reduce some of this to writing, as a sort of manual. Or what about making a series of short videotapes, each on a particular topic, that the individual can use to learn the essentials? What you do is far less important than doing something positive to shorten the time it takes a new member to become a valued, productive member of the team.

5–12

The Problem
The team gets sidetracked instead of concentrating on its mission

The Scene

Ellen: OK, how're we coming on the project for Marketing?

Sara: We've got lots of time for that. Tom and I have been trying out a new format for our reports. We think it'll look a lot more professional.

Ellen: Do I dare ask what the situation is with our backlog?

Tip: Aw, don't worry. It's not getting any bigger and we can get it caught up next month without hurting anything. Right now, I want to revise the spreadsheet we're using to make it easier.

Jerel: And I want to get everyone's reaction. Which of these new fax formats do you think looks best?

When does the team take time to get its mission done? Or does it?

Possible Causes

The team doesn't have enough work to do.

Not having enough work to keep the team busy can cause a variety of problems as the team tries to find activities to occupy the free time.

The team doesn't care about its mission.

The team may believe no one cares about what it produces or that output is frequently revised, rewritten, or discarded. It's a lot less painful to find other tasks to work on.

The team is more creative than its mission requires.

Perhaps the assigned tasks are too routine and require little thought for the capabilities of the team. The members keep inventing tasks that are more interesting and challenging.

Cures

If the team doesn't have enough work to do:

No team should ever let itself remain without a full workload. Is it in a valley between two workload peaks? That's okay, if the valley is short. If the valleys are long and predictable, though, the team might be better off finding new work to do when times are slow. Valleys also provide excellent opportunities for teams to increase their skills, acquire new skills, and find new ways to serve customers. The team just needs to be sure that it uses its time wisely.

Perhaps the lack of work is more permanent. Case 1 in this chapter deals with this situation at length. Look at it for suggestions.

If the team doesn't really care about its mission:

The core ingredient for an effective team is a clear, compelling, and worthwhile mission. Without this, no team can sustain itself for long; it will start to fall apart in a hurry. When it does, its performance will plummet and the organization will begin to look on it as an ineffective and wasteful team.

If this is what's happening to your team, it needs to act quickly, before it disintegrates beyond recovery. Get the rest of the team together and discuss the problem. They may be happy with things the way they are. If so, push them. None of you can afford to be branded as poor or unmotivated performers. Keep pushing until the team is willing to deal with the situation.

Then the team goes looking for work. Case 5 in this chapter has some useful suggestions for how to do this, and Case 9–2 is devoted to this problem. However you approach the problem, just do so quickly and get it solved.

If the team is more creative than its mission requires:

This is a real problem, but it's the kind of problem you want to have. Don't try to solve it by dampening the creativity of the team and its members.

Can you help the team channel its creativity so that it keeps increasing its value to its customers? Time spent making a report look prettier is probably wasted, but not time spent finding out what customers want in the report and giving them more of that. Or perhaps even doing away with a formal report and handling it in a phone call. Or using e-mail. As long as everyone focuses on finding out what the customer needs and providing that more and more effectively, the work will be challenging and the team's creativity well used.

What about finding new products or services to provide to customers, or even finding new customers or new tasks the organization needs done (though may not yet realize it)? You've got all this creative power on the team—now you and the team need to see that it gets tightly focused on customers and then let loose.

What if the situation won't permit this? Don't settle for this answer until you've tried the ones above and run into a few walls. If you really can't use your creativity, it's time to go to higher management and explain how it is overlooking a major resource. Use the team's creativity when you do this. After all, when you've finished the presentation you want management to *know* that one of its highest priorities is finding work that uses the team's creativity.

Team Strengthener

It's not necessarily fatal when a team spends some time on projects not directly related to its mission, if the time is spent making its products or services more valuable to customers or finding new customers. If it spends time trying to make things easier for itself, fancying up its output without making it more useful, or just following interesting rabbit trails, the time is almost entirely wasted. An effective team concentrates its efforts on its customers. Satisfying your customers (and, most of the time, your boss) is what the game is all about.

5–13

The Problem

Different functions within the team won't work together

The Scene

"So much for multifunctional teams!" Carlo exclaims angrily. "At least when I was back in the old organization I didn't have to deal with those turkeys every day. One more fight and I'm going to ask my old boss to take me back and get me out of here!" With that he snaps the pencil he was holding, throws it into the trash, and stomps away.

Carlo is the most vocal person on your team, but you know he's not the only one who feels this way. Multifunctional teams were supposed to be a way to get the different functions to work together. Instead, they've produced unending arguments and bad feelings. You don't have long to fix the situation so how are you going to do it?

Possible Causes

The team's mission isn't clear, worthwhile, and demanding.

If a team's mission isn't clear, team members in different functions will quickly disagree on what they should be doing. If the mission isn't worthwhile, individuals aren't going to commit themselves to it strongly enough to make the team succeed. And if the mission isn't demanding, it's all too easy for team members to spend their time arguing instead of creating the result the team was designed to create.

The team doesn't need all the functions it has.

No matter how strong a team's mission is, if it doesn't need all of the individuals and (especially) all of the functions assigned to it the seeds are sown for trouble. The functional individuals who are needed wonder why those who aren't needed are there; they just get in the way of the people who have a job to do. And those who aren't needed continually try to find ways to be important and useful, which irritates the others even more.

Team members don't understand each others' functional perspectives.

Every different function in an organization speaks its own language, which makes it hard for other functions to understand what individuals in this function are saying. (After all, just what is "internal rate of return?") It's far more serious when different functions use the same language with different meanings. (When an accountant looks at a proposal and says it's fundamentally sound, does she mean what an engineer or contract specialist means with the same words? Not at all.) Both the jargon and the different meanings to the same phrases get in the way of different functions communicating.

Team members don't have an incentive to make the team succeed.

So often organizations fail to consider the many reasons individuals have for not committing themselves to a team and its mission. Perhaps their performance rating and salary increases are controlled by their formal supervisors. Perhaps, especially in the case of multifunctional teams, their careers lie in their specific function. Perhaps the organization and their functions have trained them to concentrate exclusively on their functional concerns and let higher management resolve the conflicts.

Hint

More and more organizations are using multifunctional teams, and some organizations are using them successfully. Many other organizations aren't. Why? Because it's extremely difficult to create teams in which individuals from different functions work together in ways that overcome their functional blinders. If you're in a multifunctional team, remember that no one said it was easy. But the payoff is tremendous if the team does it right.

Cures

If the team's mission isn't clear, worthwhile, and demanding:

Have you and the rest of the team analyzed the mission carefully? If not, it's time to do so because the mission is seriously getting in the way of the team functioning effectively as a team. Perhaps by looking closely at the mission, the different functions on the team will develop a consensus about the mission, one that will help them work together. Or they may develop a consensus that the mission really isn't worth their best efforts.

If the team reaches the second conclusion, it has work to do. It needs to develop a careful presentation to higher management explaining the situation. (*Tip:* Don't let any of the team stresses between functions show up in the presentation.) The presentation should include both a careful analysis *and* recommended solutions. If management agrees to assign you the new mission, ensure that all the members understand it and commit themselves to it. If management believes that the mission really is as it ought to be, ask them to meet with the team and communicate to it just what the mission is and why it's important to the team and the organization.

All the cases in Chapter 9 look at problems with team missions, and the first two cases examine problems with clarity, worth, and mission demand. You might want to look at them for suggestions on solving the basic problem.

One quick final note: Nothing will make lack of clarity, worth, and demand in a mission clearer than assigning it to a multifunctional team because it gives every function the excuse it needs not to cooperate with the others.

If the team doesn't need all the functions it has:

This one can get sticky. It may be that higher management has reasons to assign individuals whose functions aren't needed, so they may resist removing them. Here's where your powers of persuasion get tested, because they do need to remove them from the team and put them where they can make a real contribution. You may need to be persistent, but that's another virtue you might as well develop. Just keep at it until the necessary changes are made.

Far more likely, higher management believes that all the functions are necessary, but the individuals in some of the functions don't share this belief. The manufacturing representative on the team, for instance, may be quite sure he doesn't need any input from the quality control representative.

The next section has some specific suggestions that can be applied here. But this cause requires another action in addition to them. Representatives of management need to meet with the team and make it clear how they expect each function to contribute. If a manager from one function can present the case for why another function is required, so much the better.

If team members don't understand each others' functional perspectives:

You've something of a chicken-and-egg situation here. Individuals in different functions get to understand one another better when they work closely together. Unfortunately, they often don't want to work closely together because they don't understand one another.

The process takes time, but here's something you might try. Take a project, or part of a project, or part of the overall task. See that each team member reads and understands it. Then have each function in turn explain how it looks at that proposal, part, or task. Encourage everyone else to ask questions and challenge statements they don't understand. It will be a slow and often painful process, but it needs to occur. (As it happens, you may want to capture each function's main concerns on a flip chart.) At the end, the functions should be able to summarize their common concerns in ways that individuals on other functions can understand and accept. Keep creating and building on experiences like this until each team member begins to get an understanding and appreciation of what each other member can add. Then synergy will take over, if the mission is a good one, and you won't have to worry with the question often again.

If team members don't have enough incentive to make the team succeed:

The *why* doesn't matter as much as *what* can be done about it. To a certain extent, the team can create effective incentives: approval by team members, the challenge of the job, the prospect of recognition for success. Other cases in the book suggest that the team can continue to create these incentives and use them even if the organization doesn't provide real incentives for team success. When different functions make up the team, though, this is far more difficult. Do your best to build commitment within the team, but don't stop there.

Get the issue out on the table with all the team members and reach as strong a consensus as possible on the incentives the team needs. Then take these to higher management. Remember, as always, to cast them in terms of management's needs, not the team's. But make them clear, and make the consequences of not having them clear. And make the recommendations as specific and easy to implement as possible. Once again, persistence counts. Organizations don't change incentives easily, but they will change them when they see a clear benefit from the change.

Team Strengthener

Without a clear, worthwhile, compelling mission to which each individual is committed no team can succeed for long. (*Warning note:* New teams often seem very successful at first because the experience is new and exciting. But newness and excitement don't last long. When they die down, only a strong mission supported by strong individual commitments can carry a team.) Whenever a team isn't "jelling," it needs to review its mission carefully and then review just as carefully—and honestly—everyone's commitment to the mission. Get these two factors in place and the team will do whatever it must to be successful.

5–14

The Problem
The team functions poorly because members have different statuses

The Scene

"What do you think, Marie?" Brady asks.

"Yes—I'd like to know, too," Angel chimes in.

"I'd really like to hear what you think first," Marie replies. "After all, you know the accounts receivable process even better than I do."

"Maybe—but you're an accountant," Becky adds. "You know more about the entire system than we do. We need to start with your best ideas."

You've been holding back and not interfering with the team. But it keeps happening: Everyone defers to Marie, just because she's an accountant. She's very intelligent, but the bookkeepers and clerks on the team know more about the details of the system than she does. Despite that, they all look to Marie for answers. The whole purpose of the team is to enable everyone to share his or her expertise. Marie's team says she's willing to listen to the others, but they don't take her up on it. If something doesn't happen soon, there's going to be no point in having the team.

Possible Causes

The team is new and still reacting to statuses instead of individuals.

It takes time for teams to jell, particularly when the individuals on them have different statuses in the organization. In the example, Marie is an accountant, while the others are bookkeepers and accounting clerks, with much lower status. But the same could happen with sales teams (combining a salesperson with assistants and clerks), medical teams (with a physician, nurses, and various technicians and assistants), and a variety of other teams. Everyone expects to defer to the high-status people because that's what they did before they became part of a team.

Team members don't understand how they're expected to perform.

This may or may not be related to the first cause. Perhaps no one really explained to the team members how life is different in a closely knit team. So everyone goes on deferring to status as they always have because they believe it's still what's expected of them.

Marie doesn't pay attention to the others' opinions.

Don't ever assume that individuals with high status *want* to be on teams with individuals from lower-status occupations. Often they don't. They may see it as diluting their importance by giving individuals with less education or lower skills the same status that they worked so hard to get. When this is the way they see the team, you can be almost certain that they will resist becoming an "equal" member of it.

The job doesn't require a team.

No wonder the team isn't working—it violates the first rule of teaming. *If work can be done by individuals and doesn't require a team, don't create a team.* Teams that perform work individuals could do independently are predictably less efficient and effective and can be counted on to have significant internal problems.

Cures

If the team is new and still reacting to statuses instead of individuals:

How likely is it that the team will stop reacting to statuses? Surprisingly likely, if the team really begins to think and act as a team and receives continuing guidance on why everyone is working together this way. No nursing assistant will ever overrule a doctor, but if there's a real team the doctor will listen carefully when the assistant talks about a particular patient's unusual behavior or a nurse describes the effect of the latest treatment. In short, even members of a team with large status differences can develop a balance and mutual respect for one another that's virtually impossible in a traditional work situation.

How do you encourage this? In part, it just takes time. The team needs to work together long enough to get to know one another and to develop trust in one another. You can help the process, of course, by helping the team work through early conflicts and encouraging everyone to listen honestly to everyone else. And you can help by noticing and recognizing each action that reflects understanding of team roles. As in so many cases, a skilled facilitator will also help if his or her skills include working with teams that have significant status differences.

If team members don't understand how they're expected to perform:

You can help team members begin to understand their new roles, as can an experienced facilitator. Probably, though, you need to take another step first. Get someone from higher management who understands how teams should work to talk with the team. He or she can make clear the expectations that the organization has for team members. Even better, get managers representing each of the functions and let them explain together how the team should operate. (This assumes that higher management has its act together and that managers are clear on the issue. You need to check this out before you invite managers in, because your organization may not have made it clear to its managers what to expect from teams.)

You can also help from day to day by recognizing and encouraging any behavior that begins to reflect the new roles. Perhaps the engineer on the team genuinely listens to a suggestion from a technician, or the salesperson makes a suggestion to an assistant and genuinely asks for his reaction. Every time that something like this happens be sure to notice it and point out how it embodies what's needed in the team.

If Marie doesn't pay attention to the others' opinions:

Having a higher manager who understands the status differences talk with Marie may help, but don't count on achieving too much that way. After all, the higher-level manager may feel the same way as the team member. What higher management can do is to make clear that teams are permanent—if they genuinely are!—and that everyone needs to adapt to that reality. Even a long-time hardhead may begin to change if he or she sees clear handwriting on the wall.

Your best bet, however, is to work within the team. Marie and her counterparts on other teams will begin to change if they see real advantages from working as part of a team. Suppose, for instance, that one of the assistants shows Marie how a particular procedure slows down the reconciliation process and how the process can be speeded up. That means Marie can get reports out more quickly, a real benefit to her. Just keep looking for occasions when other team members contribute something of real value to higher status members, then make sure that everyone recognizes the worth of this. Don't expect quick results. But hang in there, no matter how bad things seem at first. When they see the value for themselves in the change, people can change remarkably.

If the job doesn't require a team:

What do you need to do to get higher management to recognize this? If they're willing to consider abolishing the team, have the team analyze the situation and get its facts together. If there's a consensus that the team structure adds nothing, develop and make a presentation to higher management. The first presentation may not succeed, so persevere. After several attempts, management may begin to listen and reevaluate its strategy.

But there's another alternative. You can try to change the team's mission so that it does require everyone on the team to accomplish. You and the team may be forced to this alternative because higher management won't listen to abolishing the team. Even if higher management won't go along with shrinking the team, you and the other members of team may decide you'd really like to remain together and work out a way to do so.

Team Strengthener

In many cases, this book recommends dealing "straight on" with problems. That's an effective way and the one that works best with a variety of problems. It's not the only strategy, though, and the first three sections of this case suggested a different one: noticing each time individuals begin to practice behaviors that are useful for teaming and recognizing them for it. ("Brady, I really appreciate your listening so carefully to Angel even when you didn't agree with him." "Marie, you were very helpful to Becky when she was trying to express her problem with the current process.") You can also encourage team members to recognize instances like this, and to show their appreciation when someone treats them in an appropriate way. ("Angel, I really appreciate your asking me to clarify what I said about problems with the system.") Organizational recognition programs seldom accomplish anything. Teams whose members informally acknowledge and appreciate one another can accomplish amazing feats.

The Problem

The team wants to ignore its next-level manager

The Scene

"Look, we have a job to do!" Mac exclaims. "If we try to do it Mr. Marvin's way we'll never get it done."

"Mac, we just can't ignore what he wants us to do. He is our boss."

"Yeah, and if we keep doing things the way he wants we won't be a team much longer."

Several other team members nod in agreement.

Things have gotten serious. The team has been frustrated with Mr. Marvin, but never to the point of ignoring him. This is about to become a crisis.

Possible Causes

The team is taking its autonomy too seriously.

The team believes that being self-managing means that it doesn't have to take direction from anyone. The organization has never intended that.

Mr. Marvin neither likes nor supports the team.

No one asked Mr. Marvin whether he wanted to manage teams; he may have been strongly opposed to teams from the beginning. Now he has to manage a team.

He doesn't understand the team's mission.

The team includes members from several different functions performing a mission that requires all the functions. Mr. Marvin doesn't understand either the mission or the work of the other functions. And if he's not fond of teams, he may not care to learn. If on top of that he attempts to supervise the team in a traditional manner, he creates a really touchy situation.

Cures

If the team is taking its autonomy too seriously:

You must help the team accomplish two goals. First, it needs to understand that it doesn't have unlimited freedom. Among other things, it still has a boss, and it cannot ignore him. Can you get someone in higher management who understands how teams are supposed to operate to talk with the team? If so, you might invite Mr. Marvin to sit in. That way, he and the team would have a shared understanding of how the team should operate.

At the same time, you must help the members of the team avoid being discouraged. They'll almost certainly feel disappointed when they fnd that they don't have the autonomy they expected. They may also be angry and feel that they've been misled. Don't try to stop them from being emotional, but help them work through their feelings to understand and appreciate the amount of autonomy they do have. Also help them understand that if they use the freedom they have to perform effectively, they can almost certainly increase their autonomy.

If Mr. Marvin neither likes nor supports the team:

There may be a genuine survival issue here; Mr. Marvin may be quite willing to see the team fail. It may be even more important in this circumstance than in the one above to get someone from higher management to talk to the team, with Mr. Marvin there. If the team is savvy enough and asks the right questions, it can alert higher management to the problem and ensure that Mr. Marvin at least hears what the organization's intent is with the team present.

The team also needs actively to attempt to change Mr. Marvin's opinion of itself and of teams in general. It should do its job well and make sure that he knows it's doing well. It should understand his priorities and pay attention to them. Above all, it should try to make him look good without giving up any of its autonomy. Not easy, but not impossible either.

If Mr. Marvin doesn't understand the team's mission:

First of all, the team must try to keep Mr. Marvin continually involved. It doesn't give up any of its autonomy, but it does try to get him to sit in on its presentation and perhaps even on a few team meetings. This may help him understand the team's mission and performance better and be able to work with it more effectively. Or he may realize that he doesn't understand it and may let the team have more autonomy.

The team should also check to see if other teams are having the same problem. If so, the teams need to get together and prepare a presentation explaining the situation and recommending alternatives. Then, if possible, they need to get the next-level managers of the teams involved together and make the presentation to them. The better they and the organization understand the problem, the more realistic everyone can be in dealing with it.

Team Strengthener

A multifunctional team can operate most successfully when it reports to an individual with strong project management skills. What are these? They include the ability to get different functions to work together, to set realistic milestones for everyone, and to manage in terms of goals and objectives rather than day-to-day supervision. If your team is multifunctional, it should work however it can to see that the organization provides it with this kind of next-level manager.

5–16

The Problem

Team members are discouraged and performance has begun to decline because there is little career progression

The Scene

"Boy, this is the pits!" Marlene exclaims. "Human Resources just showed me the so-called career paths in the organization, and there just about aren't any. Back in my old job the work may not have been much fun but at least I could look forward to being a lead worker and then probably a supervisor and maybe a unit manager. None of those jobs even exist any more!"

You just found out a few days ago how limited are the chances for career advancement, and you've been trying to decide when to bring it up to the team. Well, it looks like Marlene just made the decision for you.

Possible Cause

We don't need to speculate on the cause; it's very straightforward. When organizations implement teams, they make part of their cost savings by cutting out the kinds of jobs Marlene is talking about. Career ladders collapse to virtually nothing, especially if there are no fixed team leader positions.

Cures

There is no cure for the lack of career progression itself, or at least no one has found a cure yet. But there are steps that teams and their members can take to develop alternatives.

Decide whether the satisfaction of working on a self-managing team is worth the lack of career steps:

In organizations that have true self-managing teams, many individuals get enough satisfaction from working as part of a team that they willingly forgo a shot at a higher-level position. But not all. Each individual must decide for himself or herself, but it will help to have a team discussion where everyone can contribute his or her ideas. If the team is mature enough, it will also help if each member shares with the others what his or her decision is so that everyone can be as helpful as possible to everyone else.

Help each member who remains on the team become expert at his or her tasks:

This should happen in the normal course of events, but the team can make sure that it happens. The team should organize to use the highest level of skills that each member has.

Help each member of the team develop strong leadership skills, particularly project management skills:

Developing and using leadership skills is satisfying on its own and is excellent preparation for any higher-level positions that do open. In particular, the team should help each member learn project management skills since it appears that these will be among the most valuable management skills for the next decade or two.

Help each member of the team learn at least the basics of as many other members' jobs as is feasible:

If the team is working under very tight time constraints, this may be difficult. Even then, it may still be possible. The more each member knows about the job of each other member, the more effectively the team will function, so everyone, including the organization, will get a payoff.

Help each member of the team get the training required to accomplish each of these goals:

Again, this depends somewhat on the time available to the team for training. Fortunately, most team-based organizations allow for significant amounts of training. Consult the organization's training department to find out what the training policy is.

Team Strengthener

Does the satisfaction of working as part of an effective team offset the lack of career progression? Each individual needs to decide for himself or herself. The team will be most effective if it recognizes the right of each member to make the decision and then supports the decision. That way, the individuals who remain on the team are there because they want to be, and that strengthens the team.

The Problem
The team wants to give up

The Scene

You walk into the meeting, expecting to discuss the team's progress on the latest project. Instead, before you even sit down, Jeff speaks up.

"We met a little early because we wanted to discuss something. We all agree that we should just give up on this team stuff. It just isn't worth it. Right?" He looks around at the other team members, who all nod.

"I'm sorry we didn't have you in the meeting," he continued, looking genuinely sorry—"but we knew you'd do your best to talk us out of it."

And you would have. You know the team has been under a lot of stress, but you hadn't realized that it had reached this point. What now?

Possible Causes

The team is new and not used to the stress of being self-managing:

Team members find themselves having to plan and take responsibility as they never did before. Because no one seems to be helping or supporting them, they don't believe they can handle the stress, or they simply may not want to handle it.

The team's workload has grown to the point that the team can't handle it:

Perhaps they can't get the work done, or perhaps they feel they can't get it done with sufficient quality.

No one seems to care about them or their work:

They can't see putting up with the stress of being a self-managing team when neither they nor their outputs seem to matter to anyone.

Cures

If the team is new and not used to the stress of being self-managing:

Here, your task is simple: Get the team past this and back at work learning how to be a team. It won't be easy; they've already indicated that they don't want to be talked out of their decision. But you must do it. Will it help to ask them to set a realistic time by which they will either change their minds or you will work with them to disband the team?

Have they really not been getting the support they need? They may have, but have been expecting the different kind of support and supervision they got on their previous job. You can help them understand how support is different for teams. But what if they've gotten poor support—little training, an unclear mission, no feedback from customers? You take their part and talk with your next-level manager and anyone else you must. If the organization intends this to be a self-managing team, it needs to support it properly.

If the team's workload has grown to the point that the team can't handle it:

As organizations continue to "rightsize," the people who do the work must do more and more of it. How do you help the team deal with that situation? You begin by trying to get them to express and then get past their frustration. Now you help them to analyze their situation. Is it really too much work, or just more work than they're accustomed to? And can they do the work but get frustrated by what they see as the low quality of their products? You and they need to find the most exact answers you can to these questions and others like them. Then you need to take them to your next-level manager and enlist his or her support.

You can find suggestions to help you with this problem in Cases 5–1, 5–3, and 5–6.

If no one seems to care about them or their work:

No wonder they want to call it quits! Your first task is to find out whether in fact this is true. Who uses the team's output, and how do they use it? Does it really matter? Find out the answers to these questions as quickly as possible.

Suppose the organization uses what the team produces and the team's customers think it's quite important. Get someone from the customer team or organization to meet quickly with the team and explain how important the team's outputs are. That should boost the team's morale significantly.

But that's not enough, even if the team's outputs are highly valued. Why didn't the team know this? Obviously the team either didn't get feedback or didn't use it. Look at Cases 5–9, 5–10, and 9–7 for specific suggestions and use them.

That leaves the final alternative—no one really does care about the team's output. Perhaps it makes sense for the team to go out of business, particularly if they haven't jelled into a team yet. What if they'd like to remain a team, despite what they said? Then the team gets all the facts together and makes a presentation to higher management. Remember to focus on the payoff of what you recommend to higher management, not just to the team.

Team Strengthener

Nothing will demoralize any of us faster than the belief that no one cares about us or what we produce. If a team begins to think it's in that situation, it needs to act quickly to determine the facts. If it and its outputs aren't valued, it needs to deal with the situation before it gets as serious as the problem described in this case. The same holds true even when the team has doubts only about part of its output. Don't waste time producing results that aren't valued—period.

The Problem
The team wants to split into two teams

The Scene

"I think the time has come to face reality," Imogene says firmly. "We need to split into two teams. I like to talk, but with seventeen people on the team either I have to rein myself in or someone else doesn't get a chance to talk."

"I have to agree with you," Lin says, nodding. "There's no way we can be a real team with this many people. As much as I like all of you—and I really do—it just isn't working."

The discussion continues, with everyone agreeing. Clearly, the team needs to do something.

Possible Causes

There might be any number of superficial causes, such as the team splitting into cliques or the same few people working projects each time. These are symptoms, though. In fact, seventeen people cannot function as a single team. It will find that the same small group of individuals do most of the talking and provide most of the leadership. A team of five to eight people is a good size. Even as many as ten people can function as a team if they see themselves as a team and look out for one another. But more people than that will virtually never act as a real team. In other words, Imogene and her teammates are right. But there is more than one way to solve the problem.

Cures

Make regular use of subteams, varying the membership on these teams:

While dividing into two teams may be an acceptable alternative, it requires the organization's okay. Can the team accomplish much the same goal by dividing the work among several subteams? If the team has a great deal of project work, the team could set up a different subteam for each project, always making sure to give different members the chance to work together on different subteams. Even if your duties are set, nothing says that team members can't switch among subteams periodically. (This could be an excellent way to accomplish some of the goals of Case 5–16.) Using subteams also provides broad experience in leadership, as well as giving members of the subteams experience in working closely with one another.

If you rely on subteams, be sure to get everyone in the overall team together regularly. Subteams can report on their projects; subteams with related projects might want to meet together for a while to compare notes. A social occasion can also help the team as a whole restore their cohesiveness. If the team decides to remain an overall team, it needs to ensure that it has periodic rituals to remind everyone that they are first of all part of that team.

Keep the single team structure but divide it into to semi-permanent subteams:

This constitutes a sort of halfway solution. If the mission can be divided in two without great difficulty, having two more or less permanent subteams can provide an answer to the problem.

Don't lose the advantage of the larger team, though. Have meetings between the two subteams periodically so they can keep up with one another. More important, have team members move constantly from one subteam to another. This keeps individual interest up, helps broaden experience and skills, and reinforces the sense of the larger team.

Ask management to let the team divide into two teams:

Asking to split into two teams has two drawbacks. First, it requires approval from management, and its interest in the matter may be very different from that of the team. Second, it breaks up the team. Regardless of what members may say to one another, the sense of the larger team will vanish quickly.

Don't hesitate to pursue this course, though, if neither of the first two solutions will work. The team needs to prepare its case carefully, separate the missions of the two teams clearly, and demonstrate the benefits the action will have for the organization. And it needs to spell out the problems for effective team organization and performance.

Team Strengthener

Calling a group of people a team doesn't make them one. A team is a group of people who need one another to accomplish a task or a goal and one that is small enough that all of the members can work closely with one another *and* have a chance to contribute. When someone creates a team with more than ten members, these conditions aren't apt to be true. Be prepared. Help reduce the size of the team if possible. If not, start thinking about how the team can be organized to work through subteams.

5–19

The Problem
The team keeps violating its norms

The Scene

"Gen, let Peter say what he needs to say. We all agreed when we first started that we'd give everyone whatever time they needed to get their point across. Now we've started hurrying people and even cutting them off."

"I know we made that a norm, but it just isn't realistic. It sounded good back then, but we didn't really understand being a team very well. Now we understand—and you know as well as I do that norm doesn't work."

Gen and Del continue their discussion, joined by Peter and several other team members. Because feelings are starting to run high, you redirect the discussion back to the original topic. But there isn't much question that you and the team need to do something.

Possible Causes

It doesn't matter in this case what has caused the team to violate this norm—and perhaps others. The problem is that they are systematically violating them. Whether a new team goes through the forming-norming-storming-performing process or not, it needs to develop and follow its norms.

Cures

A team never outgrows its need for team norms:

All continuing groups and organizations have norms. They help the group structure itself to perform effectively. They also help provide predictability in team interactions. When a team begins to ignore norm, no matter how important the reason seems for doing so, it begins to introduce confusion into its interactions. ("Hey, are we doing this or not?") Unless the situation is faced and resolved, team performance begins to suffer.

The team needs to review and update its norms regularly:

Most team norms are developed in the first week or so of the team's life. They're largely realistic then, but both the team and its situation change. If the team doesn't pay attention to growing conflicts between the norm and its situation, it can easily end up where the team in the example ended.

The team doesn't have to review the norms regularly, but it may be an excellent idea. How often? Probably quarterly unless the situation is very stable. If reviews aren't done regularly, the team has to depend on an individual raising the conflict, which many team members may hesitate to do.

The team should always respond when a member says that a member is violating a norm:

Whether the team regularly reviews its norms or not, one of its clear norms should be that any member can point out a conflict between a norm and the team's actual behavior at any time. If this norm isn't enforced, members will be tempted to let the conflict slide—and thus it will become that much harder to resolve.

When a member points out a conflict and practice, the team needs to respond to the comment immediately. Normally, it should agree to abide by the norm then and schedule a discussion of it for as soon thereafter as possible.

The team should be particularly careful about norms that prevent the team from "steamrolling" an individual or small group with the team:

Team members depend on norms for structure and predictability. But they also depend on many of them to preserve the integrity of the team and its processes. Giving everyone the right to be fully heard, to be respected, and to disagree helps ensure that a full range of ideas are explored.

In the short run, this kind of norm seems to interfere with the team's effectiveness. So it takes continuing team discipline to stick with the norms. As team leader, it's your responsibility to see that the team sticks with these norms and deals immediately with any conflict between them and practice.

Team Strengthener

We think of democracy primarily as a political system. It is, of course, but even more basically it's a set of principles that any group can use to help it accomplish the goals of its members. An effective self-managing team represents democracy in action, so its norms need to reflect basic democratic principles.

CHAPTER 6

Problems With Individual and Team Work Practices

How individuals and teams perform their work forms a critical aspect of how well the team functions. In one sense this is no different from traditional workgroups, which have the same problems. Since team members work so closely together, though, effective individual and team work practices become even more important.

The ten cases in this chapter illustrate common problems that teams encounter with work practices. The team may be too adventurous in using untested practices or it may be relectant to try unproven procedures. If you're familiar with Quality programs, you recognize these as problems.

Teams and the individuals on them may have as much trouble with change as traditional workgroups. The first four cases deal specifically with individual and team change. Between the four cases, you will find most of the issues involved in trying to create change. Read carefully, though, because individual and team reasons for resisting change aren't always bad.

Whatever the problem, the cases delve into the causes and recommend specific solutions that you and your team can apply. As you examine the causes and then find ways to deal with them, the team will become more flexible and open to different ways of accomplishing its goals. And this flexibility, after all, is one of the basic reasons why organizations use teams in the first place.

The Problem
A team member refuses to use new technology

The Scene

"Carmine, I've tried the new software out. Believe me, you can keep track of your customer contact in no time with it."

"Rosie, I know that kind of stuff works for you. But I've been using my Rolodex™ for 20 years and I've got it down pat. I don't need anything new. Just let me be and let me do it my way."

And that's where the conversation ends. Everybody on the team is either using the new software or trying it out—everybody except Carmine. He hasn't tried anything new since the team was formed. There must be something the team can do about it.

Possible Causes

Carmine's systems work fine for him.

Organizations, teams, and individuals may adopt a new technology simply because it's new and exciting. This isn't a good strategy, because it separates the technology from getting the mission done. In this circumstance, the new customer-contact software may not be much of an improvement. Carmine may spend more time learning to use it than he saves once he's mastered it.

Carmine is afraid of computers.

The fact that an organization or team puts a computer on someone's desk doesn't mean that the individual either wants to use it or knows how to use it. Carmine may be completely baffled by it. Even worse, he may be afraid that if he tries to use it he'll break it. (Don't laugh—this is a common fear.) Whether the software works or not isn't the question; he hasn't gotten that far.

Carmine is "set in his ways."

In traditional organizations, individual workers may perform the same basic job for ten, twenty, thirty years. In fact, that's what he or she may be expected to do. If you're a normal, intelligent human being, you burn out on this quickly. So what do you do? You turn it into a routine, do it, and spend your attention and energy on something else. That may be what Carmine has learned to do.

Cures

If Carmine's systems work fine for him:

What do you do? Nothing for the moment. Let Carmine continue to use his manual system, even if everyone else on the team is using the new software. If the software provides that much of an advantage, Carmine may decide to learn and use it himself. If not, let him be for a while.

When do you stop letting him be? If his manual system enables him to keep up and provide what the team needs, he can keep using it as long as he wants. But if his system begins to interfere with other members of the team, or if it's significantly slower, the time has come to act. Look at the last section of this case for specific suggestions.

If Carmine is afraid of computers:

This problem has a simple solution: some effective training. It should begin with training on how to operate a personal computer. If a course on how to use the software is available, ask Carmine to attend it also. Whether it is or not, have a member of the team experienced with the computer and the software work with Carmine and show him how to use the software effectively. This individual can show Carmine how to take what he's familiar with and translate it to the new program so that he can make the transition with the smallest possible disruption.

Do this sensitively. Carmine may have all kinds of fears and misgivings. Though computers and their software are often poorly designed for people, we tend to blame ourselves when we can't use them effectively. Carmine may feel stupid, particularly if the rest of the team is competent with computers. Take it easy; support him every step of the way. If another team member has gone through the same kind of trauma, you might have him or her work with Carmine.

If Carmine is "set in his ways":

This much is sure: You cannot force Carmine to change. In fact, the more you push, the more he will resist changing. So, what do you and the team do? You let him perform as he wants to perform, as long as he contributes fully to the team. If his manual system is really slower than the computerized one, don't attack his system as such but keep the pressure on for him to perform as effectively as everyone else.

What will happen? He may hunker down, get more defensive, and cause the team an even more serious problem. But it's more likely that he will start to see the potential of the new system and become curious about it. Then he may be willing to learn a little about it. If it really is better and if Carmine really is the kind of person who ought to be on your team, he will gradually come around and begin to explore the new system. Remember, the key is not to push him to use the system but to push him to keep contributing to the team.

Team Strengthener

Don't *ever* assume that because someone is opposed to new ideas that he or she will remain that way. This sells people short. People do change, and sometimes they change dramatically. I've seen it, and if you've been around very long and kept your eyes open you've seen it. *Don't ever treat people as though they will never change,* period. This locks them in and makes it almost impossible for them to change even when they want to. If someone doesn't want to change now, just take it as that: he or she doesn't want to change now. Tomorrow, next week, next month, or next year—well, wait until then before drawing any final conclusions.

The Problem

A team member refuses to consider new ways of working

The Scene

"Hey, Ella, it's time for the training session on continuous process improvement."

"You guys go ahead. I'm going to sit and handle this pile of paper. You can tell me all about it."

"It's not at all like being there. You know how important the Quality program is."

"Yeah, sure—just like the past dozen hot programs we've gone through. You get as enthusiastic as you want. Me, I'm going to keep on doing what I've always done."

Possible Causes

Ella sees no benefit for herself in the new program.

Organizations constantly come up with new programs that they believe will benefit the organization and, often, its workers. But then they often fail to communicate, or perhaps even consider what the payoff is for the individual worker—the person who actually has to work differently. So how does the worker react? Like you and me, she's reluctant to put the effort into a change that doesn't offer her a benefit.

Ella doesn't believe the new program will succeed.

This gets to the heart of why so many workers (and managers, too, for that matter) won't support new programs. They've seen programs like the new program hyped in the past, then discarded to make way for the new "flavor of the month." American organizations waste millions of dollars and millions of hours of time each year adopting fashionable programs that don't produce a useful payoff.

Ella has been burned when she supported programs like this in the past.

In the long run, the cynicism that "flavors of the month" create does far more damage than the time and money they waste. Many workers—perhaps most of us—begin with enthusiasm and the desire to learn and perform well. A new program comes along that promises to help us learn new and better ways. So we commit ourselves to the new program, put in extra time learning it, get excited by it, and then the company abandons it and goes on to something else. How does it feel when this happens? If it happened a few times to Ella, how do you think she feels about it? Besides her intellectual reason for ignoring new programs (they won't work), she has a strong emotional reason (I don't intend to make a fool of myself again).

Hint

The last section of the case before this one dealt with the situation where a worker refused to change simply because he was "set in his ways." You might want to look quickly at that section before reading this case, which explores some of the reasons *why* people get set in their ways. While individuals differ tremendously in their tolerance for change, few people simply reject change unless they've learned that it's a realistic strategy to do so.

Cures

If Ella sees no benefit for herself in the new program:

How do you change Ella's reluctance to look at the new program? Basically, you and the rest of the team need to show her how the change will benefit her. Will it make work easier? More interesting or satisfying? More efficient, so you can do more of it with the same effort? Might it help her develop useful new skills? She'll most likely change, or at least consider the new program, if she sees this kind of benefit for herself and the team.

What if you can't find benefits for her and the team? Then it's time to talk to higher management and try to discover them.

After all, you don't want to waste your time any more than Ella does.

If Ella doesn't believe the new program will succeed:

Start with the suggestions in the section above. If possible, show her not only that the program will benefit her but that it will likely succeed.

But suppose not only that Ella isn't convinced, but that she seems to be right and this appears to be just another passing fad? Do you join her in attempting to ignore the program? Let me get practical here. Take two steps. First, do the minimum necessary to outwardly support the program, and persuade Ella to do the same. Why? Because you don't want the team to get a reputation for "fighting progress" or even being stuck in its ways. Then, learn about the program and identify any parts of it that the team can use. There will almost certainly be something useful in it. Concentrate on these useful parts and implement them. And look at the next two cases for some more suggestions.

If Ella has been burned when she supported programs like this in the past:

Don't try to hype the program with Ella. She probably won't believe you. If she does, tries the program, and then it fails, she'll be even more hurt and cynical. Your only chance of success is complete honesty.

Look to find any benefits in the program that the team can use, even if the program vanishes. Look hard. Your goal is to make the program work for Ella, the team, and you—whether it works for the organization as a whole or not. Then help Ella see that she doesn't have to commit to the overall program, just to the parts of it that work for her and the team. If she sees that you are taking her concerns into account, she'll probably be willing to give these parts a try.

Team Strengthener

This case contains a critical insight. You aren't responsible for supporting a new program just because it's new and flashy.

But you and your team are responsible for finding how you can make the program pay off for you. Perhaps the program as a whole has benefits for you. Perhaps there are no more than one or two aspects of the program that will make a difference. Fine—concentrate on them. If you have to produce the outward appearances of supporting the program, do so, but take the minimum amount of time. Focus on the parts that the team can use to improve its operation. Then, no matter what happens to the program in the organization, your team will be more effective than it was before.

6–3

The Problem
The team refuses to use new technology

The Scene

You wait until the pressing business is over and then bring up your discovery. "Hey, I just heard about a really sharp new customer contact program that will make the whole process a lot easier and faster than it is now. And the company will pay for it."

John answers, "I know that kind of stuff works for some people. But I think the system we're using now works fine, and we've got it down pat. We don't need anything new."

You look around, to see most of the rest of the team nodding in agreement. Once again, the team's turning down the chance to use new technology that could help get the job done. There must be some way to get it to change.

Possible Causes

The team is having too much technology pushed at it.

Technology can be immensely helpful to teams. In fact, most self-managing teams need effective technology to be effective themselves. But not all technology helps. More important, even when new technology would help, people can only assimilate so much at one time. They have to learn the current technology fully and be comfortable with it before they can assimilate new technology. If a team has to spend time constantly learning new technology, it can quickly get burned out on technology in general.

The team doesn't see the benefit of computers.

Too many of us started work in traditional organizations that had traditional data-processing systems, very rigid systems that were user-hostile, took up tremendous amounts of time, and often produced few if any results that were useful. Unfortunately, many organizations still have these "legacy" systems, and this is what workers think of when they think of computers. (The first few cases in Chapter 11 deal in depth with some of the problems caused by these systems.)

The team hasn't had to change lately.

Teams, like individuals, can stagnate. The first few chapters of the book have stressed how important it is for teams to continue to grow and not let themselves get too comfortable with the current way of doing things. This approach is just as important where technology is concerned as it is anywhere else. In today's rapidly changing world, a team that isn't changing to keep up is making itself obsolete. Neither you nor the team want that.

Hint

This case parallels the first case in this chapter. That one concerned an individual who didn't want to use new technology. In this one, the entire team is avoiding the technology. This case takes a somewhat different approach, so you may also want to look at the first case for ideas that can be applied to this problem.

Cures

If the team is having too much technology pushed at it:

The short-term cure is simple: See that you and/or the organization stop pushing technology so hard at the team. Concentrate instead on fully understanding the technology already in place and getting the most from it. Then start looking, very carefully, for the next step: a technology with a clear payoff for the team.

Of course, if the push is coming from higher levels in the organization you can't control it by yourself. That's when your team and perhaps several other teams need to talk to higher management and explain the situation. Be careful; you want to be clear that you're not opposed to new technology, just to so much of it so quickly.

One more thought. Perhaps the team has trouble assimilating new technology because the members don't get effective training in it. If that's the case, you have another avenue open to you. Help the team get training. If you've decided to talk with higher management, stress the need for training to them. Training is absolutely critical to effective change, even if the change is just a new computer program.

If the team doesn't see the benefit of computers:

You can't change the organization's systems, so what can you do? You can help the team learn about the power of personal computers, especially when they're linked into local area networks (LANs) and then perhaps on to wider networks such as the Internet. Personal computers are getting easier to use every day. Macintosh has been known for its user friendliness for years, and now the Windows system on IBM-type computers is getting almost as friendly. Software has also gotten much more friendly; some programs even have built-in tutors to show workers how to use the main features.

You can encourage team members to attend courses explaining the value of personal computers and the new software. But you'll probably be more effective if you can have a few people come in from another team (inside or outside the organization) that uses personal computers. These individuals can do more to persuade your team to look into the software than a dozen courses could. And, of course, you can suggest that several team members visit that team, or another one using software successfully, to see how it actually works in practice. When they see another team like their own using personal computers effectively, they'll begin to see the possibilities for themselves.

If the team hasn't had to change lately:

Look at the last paragraph in the section above for one way to deal with the situation. If your team sees how another team uses computers effectively, it will begin to open up. This will happen even more rapidly if the other team has used computers to solve problems that are plaguing your team. No matter how opposed to change individuals and teams may be, if they see a clear benefit to themselves from a new technology they will at least be willing to look more closely at it.

Remember that the technology is only the short-range problem. The longer-range problem is the stagnation of the team. If you can use the ideas just above to get the team to look seriously at new technology, perhaps you can build on this and get the team to consider how complacent it's become. Team members may begin to realize that they've been cutting themselves off from important changes and that the team is being harmed because of it. When this happens, things will change.

Team Strengthener

Technology can be a wonderful thing, or it can be confusing, disruptive, and wasteful. How do you tell the difference? This is the easiest way: Ask yourself what impact the new technology would have on the team's ability to satisfy its customers. If it gets in the way, if it cuts down your ability to respond quickly to customers, for instance, forget it. (And if higher management is pushing it, try to get them to forget it.) If it will help the team serve its customers, look closely at it and use it if possible. But what if it doesn't have any impact on customers? Then you're probably best advised to look at a different technology until you find one that will help you serve your customers. Hundreds of organizations would be in better shape today than they are now if they consistently used this simple approach.

The Problem

The team refuses to consider new ways of working

The Scene

"Okay, guys—the first training session on team planning is tomorrow. Everybody planning to go?"

"You go ahead if you want. I don't see any point in learning anything more about planning. We've done fine so far."

"I don't have any interest, either. I've talked to several people on Marv Edison's team and none of them are very impressed by it."

"Yeah, it'll blow over—just like the past dozen hot programs we've gone through. If you want to get enthusiastic, go right ahead. I don't see any point in wasting energy."

After a few more comments, it's obvious that no one on the team intends to go. Team planning is the company's big program for now; how is it going to look when you're the only one who shows up? On the other hand, why should you even bother to go?

Possible Causes

The team doesn't put much faith in new programs.

Team members may have been around long enough to see similar programs come and go. They don't have much confidence that this one will fare any better. Even worse, in the past they may have enthusiastically supported programs that didn't succeed. Now they're gun shy about getting enthusiastic, no matter how good the program sounds. Their experience may also tell them that there won't be much of a payoff for the team, no matter how well the program goes.

The team has gotten too arrogant about its abilities.

Really good teams tend to get prideful and often downright arrogant. Because they're good, they begin to believe they have nothing to learn from others. This can lead a team quickly and easily down the primrose path of stagnation and degrading performance.

The team has worked out a good planning process on its own.

Don't accept this as the cause until you have examined the two causes above (and perhaps those in Case 2 in this chapter). But, it in fact may be the cause. Your team may be innovative enough and/or it may have faced a challenging enough situation that it did come up with a truly stellar planning process.

Hint

This case parallels the second case in this chapter. That one dealt with an individual problem, while this one concerns a team with the same problem. Since the causes listed in this are generally different from the second case, you may want to look at that case for additional ideas you can apply to this problem.

Cures

If the team doesn't put much faith in new programs:

What do you do? Your best approach is to go to the training and learn all you can about the new program. Are there aspects of the change that will genuinely help the team, whether the organization continues with the program or not? If so, get with the team and explain these parts. Show how the team can profit from them no matter what happens in the organization as a whole. If your analysis has been good and your presentation persuasive, the team may give the program a chance.

But what if you don't believe the program will help the team? You have a basically political decision to make. What will happen if you don't support the program? If it will give you a reputation as a team that doesn't really support the organization, the team needs to swallow hard and do the minimum it must to keep credibility.

One final thought: Some organizations truly go off the deep end for new programs, trying one after another without giving any of them a chance to succeed. Being productive in an organization such as this can be difficult. If your organization is that way, the team needs to develop a pair of skills:

- First, you need to get good at identifying the parts of a new program that will help the team, those which you can use no matter what happens to the program overall *and that you can learn in the time that the organization will spend on the program.* You don't want to overlook anything that will help make the team more productive.

- Second, you need to identify the motions you must go through to appear to be supporting the new program. Is it attending training? Sending in regular reports showing progress? Talking the program up with higher management? Find out the minimum that your organization will accept as appropriate support and do it.

If the team has gotten too arrogant about its abilities:

If that appears to be the real cause here, you've no choice but to bring it up with the team. Before you do, analyze the new program carefully. If you can't see any benefit from it, fall back on the solutions in the section above. If there are benefits, look at them carefully and ensure that you're being realistic. Then put the matter on the table before the entire team. If they genuinely see benefits, it may help them to realize how arrogant they have gotten.

If the team won't respond to the problem as you see it, try another ploy. Is there another team, one with which your team feels competitive, that is using the new program? Are they having good results with it? May they really improve enough to perform better than your team? If so, you may be able to persuade the team to support the program from pure competitiveness. Cooperation is generally superior to competition in a team-based organization, but there are some exceptions.

If the team has worked out a good planning process on its own:

If you can, make a presentation to higher management that demonstrates how effective your system is. At worst, they may approve your using it instead of the new system. At best, they may decide that it's a better system than they're advocating and give you the chance to train others to use the system.

Higher management may not want to hear this, so now what? Do what you have to do to provide minimum support for the new program. Your system may genuinely be better, but there still may be some elements of the new system that would be an improvement. If so, learn and use them.

Team Strengthener

Don't ever let yourself or the team get into a "not invented here" mentality. You know, the mentality that says "If we didn't think of the idea, it can't be that good." Or "Maybe it works there, but it won't work here." Perhaps it's sometimes true; perhaps, in fact, it's often true. But it will *never* always be true. The better your team is, the less often it will be true, but the better you and the team must become at evaluating the strengths and weaknesses of other programs. Remember, the better you believe you are the more you're apt to overlook genuinely useful ideas that you didn't originate. As this book stresses, no team can afford to stagnate, particularly in a pool of its own ideas. If you suspect that your team may be rejecting good ideas from outside, do this: Make planned visits to other teams (inside the organization or outside) specifically to find new ideas for yourself. If you do that regularly, you will probably find that (1) your team is pretty good and (2) other teams are using ideas that will make it even better.

The Problem
The team won't conform to company procedures

The Scene

"Look—it says right here that we need to coordinate with the customer team in Sales before we talk with a customer."

"I know what it says. I already read it. You remember what happened last time we asked them if we could talk to a customer?"

"Yeah, it took three meetings and three weeks before they agreed to it."

"You really think it will be any better this time? Besides, we need to talk with our customers this week if we're going to make any changes in the order."

"I suppose you're right. We do need to get it done."

How do you resolve this conflict?

Possible Causes

The team doesn't understand why it should follow the procedure.

Always look at this cause first. If a procedure exists, it's because someone at some time thought it was necessary. So begin by assuming that the organization needs the procedure (even though, as in the next section, it may be more complicated than necessary).

The procedure is unnecessarily complicated.

Organizations periodically rewrite their procedures. Sometimes it's to simplify them. More often, it's to add another step to take care of some problem. If your organization hasn't made changes to simplify them lately, they're probably quite a bit more complicated than they need to be.

The procedure isn't necessary.

This, of course, is the worst case. Times have changed but the procedure hasn't changed with them.

Hint

This case deals with the procedure as a procedure, not as one that affects another team. The next chapter describes several basic problems that can arise between one team and another. If another team is your problem, you might want to turn to that chapter.

Cures

If the team doesn't understand why it should follow the procedure:

The obvious step is to investigate why the procedure exists. Why does the sales team need to coordinate? What will happen if they don't? Does your team understand the issues it faces?

How do you get your team to pause and ask these questions? See if the team will agree to contact the sales team and arrange for representatives from it to meet with your representatives. You have a threefold goal. First, you want to ask the sales team the questions. Second, you want to ensure that they understand your interest. Third, you want to strengthen your relationship with the team.

Remember, what's at stake here isn't the team relationship as such. But the basic principle, talking with other parts of the organization that are affected by the procedure, applies not only here but almost everywhere. Then if it turns out that the other team(s) won't cooperate with you, look at the next chapter.

If the procedure is unnecessarily complicated:

You may have to follow it this time, unless it will truly interfere with serving a customer. (The team doesn't want to ignore procedures, but *nothing* should interfere with serving the customer.) If so, follow the suggestions in the section above.

Don't settle for following the procedure halfheartedly. Immediately set up a meeting with the sales team and anyone else affected by the procedure. Organize a joint team to look at the procedure and the process underlying it and simplify them. If the other team or teams don't want to cooperate, press hard. If necessary, enlist higher management's support, but only as a last resort.

Simplifying processes and procedures is everyone's business, all the time. If your organization doesn't believe this, start recruiting other teams you work closely with to join you in simplifying the ones that affect you jointly. Even if the organization doesn't practice Total Quality Management, your team and others can use some TQM principles to make yourselves more effective. (Case 5–6 discusses continuous process improvement. You might want to look at it for suggestions.)

If the procedure isn't necessary:

Don't conclude this until you've looked carefully at the procedure and the problems it's designed to prevent. But it may truly be unnecessary. It may be left over from when the organization used traditional management, or from a time when teams weren't as effective as they are now. Or it may reflect higher management's desire to retain control over teams.

If the procedure affects other teams, enlist their support. This time you don't want to create a joint team; you want to create a joint delegation to go to higher management. Your job, of course, is to persuade higher management that they don't need the procedure.

Suppose you try all of the alternatives. You talk with other teams and with higher management. Nothing changes. The procedure stays so complex that it gets in the way, or it doesn't accomplish anything. Here you and the team have to make a decision, and you have to make it carefully. As someone said, "It's easier to ask forgiveness than permission." You can just ignore the procedure, do what you have to do, and see what the consequences are. Should you? That's your call.

Team Strengthener

In a traditional organization, procedures are a part of everyday life. The larger and more bureaucratic the organization is, the more it operates by means of these procedures. When an organization successfully bases itself on self-managing teams, it needs many fewer procedures (and far more cooperation between teams). When the organization attempts to convert to teams, it needs to examine its existing procedures carefully. Some, such as approval for major capital equipment, it will want to keep. Others, such as rigid work hours, it will probably want to drop and let teams manage for themselves. Yet others will have to be examined carefully and rewritten or simplified. Has this happened in your organization? If not, you probably want to enlist the support of other teams and start pushing to make it happen.

6–6

The Problem
The team keeps trying new methods that no one has approved

The Scene

Kyle: See, this is what I was talking about. We can avoid these three steps if we do it this way.

Li Wan: It looks as if it would work. But that's not the way we're supposed to do it.

Kyle: What's more important—doing it by the book or doing it the best way? Don't they keep preaching at us to be efficient and find better ways?

Wanda: Sure, but I don't know if we should just disregard established procedures. We might be fouling somebody up . . .

You walk away from the discussion, not sure how you feel about it. Management expects your team to be innovative, but how would they feel about your ignoring the way things are supposed to be done? What should you do?

Possible Causes

The team doesn't understand the proper procedure.

This happens more often than you may think. The procedure is buried in an old manual no one ever reads. Or it hasn't been updated lately. Or the organization assumes that everyone knows it. Or it's complicated and no one has gotten the training in it they need. As a result, people do what seems to work and let it go at that.

The team has gotten too independent.

Teams are supposed to be autonomous and self-managing, right? Right—but they also need to coordinate their actions with the rest of the organization. Effective teams are independent, but they are also *inter*dependent; they must work effectively with other teams and with the organization as a whole to succeed. Your team may be tuned to its independence but not its interdependence.

The team is doing exactly what it should be doing.

Organizations create autonomous, self-managing teams so they can deal rapidly with changing conditions. This includes improving current procedures and processes whenever they can. Traditional organizations established their procedures and processes expecting that they would work for months or years. Team-based organizations can't share these expectations. They must be open to continuous change and to continuous improvement of their processes and procedures.

Cures

If the team doesn't understand the proper procedure:

Procedures are always established with a reason. Someone, somewhere, expects them to make work easier or higher in quality or faster or more efficient. In other words, there's always a reason for a procedure. Before a team changes the procedure, it needs to understand the reason behind it. Once it understands the reason it may not want to change the procedure, or it may want to change it in a different way.

It's hoped that your organization has open communication. If it does, suggest to Kyle that he talk to the individual, group, or team that developed the procedure in the first place. What was the goal? How did the procedure improve things? What would happen if Kyle made the change he wants to? Once Kyle has that information, he's in a better place to decide what change, if any, he needs to make.

If this level of communication doesn't exist? If the procedure was established by a staff office that no longer exists or that doesn't appreciate questions from operating people? If the group that established the procedure insists you do it their way, period? Does the organization really intend for your team to be autonomous and self-managing? If yes, look at the last cure in this case. If no, remember that it's easier to ask forgiveness than permission, and look at the last cure.

If the team has gotten too independent:

Was the procedure worked out by another team, and do they depend on your doing it the way they described? Get someone from that team to talk with your team and explain why the procedure is the way it is. This gives Kyle and other team members the opportunity to question the procedure and either satisfy themselves or suggest improvements to the other team. This is the best way to deal with situations such as this one.

Suppose the team has the same problem finding who developed the procedure, and why it was developed, that the first section described? The team needs to work together to decide whether it should follow the procedure. Let Kyle present his analysis and why he believes his way is better. Let the team play "devil's advocate," trying to find ways that his change might handicap other teams. When the team has reached a decision, turn to the next section.

If the team is doing exactly what it should be doing:

Kyle has found a new and better way. The team should congratulate him for that and then use his new way.

Then the team should analyze what Kyle did, for two reasons. First, by using his approach it may find other procedures that can be improved. Second, it may find that other teams could use the new method. If it does, it should write up the method and the reasons and present them to the other team(s), preferably in person with Kyle taking the lead.

Team Strengthener

Your team should understand that a new method can be valuable whether the team developed it or not, and it should actively look for improvements made by others. That's lesson number one. Then it should assume that other teams have learned the same lesson and be willing to share its improvements with these teams. That's lesson number two. Organizations that use empowered teams can thrive only if these teams constantly share their improvements with one another. Neither your team nor another team can afford a "not invented here" attitude. Good ideas are good ideas; it doesn't matter who found them first.

6–7

The Problem
The team always seems to be disorganized

The Scene

"Are we ready to change over to the new method we came up with?" you ask hopefully.

"Well," Ellen replies, "We're definitely on our way. Bob was going to copy the details of it for us, but he got involved in a customer's team meeting, which doesn't matter too much right now, since the change that Maury made in it conflicts with the new policy. And Josh hasn't finished coordinating the details with the team we developed the method with. Which reminds me—they're ticked off with us because we were all supposed to have it in place by last Friday . . ."

So much for being hopeful. Once again, the team can't seem to get organized to accomplish what should have been a simple change.

Possible Causes

The team concentrates on "important" tasks.

Almost every one of us draws a distinction between "what's really important in a job" and everything else. We prefer to concentrate on what's important. We do the rest when we have a chance and often don't do it willingly even then. Teams are no different. Unless a team pays close attention and disciplines itself, it can easily let tasks such as implementation of new methods draw on and on.

The team is poor at follow-through.

Many individuals and teams enjoy the challenge of developing new ideas and approaches. (See the next case.) Unfortunately, many of these same individuals and teams lose interest when the time comes to move from having ideas to implementing them. Actually putting a new method into practice requires detailed, often boring work. A team can all too easily find reasons why it "doesn't have time" for this work, leaving the job half done. The result can look like disorganization, since no one is spending the time and effort to complete the task.

The team is disorganized in everything it does.

It may not have learned how to organize its work as a team, probably because it's been able to get by without good organizing skills.

Cures

If the team concentrates on "important" tasks:

All of us need to concentrate on the important tasks before the less important tasks, but not instead of them. And the best way to accomplish this is to be well organized. In fact, good organization is the only way that a team can both focus on the most important work and still get the rest of the work done.

The team as a whole needs to work and solve this problem. You will probably have to bring it up. Do so, but be sure to raise it as a matter for the entire team to examine and solve. (You need to walk a fine line between acting occasionally as the team's conscience and taking responsibility for its performance.) If nothing else motivates the team, point out the impact the team's disorganization is having on the other team.

What if none of that works? The problem is much more serious: The team has gotten sloppy and perhaps self-centered. It has quite a job to do before it becomes an effective team again. You'll hope that at least another member or two sees the problem being raised by the sloppiness. You can enlist them and together try to gradually bring the team around to the point where it's willing to discipline itself again. Sound like hard work? It is. The best remedy is for the team to stay sharp and not have to face the problem.

If the team is poor at follow-through:

Bring the matter up to the team. Here you're acting not so much as the team's conscience as presenting an opportunity for the team to look at what it wants and what it actually does. Choices need to be made, and whatever choices are made need to deal with the issue head-on.

Here are some of the options:

- Is there another team that's particularly good at implementation but not at idea generation? (See Case 6–9.) Could your team form an alliance with it in which each of you does what you're best at? If so, don't count on being able to throw your ideas "over the wall" and have them implemented effectively by the other team. One reason your organization has teams is to prevent this kind of isolation. Instead, plan on meeting regularly with the other team and working the situation as a partnership.

- Are one or two team members particularly good at implementation and willing to do it? The team could negotiate with them to do most of the implementation. *Warning:* Don't make an absolute distinction, where they are the ones always doing the implementation. That builds walls within the team, between the people who come up with the ideas and the ones who implement them. In return for these individuals doing most of the implementation (60–80 percent?), the rest of the team should be willing to (1) include them fully in idea generation and (2) do the implementation the rest of the time.

• If neither of these alternatives works, the team has at least two more. It can try to get higher management to change its mission so that its responsibility for implementation is limited. This may work, but don't count on it. So the team will simply have to stiffen its collective upper lip and decide to do implementation effectively. It needs to develop an internal process to ensure both that the implementation gets done and that the burden falls evenly on everyone. Then it needs to stick to its resolution and spend the time and effort needed to implement effectively.

If the team is disorganized in everything it does:

The team needs to stop abruptly and take a hard look at itself. And it's not so simple as "Why are we disorganized?" An equally important question is "*How* are we disorganized?" Until you answer both these questions and then answer "How can we solve the problem?" you'll remain caught where you are. And you don't want to create a reputation for being disorganized; you can easily see what that will do to the team.

One place to start is by analyzing some fundamental team processes. They may be long and cumbersome. They may be ill-suited to get things done. Or the processes may be weak, so that each team member is basically doing his or her own thing. If you need outside help to look at your processes, by all means do so.

When an individual, team, or group is disorganized, it has one predictable outcome: There's never enough time. The team can easily conclude that there's not enough time to analyze the situation, not enough time to find solutions, not enough time to implement the solutions. *Don't get caught in this trap*. The team must *make* time to analyze, solve, and implement. If necessary, let a subteam do the analysis while the rest of the team gets the work done.

No matter what the cause is:

Begin dealing with the problem immediately. A team that gets the reputation that "it just can't get anything done" (on time, or well, or inexpensively) is in serious danger of ceasing to be a team. Management can decide to break up the team and put its members on other teams that are better organized.

Team Strengthener

An effective team develops a flowing, changing balance within itself of who does what when. The different leadership roles move from individual to individual. Individuals act with concern for themselves, for other members of the team, and for the team as a whole. This flexibility can degenerate into disorganization, but it need not do so. Instead, it can become a way of ensuring that even less desirable tasks get done, but that they don't get "dumped" on one or two individuals.

6–8

The Problem
The team is very creative but not very productive

The Scene

"I think you know why I called you in."

"I expect so, Mr. Samuels. It's because we're behind on our milestones again, isn't it?"

"It is. Look—your team is one of the most creative ones we have. You guys can come up with more good new ideas in a week than most other teams can manage in a quarter. And I appreciate that. But I don't appreciate the fact that you're one of the least productive teams we have. You and the team are just going to have to find some way to change that; we just can't afford to carry your low productivity much longer."

"That's certainly clear," you think to yourself as you walk back to the team's work area. "Now if I were only as clear about what to do about it."

Possible Causes

The team is undisciplined.

Individuals and teams that are both creative and effective are highly disciplined. Your team has half the requirements—creativity—but lacks the other. Its task is to develop discipline and control its creativity without squashing the creativity. This can be done, as long as the team genuinely intends to do it.

The team doesn't know how to produce effectively.

All of us prefer to do work we like. As we do it, we get better and better at it, and another preference comes into play: We prefer to do what we do well. As a result, we get better and better at what we like and never develop skills at the tasks we didn't like in the first place. That may be exactly what has happened to your team. Because members are effectively creative, they prefer to do "creative" tasks. So they haven't learned how to do "noncreative" tasks well. (And their performance and attitude may be tied up with the attitude described in the section above.)

The team is mismatched with its mission.

Don't reach this conclusion until you've looked closely at the two causes above. However, the team may be genuinely mismatched with its assigned mission. If it is creative with a mission that limits it to routine work, it will continue to be nonproductive.

Cures

If the team is undisciplined:

The team needs to begin with an honest assessment of its strengths and weaknesses. This may be difficult, particularly because "creative" people often look down on uncreative, routine work as beneath them. One of your tasks is to help the team work through these feelings. It doesn't matter whether the routine work is beneath the team; for its own sake, it must do this work well. Look at the section below this one for some suggestions on how to proceed.

Because the team is so creative, its members are probably intelligent and highly motivated. Now they need to turn this motivation to the effective performance of the whole mission of the team. As the team begins to discipline itself, it will face two dangers. First is the attitude reflected in the paragraph just above, reflected in comments such as "Why are we bothering with this crap anyway—let somebody else do it." The second is the fear that by doing routine work individuals and the team will lose creativity. This latter is a real fear, and probably a deep-seated one for the team. You need to help the team learn that it can become productive at "noncreative" work while still remaining creative. Help keep it pointed toward this goal: The better the team is at the routine, implementation work, the more impact its creative ideas will have.

If the team doesn't know how to produce effectively:

One approach will almost certainly work better than any other alternative: Can you convince the team that learning to do routine work effectively is a creative challenge? Routine work may be boring to someone creative, but arranging it so that it takes the least possible time can be a creative challenge. It may also be possible to generate some friendly competition among team members to see who can learn to do the routine work fastest. (The team might even decide that for a while the most creative tasks will be assigned to individuals who work most diligently and effectively at routine tasks.)

Watch out for one danger here. When creative individuals begin to use their creativity to work routine problems, they often become involved in the minutiae of the routine problems. Then they begin "tinkering"—changing this and that to make them a little more effective or a little quicker. This is a tremendous waste, for the individuals, the team, and the organization. Help the team watch for it and become aware if team members begin to get caught in it. The goal is to get the routine work done quickly and effectively and save the real creativity for generating valuable ideas.

If the team is mismatched with its mission:

The team needs to evaluate its situation closely. Perhaps, as the previous case suggested, it can work out a swap with another team that must attempt to be creative but prefers more routine work. (See the next case.) If not, it must take the initiative and go to higher management.

How good is the team at making a persuasive presentation? This situation will answer that question. Prepare carefully. Higher management will disrupt operations by reassigning significant duties only if it sees a real payoff from the action. Your team's task is to make that payoff clear. Remember, you need to make it clear what the payoff is for the organization, not for the team. If you can show higher management that the organization will gain specific benefits from a change in mission, you at least have a fighting chance to get the change.

Team Strengthener

Matching individuals to jobs is both necessary and difficult. Matching teams to appropriate duties and missions is at least as much so. Organizations often begin implementing teams by assigning individuals to them without thorough consideration of these individuals' skills and preferences. First, the team has to work out an internal balance, using the skills of individuals on the team and, when necessary, finding other jobs for individuals who don't fit in. (Earlier chapters dealt with this in some detail.) But the team also has to ensure that its mission is matched with its talents. The best time to accomplish this is as soon after the organization forms teams as possible. But never be afraid to try to get the team's mission changed when you believe there's a valid reason for it.

6—9

The Problem
The team is very productive but not very creative

The Scene

This morning, Mr. Samuels stopped you in the hall. "I really appreciate the way your team sticks to its deadlines."

"Thanks—but why do I think I hear a question mark at the end of that?"

"You're very perceptive. Frankly, I'm disappointed in the team's performance. With all the talent there is on the team—including yourself—I had expected a lot more creativity from it. It's not that all of you don't do good work; you do. But you never seem to come up with the kind of innovative solution many of the other teams do."

Don't you know it? The team has discussed this shortcoming several times. But how can it become more creative?

Possible Causes

The team doesn't believe creativity is important.

Few traditional organizations value creativity except in certain departments (R&D, product development, package design, and so forth). Everywhere else, they value predictability and efficient execution of routine processes. At least that's how it used to be. Today, though, even traditional organizations have trouble competing successfully unless the people on the line are creative. Organizations that use teams have an even greater demand for creativity because a basic function of teams is to respond quickly to changing conditions.

The team doesn't understand how to be creative.

Individuals and teams who don't see much need for creativity often don't understand how to be creative—how to loosen up and open up to new and innovative ideas. They also often don't understand what to do when they get ideas, how to develop and

231

refine them and then to move from the idea to its implementation.

The team is mismatched with its mission.

When the team was established, the organization may not have realized how important creativity would be in getting its mission done. Or the match may have been fine initially, but the situation has changed. Whatever the cause, the organization needs more creativity from the team than the team can provide.

Cures

If the team doesn't believe creativity is important:

Evidently the members of your team haven't made the transition from the requirements of more traditional organizations to the requirements of a team-based organization. They believe the organization still values predictability and effective routine action above all. They don't see the need for creativity. Here is another situation in which you need to take the lead. Begin by describing your conversation with Mr. Samuels. If your boss believes the team should be more creative, it's time to listen. You ask him to speak to the team, to share with them his ideas on why it needs to be more creative.

Can you get some products from other teams that are similar to the products of your team but show significant creativity? You could show them to your team side by side and help them to understand the difference—the "value added" of the extra creative touch. You could have an individual involved in the other team's products and have him or her explain how the team came up with its ideas. If these won't work, find another way. Do what's necessary to have the team actually see the difference that creativity makes.

If the team begins to see the difference, you might have a consultant come in and show the team some basic creative techniques, or send the team as a group to training in creativity. Have representatives of the team meet with a team that has a reputation for creativity and that can describe how they get new ideas.

There's one last option, perhaps the most effective of all. The team can pick a specific project and commit itself to exploring a range of creative ideas before selecting the one to use. Use this as a springboard to a general practice of finding and implementing innovative ideas in a range of products.

If the team doesn't understand how to be creative:

The ideas in the previous section will help a lot. But concentrate on the *how* of generating ideas; be sure the team understands not just what to do but how to do it. Watch, though, that team members don't approach being creative in the same systematic, detailed way they approach their other duties. Help them understand that this is something new that requires them to respond in new and different ways.

Remember, in both this circumstance and the one in the previous section, individuals need to make significant changes. These changes will be disruptive. Team members will feel awkward and incompetent. Be sure that the atmosphere remains open and accepting. Don't criticize poor ideas; encourage the individual and the team to build on them. (Most good ideas are built on not-quite-so-good ideas that are, in turn, built on not-even-that-good ideas.) The greater the freedom that team members have to experiment, the more quickly they will become creative.

One last, quick thought. Individuals and teams become most creative when they must solve problems that require this creativity. It may be that the team's mission doesn't require it to deal with problems that really challenge it and call forth its creative abilities. It might be able to negotiate for more demanding tasks, ones that call forth the creativity it didn't realize it had.

If the team is mismatched with its mission:

As usual, don't conclude this until you've explored the other alternatives. Then look at the corresponding section in the previous case, but reverse the goal. You're looking for a team that wants to do the creative work and will appreciate your ability to implement it quickly and efficiently. Or you're looking for a changed mission that will let the team concentrate on efficient implementation.

If the team concludes that it is not as creative as its mission demands, it may get discouraged. While we often think creative individuals are strange and unusual, we also often look up to them and see them as "special" people. They are. But so are the people who know how to get things done, who are reliable, whom everyone can count on to do what needs to be done, day after day. See that your team understands this.

Team Strengthener

All effective teams are alike in some ways. They work together well; they share leadership tasks; they support one another; they surface and deal with conflict; they get their mission done, even when times are tough. They also differ from one another in significant ways, and one of these ways is the kind of work they do well. Some are excellent at projects, while others do the same job over and over well. Some are creative; others shine at implementing others' ideas. And on and on. Every team needs to understand its strengths and weaknesses and to work in ways that maximize its strengths. Of course, if the team is good it also works at overcoming its weaknesses. Truly outstanding teams strive constantly to do *everything* well. They don't ever make it, but it gives them a goal that keeps life exciting and challenging.

6-10

The Problem
The team is always wrangling over how to do things

The Scene

Tom: I tell you, there's no reason to go into this kind of detail. We just summarize what we found and let it go at that.

Isabel: Sure, and leave out the really important stuff. I had to do night and weekend work to dig that up!

> *Arlena:*   I disagree with both of you. We ought to be wor-
> rying about what we got from the interviews
> instead of this.
>
> *Brian:*   Sure, the interviews make a difference. The real
> value we can add, though, is to take everything
> we've got and do a really deep analysis of it—not
> spend time just summarizing the data.

Same song, hundredth verse. Every time the team has an important project to complete, the members end up arguing with one
another about what they ought to do. If they just took half that
energy and worked together, they could get the job done in a
hurry. But they can't see that.

Possible Causes

The team hasn't learned to manage conflict.

As earlier chapters pointed out, a team must learn to deal
with conflict if it is to become really effective. When it can't
manage conflict well, the team may run into trouble at any
point, such as the inability to reach a consensus on how to do
the team's job.

The team is rushing to finish a project and the stress shows.

If the team doesn't plan well and ends up having to rush to
finish its job, it puts tremendous pressure on itself. Most individuals operate poorly under this kind of pressure. Small things
irritate them. They get their feelings hurt more easily. They tend
to get angry at criticism instead of using it.

This is a symptom of a deeper problem in the team.

As earlier cases have shown (especially those in Chapters 2
and 5) underlying conflict in a team can show up in a number
of ways. Often, unfortunately, the way it shows up doesn't
reflect the real causes. For instance, team members may wran-
gle with one another when what really upsets them is the way
work is assigned, or the way they treat one another, or a hundred other reasons. That may be what's happening here.

Hint

Cases 2–2 through 2–7 deal with conflict within teams. If none of the causes in this case seem right, take a look at those cases for ideas.

Cures

If the team hasn't learned to manage conflict:

What the team needs is effective training in conflict management. If the organization offers it, get it as soon as possible. If the organization doesn't offer it, find another source. And if you can get a facilitator who understands conflict management to help the team, do so.

In the meantime, do your best to help the team deal constructively with the conflict. The team members should agree to a few basic ground rules, such as:

- No name calling or personal attacks. Keep everything focused on the issue.

- Everyone has the right to be heard. No one has the right to be agreed with. After everyone has been heard, the team decides.

- If wrangling takes too much time, delegate some issues to individuals or subteams and let them make the decision for the team. (This may make the team nervous at the beginning. After it works a few times, it may become their established way of dealing with this kind of situation.)

If the team is rushing to finish a project and the stress shows:

If the problem is poor planning and/or execution, there's no point in trying to treat the symptom. Go for the cause. The team needs to get control of its processes. If it's not planning well, it may not be sure what its processes are. If the plan is okay but the execution is sloppy or disorganized, it needs to learn how to translate the plan into action. (Cases 5–2 and 5–6 have some ideas that might be helpful.)

You need to help the team face the root problem openly and honestly. You'll hope everyone is fed up enough with the wrangling that they'll be motivated to do this. If the team is uncomfortable looking at its own performance, a facilitator may be helpful. But everyone needs to understand the situation before it can be cured. Once everyone has accepted the problem, some training is probably in order. If your organization has a preferred planning process for teams, get training in it. If not, find effective training through a commercial provider or a community college.

If this is a symptom of a deeper problem in the team:

This is a variation of the first section in this case: For whatever reason, the team can't surface and resolve (manage) some real conflict on the team. Training in conflict management will probably help, but unless it's intense it may not lead the team to face this buried conflict.

Here's where a good facilitator can make a significant contribution. In this case, it's probably best to bring the matter up with the team first. If the team is determined not to face the real conflict, don't force it to accept a facilitator. You'll hope, though, that they're tired enough of the conflict that they want to get it behind them, particularly if they believe the facilitator can help them accomplish this. Whatever the team decides about a facilitator, you need to keep pressing on the issue until the team comes up with an acceptable way to deal with it.

Team Strengthener

One of the roles that most teams find useful is an internal facilitator or monitor who keeps his or her hand on the "pulse" of the team. On an immature team, or on any team involved in a hot and heavy discussion, it's easy for someone to get resentful or upset and not verbalize it. If other team members don't notice what has happened and make a point of dealing with it, the individual may walk out of the session still resentful or upset. If this happens often and to many team members, it begins to eat at the team as a whole. It's useful to have someone retain enough of a distance from the discussion to notice these incidents and then bring them up to the team as a whole.

CHAPTER 7

Problems Among Your Team and Other Teams

Traditional workgroups often have problems working with one another, but these problems can be much more serious for teams. Why? One of the functions of a traditional manager is to solve the problems that workgroups bring up. Self-managing teams, though, are often expected to resolve any problems they have with other teams.

In fact, the more that your team is self managing, the more that solving problems with other teams becomes one of its basic responsibilities. When the organization finds that the team can work effectively with other teams, it is willing to let the team work with increasing independence. Unfortunately, the reverse is also true.

This chapter contains a variety of problems that teams have working with one another. Each problem is different, but each problem brings up the same issue: How does your team work effectively with other teams to produce a smooth work flow and get everyone's job done?

Each case provides specific recommendations on how to deal with a problem in ways that not only strengthen your team but strengthen its relationships with other teams. That's the goal. You don't want to be a doormat for other teams, but neither do you want them to be doormats for you. Use the ideas in these cases to work out cooperative relationships in which both your team and others prosper.

238

The situation isn't dramatically different from that in Case 1–9 and in some other cases where conflict occurs within a team. Here it's between teams, not between members of the same team. The solution is basically the same, though. The two teams must come together, put the issues on the table, resolve them, and walk away from the past. If the event that caused the bad feelings was relatively recent, it will be easier to accomplish this. No matter when the incident happened, though, it needs to be surfaced and the feelings dealt with.

First, you need to persuade your team of this. Team members may not even know what the incident was, but that doesn't matter. They need to see how harmful the current situation is, to the point where they'll try anything reasonable to resolve it. Then the team needs to persuade the other team that the two teams need to meet and resolve the issue or issues.

If both teams are mature, they can probably resolve the issues themselves. Unless you're sure of this, though, try to get an experienced facilitator. He or she needs to be a good one, used to letting teams manage conflict without repressing it. Then go to it. Find the time to meet as often as necessary to get the past settled and out of the way. Both you and the other team will come out way ahead.

Team Strengthener

Two teams, or two individuals, should compete only when they don't depend on each other to get their own work done. If your team supplies work to the other team and/or gets work from them, competition is positively harmful. Your team should never let it develop, and it should do its best to discourage the other team from it. If higher management is pushing the teams into a competitive situation, you need (if possible) to bring the situation up with management and explain how it's hurting productivity. Remember, competition doesn't work between two teams that depend on each other. There are almost no exceptions to this rule.

The Problem
Your team doesn't want to work with other teams

The Scene

"We'd really rather do the whole project ourselves," Martina says earnestly.

"Yes," Chang adds. "We don't have anything against any of the other teams, but we think we can do this one by ourselves."

"And get it done on time, which may not happen if we have to work with other teams." Liann is just as intense as the others.

Everyone else on the team seems to feel the same way. Whatever the reason, the whole team wants to do this one by themselves. But should they?

Possible Causes

The team is overconfident, perhaps even a little arrogant.

Good teams tend to get very confident and often arrogant. They know how good they are, and this often turns into the suspicion, or even the conviction, that no other teams are really as good. To a point, this is healthy. But when it interferes with the team working with other teams, it becomes hurtful.

The team has had problems working with other teams.

While team members may work well with one another, that's no guarantee that the team as a whole has the skills to work with other teams. Your team may not know how to go about cooperating with another team.

The team can handle the project by itself.

One of the strengths of teams is that they have multiple skills and can do a variety of tasks by themselves. This may be the case with your team now.

Cures

If the team is overconfident, perhaps even a little arrogant:

Curing this isn't as simple as convincing the team to work with another team. If that team isn't as competent as your team, working with them may make your team even more arrogant. On the other hand, if that team is good, they deserve to work with other good teams like your own. (And if that team is good enough, your team may learn that it's not quite as exceptional as it thought.) If your team decides to work with another team to help them become more effective, that's different. It's also different from the situation here.

Suppose the team will be better off working with another team on the project. You have a real sales job on your hand. Part of this is building up the other team. You can point out to your team the strengths the other team has and how these will help your team. If possible, get several members of your team to meet with representatives of the other team and discuss how they might help one another. If the other team is good, this gives your team a chance to find it out firsthand. Keep the team focused on the mission. Then, if working with the other team helps accomplish the mission, the team will probably be able to recognize this and agree to it.

If the team has had problems working with other teams:

If possible, get your team together with another team it needs to work with closely. Let the other team tell yours what it needs from you. You'll hope this will suggest contributions the other team can make to your success. If the mutual benefit is clear enough, you'll find ways to work together. (If rough spots develop, you may want to use a facilitator a few times when the teams meet together.)

While facilitation and training in working with other teams may help, the real key is finding ways that other teams can genuinely help your team accomplish its mission. Concentrate on finding these ways, as well as on ways your team can help others. Use this as the basis on which the team builds competence at working with other teams.

If the team can handle the project by itself:

Before you conclude this, hold a team meeting. Help the team evaluate (1) whether it has some reasons it's not facing for working with other teams and (2) whether it really has the skills to do the project by itself. Even if the team isn't sure, it may be worth doing the project independently to help it grow and develop. (Even the best team needs to do a "stretch" project occasionally.) If it does seem justified for the team to do the project by itself, make sure that higher management agrees with this. (It might have definite expectations that you'll work with another team.) Make sure as well that higher management understands why the team wants to work independently. Then go to it.

Team Strengthener

Case after case has stressed the need for a team to objectively and honestly assess itself, its motives and its capabilities. The ability to do this is one of the fundamental capabilities of an effective team. It isn't easy, and no team can do it perfectly. But good teams understand how important it is so they learn to do it, and to do it as well as possible. From the beginning, you should take helping the team assess itself honestly as one of your most important leadership responsibilities.

7–3

The Problem

Other teams are constantly trying to take over some of your team's functions

The Scene

"Hey." Roosevelt runs up to you. "They're at it again!"

"Okay, okay. Calm down. Now—who's up to what?"

"Johnson's team—they're trying to talk our boss into letting them be responsible for all of our quality analysis work."

You frown. That's the third team this month that's tried to take over some of your responsibilities. What in the world can you do about it?

Possible Causes

Your team isn't performing well.

Its performance is substandard enough that other teams see it and believe they can capitalize on it.

Your team has work that should be given to other teams.

Your team may be performing functions that fit the mission of other teams more logically. Why? Perhaps when the organization started using teams it made mistakes in allocating functions among them. Perhaps everyone started out with functions that fit together, but things changed and now a different arrangement would be more effective. It doesn't matter why. If your team performs functions that fit more logically with the functions of another team, changes need to be made.

Your team has work it wants to get rid of.

This cause doesn't rule out the one in the section above. You may want to get rid of work because it doesn't fit your mission. Or you may want to get rid of it because it's boring or the team doesn't like to do it. In this case, other teams attempting to take over a function may provide you just the excuse you need to get rid of the work you don't want.

Hint

Don't assume automatically that you need to hold on to all your team's work or all its functions. That isn't an effective approach because others see you as being defensive. Besides, trying to hold on to everything may keep you from identifying both problems (your team's poor performance, for instance) and solutions (letting other teams have certain functions).

Cures

If your team isn't performing well:

Why isn't it performing well? Chapter 5 has descriptions of ways that teams don't perform effectively. Look at it for help in identifying the causes and cures of poor performance.

The key, of course, is for the team to be willing to look critically at its own performance. As the book has stressed, it's never the best strategy to begin by looking at what others are doing. Effective teams begin by looking at themselves, to see what they're adding to the situation. Then they look outside.

When you identify *how* the team is performing inadequately and *what* it needs to do to improve, do it. But also talk with your boss. Explain to him or her what happened and how you're going to fix it. Ask for support for the short term, as the team solves its problems. Then solve them, and keep your boss abreast of every improvement you make.

If your team has work that should be given to other teams:

Where do you start? The team begins by doing some intelligence work. It needs to become familiar with the missions and functions of all of the teams performing similar work. Then it needs to analyze the missions and functions, to see where the dislocations are. Finally, the team needs to determine how functions might be swapped among teams to produce more logical combinations. And it needs to do this in such a way that its mission and functions aren't diminished and are enhanced.

Now the team is ready to take its recommendations to higher management. Remember, you're not selling this as something your team wants (even though it does). You're selling it as a solution to a management problem. This lets you recognize the validity of other teams' attempts to take over your functions and then respond to it with a solution that solves the basic problems. You may not get quite what you want, but you will get more of it than if you leave it up to someone else to make the recommendations.

If possible, the team shouldn't do the selling, or even the deciding, by itself. If relations among some of the teams involved are basically good, you may want to work with them to identify the problems and develop the solution. If you can't do that, you may be able to work with another team or two so that the recommendations represent the consensus of teams rather than just your own. The more teams that are involved and concur in the recommendation, the greater the chance that the recommendation will be accepted as made.

If your team has work it wants to get rid of:

The team needs to discuss this option carefully. It may have work it doesn't like but that is absolutely essential to its mission. Or that might form the basis of new and more interesting work. If you decide to get rid of work, be sure that letting it go won't hurt the team. Then pick the right time and volunteer to your boss to let another team (or teams) have it.

Once again, try to get the support of the other team(s) involved. If you and one or more other teams walk in with an agreed-on plan for moving duties around, the plan has a much greater chance of success than if your team alone presents it.

Team Strengthener

In a team-based organization, you'll almost always come out ahead by working with other teams to solve problems. Your team needs to develop the relationship with them that permits this. How? By being sensitive to their needs, supporting them, and dealing openly with them about disagreements. Then when problems arise the teams can work and solve them without higher management intervention (except, perhaps, to ratify the teams' agreements). The better the relationship between your team and others, the greater flexibility you will have. If another team wants to take over one of your functions, for instance, the two of you can work the problem openly. You can try to come up with a solution that meets both of your needs. Perhaps you might even involve yet other teams, then agree on a solution that realigns functions among several teams. Cooperation and mutual trust win every time, for everyone.

The Problem

The team often argues with other teams over who should do what

The Scene

You and Ray have met to plan how your two teams will work their new joint assignment. The meeting has gone on for half an hour, and the two of you are no closer to agreeing on which team performs several key tasks than you were when you met. In frustration, you call off the meeting, wondering how you're going to get the problem resolved.

Possible Causes

There are genuine personality conflicts between members of the two teams.

Most problems labeled "personality conflicts" occur because of deeper problems (conflicting roles or missions, for instance). But there are real personality conflicts, individuals who approach situations so differently that they just can't deal with one another. This may be happening here.

The teams aren't concentrating on the outcome they must produce to be successful.

Individuals and team can quickly lose the ability to work together when they concentrate on something other than their mutual goal. Team A is still griped because Team B didn't cooperate last time and wants to make a point. Or Team B wants to make sure it has an important part in the new project. Or one or both teams may have a dozen (or hundred?) other reasons for looking at something other than the result they need to get.

One or both teams believe they don't need the other to produce a successful outcome.

Who decided that the two teams needed to work together? Did they analyze the project and what each team has to con-

outcome means that the work gets done expertly and each team makes a contribution it is happy with.

- Deal with every issue as openly as possible. Don't go in trusting that the other team will look out for your team's welfare; if there's not a strong relationship, it probably won't. But don't try to "put one over on them" or pressure them. Be clear about what you want and go for it.

- Do everything you can to encourage the other team to deal openly. If you believe that it's working a hidden agenda, say so. Try to get all the agendas on the table. Make it clear that if the team will deal openly with yours you will respect their needs and try to help them achieve them.

- And keep testing everything against the first point—the requirements of a successful outcome.

Team Strengthener

The better the relationships your team has with other teams, the more effective it will be, both at accomplishing its mission and at getting what it wants for itself. In an ideal team-based organization, almost all decisions affecting teams would be made by the teams themselves. Most organizations aren't ideal, but that shouldn't keep you from getting as close as possible. What if the organization doesn't want teams making decisions? You have at least two choices. If the decision isn't a major one, the teams should go ahead and make it and get on with life. If it is major, or if you know higher management will be concerned about it, meet with the teams concerned and reach a consensus. Then present the consensus to higher management and demonstrate why it's the best decision. Do that effectively a few times, by the way, and management may decide to let the teams make their own decisions.

The Problem

Another team keeps blaming your team for mistakes

The Scene

You walk back into the team's work area just in time to hear Charlotte, from the team you work with regularly, explode at Erik.

"Dammit, can't you guys ever do anything right? It's two days past the due date and you still don't have all your input to us. We've covered for you in the past, but this one goes straight to management. We took a vote, and if you don't get your act together in a hurry we're going to refuse to work with you!"

Wow! You knew things were bad with that team, but not this bad. This situation has to be fixed, and quick!

Possible Causes

Your team really did fail to deliver what it promised.

It's painful when someone else blames you for a failure, and it's doubly painful if you deserve the blame. Unless your team is very mature, it will probably react defensively to being blamed. It will think of all the reasons why the fault was on the other side. This may be a phase the team goes through, but it needs to get through it as quickly as possible and drop its defensiveness.

The two teams miscommunicated with each other.

Unfortunately, different individuals and different teams often understand the same language in different ways. The two teams may have different functional backgrounds; perhaps yours has a strong engineering bent while the other is made up largely of marketers. The teams may have miscommunicated because they were concentrating on different aspects of the job or even because they tried to hurry the agreement.

Your team agreed to unrealistic deadlines.

Many traditional organizations try to control operations by imposing very tight deadlines on subordinates at all levels. This approach is completely out of place in a team-based organization, which must operate on a high level of trust to succeed. Even when this trust exists, a team may be pressured to agree to an unrealistic deadline because it knows management needs a quick result or because the other team needs their product. None of these reasons is a good one.

Cures

If your team really did fail to deliver what it promised:

The team needs to look as objectively as possible at *what* happened, *why* it happened, and *how* it happened. Does the team not consistently do a good job? Does it fail to perform effectively under pressure? Did it not care about this project? Was a key member missing, with no one else to take over his or her tasks?

You may find ideas to help answer the what, why, and how in Chapter 5. You will also find suggestions for dealing with the most common causes of poor performance there. Then start doing what you need to do to ensure that the poor performance doesn't happen again. Explain to the other team what happened and why they can count on it not happening again. If the team really did mean its threat to go to higher management, you go to higher management as well. Then see that the problem is fixed and remains fixed.

If the two teams miscommunicated with each other:

What do you do? First, you and the team need to find out why the miscommunication occurred. The three different examples in the paragraph above had different causes, and you would solve each problem in a different way. Once your team believes it has identified the causes, it needs to meet with the other team and see if both teams can reach agreement on the problem. Be prepared for the meeting to be stormy in the beginning. After all, the other team thinks you're to blame, so they probably also think you want to meet with them to make excuses. Just stay calm, accept their feelings, and present your case. If you've done the job right, the other team will end up accepting your conclusions or even modifying them in a helpful way.

Once the two teams have agreed on the cause, they can develop the solution. At least in the beginning, any solution will probably involve spending more time in reaching an agreement. Each team needs to understand where the other team is coming from and what its basic concerns are. Once this happens, the necessary communication will flow much more smoothly. Just as important, each team will understand where the missed communication is apt to occur and to be on the lookout for it.

If your team agreed to unrealistic deadlines:

Several cases point out that a mature team needs a clear idea of its strengths and weaknesses. It also needs a good sense of what it can accomplish with given resources in a given period of time. Your team should not only know but be able to demonstrate what kind of product it can produce by a particular deadline. It should cooperate with other teams and higher management in every way, but this doesn't require it to promise what it knows it cannot deliver.

So, what do you do when another team (or management) faces you with a deadline you know is unrealistic? You don't say "We can't do it" and end things there. You might

- explain what you can do by the deadline and how much longer you would need to produce all of what they want or
- suggest something that would be equally (or almost equally) useful that you could produce by the deadline or
- describe what additional resources the team would need to meet the deadline and ask another team or management to provide the resources.

Do none of these seem practical in your situation? Then find your own solution, one that doesn't commit the team to an unrealistic schedule but that responds to the needs of other teams and/or management.

Team Strengthener

A critical characteristic of successful individuals, teams, and organizations is this: They have high credibility. They keep their word. They tell clearly what they will do and then they do it, just as they said. This can't happen unless the commitment is made intelligently. If your team commits itself to a deadline that it believes it cannot meet, it sets itself up to ruin its credibility. It's painful to say, "We just can't do that by then," but it's far more painful to say, "I know we said we would do it, but we haven't."

7–6

The Problem

Another team asks you to tell your manager that they gave you a report two days earlier than they actually did

The Scene

"I need a favor from you."

You turn around to see Wanda, a member of one of the marketing teams.

"Here's the report we promised you day before yesterday. We promised our next-level manager we'd get to you on time, and we're going to be in a world of hurt if he finds out. If your manager or anyone else asks, could you just tell them that you got it on time? We'd really appreciate it."

"Let me think about it," you reply. "And thanks for the report."

Wanda walks away, leaving you with the report and a problem. She asked you to cover for her and her team. What do you do?

Possible Causes

In this case, the causes don't really matter. Wanda has a problem and is asking you to cover for it. The issue is not what caused that, but what your response will be.

Cures

If Wanda's team has never asked for a favor like this before:

Teams do favors for one another, and this kind of favor isn't out of line. You may feel free to make the decision, or you may want to let the team make it. If you make it, inform the team as soon as possible. If they should make it, bring it up to them as soon as possible.

No matter how uncomfortable you and the team are with covering, it's probably best to do it in this situation. Then the team should decide whether it needs to talk with Wanda's team about the situation. Perhaps it needs to say that it won't be willing to cover again. Perhaps it needs to say that it was willing to do it and would be glad to help the other team avoid the situation if possible in the future. Perhaps it requires something as simple as your assuring Wanda that you will help her team.

Again, teams often do favors for one another. As long as the favors are rare, everything is fine. When the favors get to be too frequent or too one-sided, however, they raise some sticky questions. The next section deals with some of those questions.

If Wanda's team consistently asks you to cover for it:

If this is a pattern, whether it's one-sided or just reciprocation for its covering for your team, you are in the middle of a problem. If the situation consistently requires this kind of cover-up, something's wrong.

As always, your team needs to look at itself objectively and realistically. Has it been forcing too-tight deadlines on Wanda's team to make its own life easier? Has it refused to be flexible in working with that team? Is its own performance less than it should be, so that it forces other teams to take up the slack? You need a clear idea of what your own contribution to the situation may be before you can talk with Wanda's team.

Then you and/or other members of your team need to talk with her team. The two teams need to be just as objective and realistic together about the situation as your team has been. If there's a performance problem, look at earlier cases in this book, particularly those in Chapter 5.

If you owe her team a favor:

Like individuals, teams that work together often do each other favors. And when a team does a favor for someone else, it often expects a favor in return. But a problem occurs with this arrangement if either party starts to push for more questionable favors, especially if it uses its past favors as the justification for these new favors.

Let's suppose that the situation with Wanda's team is more serious than it appears on the surface. Suppose your team made a serious mistake in some data it provided Wanda's team and then blamed that team for the final error in their calculations. Wanda's team took its lumps, but now it wants to collect for what it did. Not getting you the report was a major problem, because that team has been in continuous trouble lately because of its inability to meet schedules.

Now the favor is a lot more serious. Your team probably has no alternative but to support Wanda's team—this time. But now you and the team need to get your collective act together. Letting others cover for you when you have fouled up is a serious matter on its own, and the obligation it creates on you is dangerous. Your team's goal should always be to perform well enough that it needs few favors from others. If it fails at this every once in a while, okay. But if it consistently needs favors, it needs to look long and hard at itself. It may be taking itself down a path that has some very unpleasant turns a few feet ahead.

Team Strengthener

Other chapters have pointed out how important it is to have good relationships with other teams. There's a catch in this, however. When teams have high trust among each other, good relationships are easy and profitable. But what happens when another team is willing to take advantage of yours? Or willing to "cut corners" that make your team nervous? Your team must get these problems out on the table with the other team, as frankly and openly as it would if they were internal problems. If the bond of trust begins to erode, your team needs to move toward an open, productive but *arm's-length* relationship with that other team. In short, your team needs to do whatever it takes to maintain its own integrity.

CHAPTER 8

Problems With Team Leadership

As a team becomes more self-managing, its leadership roles become more flexible. Different individuals become leaders at different times and for different purposes. Even if you remain the overall leader, you may want to use other team members as leaders for specific projects. So leadership issues become important for teams in a way that they never do for traditional workgroups.

The cases in this chapter describe problems that you and the team can encounter when you attempt to use flexible leadership. You may be ready to let others assume leadership roles, but your next-level manager or the team (or both!) may want you to remain the leader. And when you do pass on leadership functions to other members of the team, they may not be as successful as you and the team want.

If you encounter some of these problems, don't worry. It takes teams, and the individuals on them, time to learn about shared leadership. After all, most team members come from traditional workgroups where the supervisor exercises the leadership—period. What matters is not that you and the team succeed the first time you share leadership but that you learn as much as possible from each experience.

When your team has a problem like one pictured in this chapter, look at the case carefully to make sure you and the team understand the basic cause(s) of the problem. Then use the recommendations to resolve the problem. It will not always be easy, but learning flexible leadership skills will pay tremendous dividends for the team and for you.

The Problem

The team wants to be told what to do instead of deciding for itself

The Scene

"As I see it, then," you say, "we have the three choices we've talked about. So which one do we decide on?"

The discussion that follows is brief and clear. Bruce summarizes it when he says, "Look—you're the leader, and the leader's job is to make these decisions. You tell us what to do and we'll do it."

You thought this was supposed to be a self-managing team, so how do you help them get to the point that the team as a whole is willing to make decisions?

Possible Causes

The team doesn't understand how teams are different from traditional organizations.

As this book stresses, teams operate in ways very different from the ways that traditional organizations operate. In most traditional organizations, supervisors make all the important decisions, even when supervisors ask their workgroup for input. The members of your team may be acting the way they've always acted, and they expect you to make the final decision.

The team is afraid to make decisions.

Why would your team members be afraid to make a decision? Because in the organization they came from good decisions weren't rewarded, but "bad" decisions were punished. Sad to say, that's how many traditional organizations operate. That may be how your organization currently operates: Teams are free to make their own decisions, but if they make the "wrong" decision they hear about it loudly. They may even get punished for it, in terms of future assignments, promotion opportunities, or an unmerciful chewing out.

The team hasn't matured enough to make decisions.

Even when team members aren't tied to the way traditional organizations operate, even when they aren't afraid of the results of a decision, it still takes time for them to get used to making decisions as a team. It is a different way of working; it isn't how things used to be. Even the most enthusiastic team needs time to learn the new ways.

Hint

As you'll see, all three causes are different but closely connected. Also, this case is similar to the next three. If none of the causes and cures listed here seem quite right, look at one of the following cases for suggestions.

Cures

If the team doesn't understand how teams are different from traditional organizations:

What do you do? You don't attempt to force them to make the decision, nor do you refuse to make it. Instead, you try to lead them to take more responsibility for the decision without forcing it on them. Here are two ideas you might try:

- If the team appears to lean toward one alternative, you can test for this. You might say something like this: "It sounds to me as if you'd be most comfortable if we did _____. Is that right?" You may get some resistance, but you also may get some agreement. If there's agreement, you can then say "Okay, I'll make the decision, and this is the decision I'll make."

- If there doesn't appear to be a consensus, you might try this approach. "Who'd really like to see me decide for A? What about B? C?" If you make it clear that you'll make the decision, you may get the team to vote. Then you can either abide by the majority or make a different decision and explain why.

Remember, *you're* making the decision. You're trying to encourage them to provide you input, but you need to make clear that you're not going to hang the decision around their necks. If you do this a few times, you begin to make it easier for the team to take over more of the decision process. Then the day will come when all it means for you to make the decision is to ratify the team's decision.

If the team is afraid to make decisions:

If the problem is the organizations team members came from, you can deal with it as the section above suggests. You help the team understand how the current situation is different, then lead them to begin making decisions.

But what if the current situation isn't different? What if "poor" decisions are still punished? Then you and the team have a real problem. If you have sufficient influence with higher management, you can try to persuade them to operate differently, to give teams the chance to take risks, and to treat a "poor" decision as a learning opportunity.

You'll hope that higher management will at least give this a try. If not, try to strike a deal with the team. You'll encourage them to make decisions, but then you'll take responsibility for the decision. If you do this, remember that you are only one member of the team during the decision-making process, but you will support the team's decision whether you believe it's the best solution or not. You must absolutely avoid letting the team decide and then second-guessing the decision later on. (That will reinforce team members' belief that decision making isn't worth the risk.)

If the team hasn't matured enough to make decisions:

You can use the suggestions in the first section to help them mature as a team. You can make it clear that you will support the team's decision without reservation. Most of all, though, you use the ideas scattered throughout this book to help the team mature. You want to help them see that they are a unit, a close group that will support one another and that wants to take responsibility for its actions. Be patient, keep at it. It will happen and probably sooner rather than later.

Team Strengthener

Books on teams often talk as though teams will rush to make decisions. Sometimes they will. But sometimes they won't. They remember how it was in the organizations they worked in, that bad decisions were punished and good decisions got no one anywhere. *Don't try to force them.* When supported in these decisions, almost all people prefer to make the decisions that affect them; you can count on that. You need to help them see that teams are different, that they have the opportunity to participate fully in decision making, and that you will support them completely. That's a fundamental job of a team leader during the early stages of a team. Do it.

8–2

The Problem
The team permits only two members to assume leadership functions

The Scene

After the team decides how to handle the new project, you ask, "Okay, who's going to take the leadership role for this?"

Marie turns to Lorne: "Do you have time to do it?"

"Well, I guess . . ."

"Good. Wouldn't we all like to see Lorne take the lead?" Everyone nods—and that's that.

It's not that you have anything against Lorne; he is a good leader. But every time anything important comes up, the team asks either him or Belle (who's also good) to take the leadership role. You're sure that several other team members could also be effective leaders, but how do you get the team to see it?

Possible Causes

The team is still unsure of itself.

Teams take time to develop self-confidence, just as individuals do. While your team may be developing well, it may not yet have become confident that it could succeed by sharing leadership roles among many different individuals.

When other members led a couple of projects, they made mistakes.

As teams grow, they need to experiment, and experimenting often leads to "mistakes." Why do I put mistakes in quotation marks? Because only these "mistakes" permit growth. Both individuals and teams have to find out *what* doesn't work and *why* it doesn't work. The job of a leader when the team is growing is to help it avoid major mistakes and then help it learn from the minor ones it makes.

Lorne and Belle perform well only if they are leading.

It's often been said that a good leader must also be a good follower. In traditional organizations, being this good follower generally means doing what the boss says. Being a follower in a team no longer means that (though the team as a whole needs to know and support higher management's goals). Instead, being a follower means sharing the leadership role with other team members and supporting them as they act as leaders. Lorne and Belle haven't learned how to be effective followers yet.

Cures

If the team is still unsure of itself:

How do you deal with this lack of confidence? You might try this: Help the team identify two or three other leadership roles besides that of the overall leader. The Team Strengthener at the end of this case describes two of these. There are others. For instance, the team might select someone to be responsible for seeing that all timetables are met. That's a genuine part of the leadership role. When team members perform it, they begin to develop confidence in themselves, and the team begins to develop confidence in them.

Along with developing confidence, the team needs to make a mental shift. In a traditional organization, the supervisor is responsible for the performance of the workgroup. Not so in teams. A fully effective team knows that the team as a whole is responsible for its mission. It appoints leaders for certain tasks and functions, but it still remains responsible.

If other members made mistakes when they led projects:

If the team is still gun-shy because of mistakes some members made when they served as leaders, it's clear that it hasn't learned from the mistakes. If the incidents were recent enough that everyone's memory about them is clear, put the matter on the table for the team to discuss. Let the individuals who made the "mistakes" take the lead and describe what happened and what they learned from it. Then help both them and the team increase their learning.

If the "mistakes" were painful enough, you may want to talk, individually or together, with the individuals who made them. They may have bad feelings about them and not want to talk about them, especially with the team as a whole. You need to make your view of the "mistakes" clear and make equally clear that you will support them fully in the discussion.

The team should make this a regular process. Whenever a project is completed or a "mistake" is made in the course of the team's work, the team as a whole should look at what happened and find the learning in it. But what if the project was successful? It's just as important to look at it, both to see why it succeeded and what happened that got in the way of its success.

But back to the present. After the individuals and the team have learned from the "mistakes," the team should put these individuals back into leadership roles at the first opportunity. You may have quite a selling job to do; if so, do it. And unless there are strong reasons otherwise, put the person in the same kind of role. Do this for a few times and both you and the team will begin to discover how talented the members of the team are.

If Lorne and Belle perform well only if they are leading:

Begin by meeting with Lorne and Belle. If they have a good relationship, meet with them together. Why do they not perform well if they are not leading? Do they distrust others' abilities? Do they enjoy leading and dislike following others? Instead of making judgments about them, find out what the situation is.

Now you can work with them and help them change. Ask them to help you develop leadership skills in other members of the team. They may never have thought of doing this, and they may be excited by the idea. Suggest, though, that they serve more as mentors than as teachers; they want to help others find their own abilities, not tell them what they should do.

Do you talk with the team about your conversation with Lorne and Belle and tell it what you've decided? Preferably. If there's resentment of Lorne and Belle because they haven't been effective except as leaders, you may want to hold off for a while. Let the team see that they have changed and that they genuinely want to be a resource for others. It probably won't take long before the team itself wants to discuss what's happening.

Team Strengthener

There are many different leadership roles on an effective team—many different forms of leadership that different members of the team can exercise. While one member may be responsible for the overall project, for instance, another may take responsibility for keeping the team focused on its goal, and yet another may ensure that any conflict gets surfaced and dealt with effectively. Each is a true leadership role, and on an effective team members often trade these roles around so that everyone gains skills in most or all of the roles. Don't just concentrate on the formal leadership role, but help your team to understand the other roles and use them.

The Problem
The team constantly defers to one of its members

The Scene

"Well, shall we go ahead and implement the revised process?" Beth asks.

"It sounds good," Nguyen replies. "But I'd like to hear what Kevin has to say before we make up our minds."

"Yeah, me too," Greg chimes in. "Kevin, what do you think?"

"I like the idea, and Trish has done a lot of good work getting it together, but a couple of things about it bother me . . ."

From that point on, everything is predictable. Kevin goes over his objections point by point. Trish tries to explain why each change was the way it was, but no one really listens to her. As usual, the team ends up deciding to do just what Kevin thinks it should. He has very good ideas, but still. . . .

Possible Causes

The team is still thinking like a traditional workgroup.

Once again, the root of the problem may be that team members don't see themselves as a real team, but instead just another workgroup. In a traditional workgroup, the final decision on a matter is almost always made by an individual. It may be the person who was assigned the duties. It may be a senior worker. Or it may be the manager. Almost never does the group as a whole make the decision. Team members may not have learned that effective teams don't operate that way.

The team hasn't developed confidence in its abilities.

This cause may go hand in hand with the section above (and perhaps even with the one below). In this case, it's not that the team insists on making Kevin an expert. Instead, other members of the team recognize that his ideas are good and they aren't confident of their own. (In a traditional organization, most people most of the time don't get the chance to have their ideas taken seriously.)

Kevin is different from other members of the team.

This heading covers several different situations. Kevin may be significantly more intelligent than other members of the group. He may be much more highly educated (an engineer, for instance, when other members are technicians). Or he may have a much higher position than the others (he might be an ex-manager or a senior worker). Whatever the reason, it objectively makes him different from other team members.

Cures

If the team is still thinking like a traditional workgroup:

You need Kevin as an ally (just as you will in each of the following cures). He probably believes it's natural for the team to ask his opinion and follow it, and he probably enjoys this role. You don't want to attack him, for two reasons. First, both he and the other team members will probably resent the attack and oppose you. Second, and more important, you don't want to lessen either his motivation or his contribution to the team.

Instead, you need to talk with Kevin. How does he see his role on the team? Does he understand how a team needs to be different from a traditional workgroup? He may even feel that the team should not treat him as an expert, but doesn't know how to accomplish this. Whatever the situation, your goal is to reach agreement that his role will change. He will still be a strong member of the team, but he will work actively to involve everyone in the decision making.

It's best if Kevin brings up the matter with the team. He can explain the situation as he sees it. The rest of the team should have every opportunity to respond to what he says. (Their answers are likely to be along the lines of "But we value your opinion" or "Your ideas are so good.") Then very gently you and Kevin need to encourage the rest of the team to start voicing their ideas and to be willing to disagree with Kevin. And Kevin needs to respond by encouraging their ideas and refraining from offering his own whenever possible. Then both you and he will have to act out these commitments again and again, until the team becomes comfortable without him in an "expert" role.

If the team hasn't developed confidence in its abilities:

Use basically the same solution described in the previous section. You need Kevin's help. In this case, though, you want him to help you encourage ideas from others even more. The other team members need to see that they do have good ideas and that as they continue to offer them and discuss them, their ideas will get better and better.

One thing to watch out for: Initially the ideas of other team members will be expressed tentatively and often incompletely. It will be easy for you or Kevin to correct them or reject them. *Don't.* If you encourage the ideas and help individuals develop them, you will find that the strength and completeness of the ideas begin to rise rapidly.

If Kevin is different from other members of the team:

First answer this question: Is it appropriate for him to be on the team? Should he be on a different team, one made up of others largely like himself (other engineers or senior workers, for instance)? If he should, is it practical to help him get reassigned? If so, work with him to help him understand the situation, which he may understand very well already, and then work out the reassignment.

But it may be appropriate for him to be on the team, or it may not be possible to reassign him. In these cases, you need to follow the suggestions in the first two sections of this case and work with him to balance the team out as best the two of you can. However, the most effective solution may involve a special role for him, one that uses his particular qualifications. The team might agree, for instance, that in certain matters he is the expert, and other members will use him as the resource person in these matters.

Team Strengthener

When an individual (such as Kevin) is consistently treated as an expert, he begins to develop expertise in presenting ideas. He presents his ideas often in complete and polished form; they sound good "right out of the box." But he didn't begin that way, and neither will other members of the team who are just learning to express ideas and opinions. Their ideas will be much more fragmentary and incomplete. This represents a key transition point; every member of the team needs to help every other member develop his or her ideas, so that the individuals become expert at expressing them. How do team members help? By listening. By asking good, leading questions. "Do you mean that. . .?" or "Can you tell me more about. . .?" Both effective listening and effective questioning are significant skills, so that everyone who uses them also becomes more skillful—including, probably, Kevin.

8–4

The Problem

The team is ready to be self-leading, but your boss wants you to perform all the leadership functions

The Scene

"Are you telling me that you let the team decide how to do the Quality Renaissance project without you and that Mark Taggert is going to lead it?"

"It really wasn't that big a deal, Mr. Bakkurian. Mark knows at least as much about the program as I do, and the other people on the team with him are first rate. You don't need to worry about . . ."

"I'll decide whether to worry or not, and when you're the leader I don't, but when you don't lead I worry. Now I want you to go back and take that project over yourself. Use Mark as your assistant if you want; that's fine. But as long as you're the leader you're going to personally direct any project as important as the Renaissance. Got that?"

You got it, because Mr. Bakkurian is loud and clear. But he's wrong. The team is ready to be self-managing and your taking back over is really going to disappoint it. And if you don't find a way to change Mr. Bakkurian's approach, morale is going to start heading for the cellar in a hurry.

Possible Causes

Mr Bakkurian believes that team leaders should act as supervisors.

Mr. Bakkurian may be managing teams, but he's still thinking in terms of traditional workgroups. In a traditional organization, it's important for every workgroup to have one designated leader or supervisor who is responsible for everything the team does. If there's a problem, higher management goes to this individual. Unfortunately, team-based organizations can't operate well this way. A team doesn't really hit its stride until everyone acts in leadership roles of one kind or another.

Mr. Bakkurian doesn't believe in teams.

Mr. Bakkurian may have had many years as a traditional manager. If so, no wonder he's most comfortable with established procedures and chains of command and with individual rather than team responsibility. When he looks at a team, he sees confusion and blurred responsibility. He's never really become comfortable with that way of organizing.

He's afraid he'll lose control if you aren't the permanent leader.

Control is a critical issue for managers in traditional organizations. One of the greatest fears of many managers is that they'll lose control in one way or another. Team-based organizations can't operate in this way, but that doesn't necessarily change managers' view of managing. Mr. Bakkurian is used to the traditional environment. He wants to maintain control, and he doesn't see how he can do this unless he has just one permanent leader—you.

Hints

This case is similar to several others in which higher-level managers are still thinking in traditional management terms. (See Cases 10–3 and 10–7.)

The three causes don't exclude one another. One, two, or all three of them may be contributing to the problem.

Cures

If Mr Bakkurian believes that team leaders should act as supervisors:

How do you begin communicating this to Mr. Bakkurian? First, make sure he has confidence in you and the team. If the team has been producing so-so results or missing deadlines or otherwise failing to perform at its best, start by correcting this situation. Mr. Bakkurian will never begin to change until he has confidence that the team is both talented and motivated and that it produces consistently high-quality results.

When the team is clearly performing effectively, start negotiating with Mr. Bakkurian. Will he accept it if you lead a project but delegate most of the actual leadership up to the team members on the project? Will he let you permit someone else to lead a project if that person and you report to him on a regular basis? What else can you suggest that will enlarge the team's freedom to rotate leadership and at the same time reassure him that everything is going well?

If Mr. Bakkurian doesn't believe in teams:

How do you change this? Follow the first step in the section above: Make sure the team is performing effectively. And make sure Mr. Bakkurian knows that it's performing effectively. If he sees that despite his dislike of teams your team gets its mission done efficiently and effectively, his attitude may start to soften.

Then you can start negotiating more freedom for the team, as in the section above. Rather than making leadership an issue, stress how high morale is, how economically the team goes about its business, how satisfied its customers are. (Perhaps you could get a customer or two to contact him and say that.) Stress how these results come from the team organization itself and suggest that the more freedom the team has to develop its own leadership the more effective it will be. Your basic goal in all this is to demonstrate that the team is superior to a traditional workgroup. If you do this, he will probably be willing to loosen up and see if the team can handle its new freedom. It's then up to the team, of course, to demonstrate that it can.

If Mr. Bakkurian is afraid he'll lose control if you aren't the permanent leader:

Your task is clear, though it may be very hard and take quite a while. You need to show Mr. Bakkurian that he can have all the control he needs even though the team is self-managing. As always, this begins by the team performing effectively—he won't have any motivation to change unless he sees that the team is consistently good at what it does.

The critical issue for Mr. Bakkurian is control. He needs to see that the team stays focused on its mission even without a permanent leader. Perhaps even more, he needs to see that he can get quick, responsible answers to his questions, whether he gets them from you or from someone else. One way to begin moving in this direction is to let other team members report to him on important milestones. You might need to be there as the team leader, but the other individual handles the session. If Mr. Bakkurian sees that other team members are competent and responsive, his attitude toward them will probably begin to change. He might even suggest that "so-and-so really looks like a performer—he needs some more responsibility."

Team Strengthener

What does it mean to satisfy a customer? It means to help the individual, team, or organization become more successful at their mission. You can apply the same logic with your higher-level manager and, indeed, with all higher-level management. Managers have goals, which range all the way from wanting quick promotions to simply staying in their job and staying out of trouble. The way you satisfy your manager is to find out what his or her goals are and then act in the ways that help him or her to achieve these goals. Why does Mr. Bakkurian want to keep control? What is his basic goal? The team should find the answer to that question and then do what it can to help him meet this basic goal. Then, with patience and skill, it can show him how to meet the goal without having to maintain tight control.

8–5

The Problem

When you encourage others to lead the team, they don't do very well

The Scene

"Can I talk with you for just a moment?"

"Certainly, Mr. Dana. What's up?"

"I really wasn't very happy with the way your team handled the project you gave me earlier this week. It wasn't a first-rate job. What happened?"

"I meant to warn you—and I'm sorry I didn't. I've been trying to spread the leadership around, and frankly it's not working that well. Chris headed the most recent project, and you've seen what happened. I really want others to be leaders, too, but not when we get these kinds of results."

"Well, keep working on it. I can live with your spreading the leadership around, but only if we get better results."

"I understand. I just need to figure out a way to improve the situation."

Possible Causes

The team isn't developed enough to share leadership.

Teams take time to "jell." Team members have to get to know one another and feel comfortable with one another. Since most team members come from backgrounds where leaders were almost always managers, they didn't get a chance to develop leadership skills. Because of this, they don't have confidence in their abilities to lead. The combination of lack of experience and lack of confidence makes it difficult for team members to perform effectively in leadership roles.

You're not helping other members learn leadership roles.

Did you select a team member (such as Chris) to assume a leadership role and then not help him perform the role effectively? You may have been a manager or leader for so long that knowing what to do is second nature to you. But it's not to workers who've never had the experience. For all practical purposes, you've given them a job requiring skills they've never used before, then expected them to do it competently.

You've been too strong a leader.

Traditional organizations often stress that managers should be "strong" managers and "strong" leaders. Having a reputation as a strong manager is often a necessity for promotion. You've apparently brought those ideas over to the team with you.

Hint

Once again, one, two, or all three of the causes may be part of the problem. Pay particular attention to the third cause.

Cures

If the team isn't developed enough to share leadership:

Each of the next two sections may have useful suggestions for dealing with this, so look at them. Your primary goal at the moment, though, is to help the individual members come together as a team. They need to mature so that they begin to think of themselves as a true team. How does this help? When an individual is asked to take a leadership role, he or she can count on everyone else being supportive. This makes it much easier for the person to perform as leader and to ask for help when it's needed.

Since mature teams understand the strengths and weaknesses of their members, the team (and you) can do a much more effective job of picking the right leader for the right project and then supporting this individual with other team members who will help him or her succeed.

If you're not helping other members learn leadership roles:

This doesn't work. Individuals can be more effective leaders when they're part of a mature team, but that's not the whole picture. They also need to be coached or mentored by other individuals, such as yourself, who have the skills they need to learn.

Now you have a clear course of action. When an appropriate project comes along (preferably as soon as possible), select a team member to be its leader. Then meet with the individual and help him or her develop an effective plan. Have the individual talk through the plan, outlining what should happen at each point. Arrange milestones, where the individual will meet with you to discuss progress. There should be frequent milestones at the beginning (perhaps every few days) but less frequent ones as the individual performs successfully. Don't ever take responsibility back; let the individual retain it no matter how tough things get. Just keep coaching.

Things may be a little rocky for a while. After all, the individuals are just learning some demanding skills. But if you stick in there and devote yourself to helping them, they'll pick up the skills. And because you're backstopping them, you won't have any more mediocre products, which will make your next-level manager happy.

Take a look at the third section of Case 8–9 for some more suggestions.

If you've been too strong a leader:

Well, the time has come to get rid of your old ideas of what makes a strong manager and adopt a style more suited to effective team performance. What's that style? A team leader makes the greatest contribution to the team when he or she becomes a teacher and a coach. You teach when you *tell and show* other team members how to perform effectively. You coach when you help them actually perform effectively. And the more you act like a coach, the faster other team members will acquire leadership skills.

The section above explained the rudiments of coaching; read it. Most important, though, make the mental shift required. Think of yourself differently. You may have difficulty making the transition—most managers do. Go to a course in coaching, watch videos on coaching, read a book on coaching. Get the role clear in your mind. Then act out the role. And as you learn more about what it means to be a coach, explain it to the team. As team members become more proficient, they will need to become effective coaches to other members.

Team Strengthener

When a manager moves from being a supervisor to a team leader, coach, and teacher, the individual doesn't move from being a "strong" manager to being a "weak" one. Weak managers do no good for anyone in any situation. Instead, the individual changes roles and contributes different activities and skills to the team. The heart of the skills is this: An effective team leader *passes on to the team* all of his or her skills. On an effective team, no one is *the* leader. Everyone is a leader in some ways and at some times. That's your goal.

8–6

The Problem
The team won't support the leaders it picks

The Scene

"Can I talk with you for a moment?"
"Sure, Carl. What's the matter?"

"You know the team asked me to look at the different word processors we could use and recommend the one we should pick, right?"

"Yes. Are you having problems?"

"I just can't get anyone to help me. I wanted to have two or three of the other people on the team use it so I could compare their reactions to mine. But everyone says they don't have the time."

"Okay, Carl—I'll bring it up at the next meeting. If they want you to take the responsibility, they need to support you."

Possible Causes

The individuals don't yet think of themselves as a true team.

It takes time for a team to mature so that leadership roles can be taken by different team members. The case before this one stressed maturity from the point of view of the leader. It's just as important from the point of view of the team itself.

Carl and other team members don't have good leadership skills.

Workers in traditional organizations don't get much opportunity to learn and use leadership skills. And these skills can't be developed overnight.

The team gave Carl the project because the rest of the team didn't want to be bothered with it.

In this case, it's neither Carl's lack of leadership nor the team's failure to support him. The team asked him to take the project so that it wouldn't have to be bothered further with it. The failure of other members to support him results from this.

Hint

The leader makes a serious mistake in the comment at the end of the scene that opens this case. Can you identify why it's a mistake? (See the Team Strengthener for more information.)

Cures

If the individuals don't yet think of themselves as a true team:

It takes time for a team to mature to the point that members feel committed to one another, and this commitment is even more difficult when one of the members is in a leadership role. You need to help the team develop this maturity.

In the meantime, you may need to keep the leadership role for yourself most of the time. What you can do, though, is to select one team member as your assistant on any of the significant projects. Then involve this individual as much as possible in the project, so that he or she begins to pick up the necessary skills. If you do this for a period of time and you see that everyone gets the opportunity to help lead, you will develop leadership skills at the same time the team matures. And since the individual you select is your assistant rather than the leader, it may be easier for the team to accept him or her.

If Carl and other team members don't have good leadership skills:

Ask yourself if you're carrying over attitudes toward leadership from experience in a traditional organization. If you were the manager there, you remained the manager. You had no responsibility for developing leadership abilities in others. Are you perhaps still thinking in those terms? It's time to change. Helping other team members become effective leaders is now one of your core responsibilities.

How do you help team members develop these skills? Look back at the second section in Case 8–5. It has several suggestions for developing leadership in individual team members.

The last paragraph of the section above, concerning appointing an assistant rather than a team leader, also contains a useful suggestion for developing individual ability to lead. When you feel that you need to keep the leadership of a project, use its suggestions to help develop other leaders on the team.

Don't feel confined by these suggestions. Draw on any resources you can find. Do whatever it takes to help other team members develop into leaders.

If the team gave Carl the project because the rest of the team didn't want to be bothered with it:

What's the problem here? The team wasn't clear with Carl or Carl didn't listen closely enough—or both. He didn't get the word that the project was his alone, that no one else wanted to be concerned with it until he came back with a recommendation. If possible, have Carl bring the problem up with the team. Let them work it out. If you don't feel Carl and the team have developed enough to do this successfully, bring it up yourself. Then guide Carl and the team to resolve it.

This may provide an excellent teaching/learning opportunity. If the team hasn't learned how to be clear when it assigns leadership responsibility, it can learn from its failure to do so in this case. If Carl and others haven't learned to listen carefully to what they're accepting, and to ask the right questions, this is their opportunity to start learning to do so.

Team Strengthener

What did the team leader do at the end of the case? She rescued Carl. That is, she took over responsibility for solving the problem. Unless there's a crisis and this is the only way out, rescuing a team member who's acting as a leader is counterproductive. Carl needs to confront the problem. The assignment was his, and he needs to finish it, though a good team leader will work with him and help him decide how to do so. Once you delegate a project, though, let the individual stick with it. That's the only way team members will be able to develop self-confidence in their abilities.

8–7

The Problem

A team member won't take a leadership role but constantly criticizes those who do

The Scene

"Charlie, I'd never do it that way," Mario says pointedly.

"Well, it's too late to tell me now," Charlie responds. "This is the way we're going."

"Everybody to his own tastes, I guess, but I think you're wasting all kinds of time."

"Mario," Evelyn joins in, "why don't you lay off Charlie. You had a chance to lead this project, but you turned it down."

Mario responds with a shrug: "Yeah—I'm too busy. I just don't like to see somebody screw up what could have been a good project." With that, he turns and wanders away.

Mario could probably be an effective leader, but he won't accept leadership positions in the team. Instead, he always criticizes the way anyone else leads anything. How can you get him to stop criticizing and start trying to lead?

Possible Causes

Mario lacks confidence in his leadership ability.

Sometimes individuals get caught in an internal trap. They lack self-confidence in their ability to do a job, so they avoid doing the job but can't let themselves appreciate those who can. Mario may be caught this way. He'd probably like to take a try at being a leader, but isn't confident he could pull it off. So he maintains his self-esteem by criticizing those who try.

He habitually criticizes leaders.

In traditional organizations, many workers feel as though they have little or no power, no part to play in making significant decisions. It becomes easy for an individual in that situation to turn negative about those who do make decisions and to constantly criticize them. Mario may well have come from such an environment.

Mario is unhappy with the team.

Mario's critical attitude may conceal a deeper dissatisfaction. He may feel the team isn't treating him right or that he doesn't belong on the team. He may feel that he's not getting the recognition he's due. He may prefer to be an individual worker. It doesn't matter, though, what the cause is.

Cures

If Mario lacks confidence in his leadership ability:

This approach is harmful both for Mario and for the rest of the team. What's the best way to deal with it? If the team has enough maturity to confront Mario without attacking him, that's the best route. The fact that it doesn't attack Mario, though, doesn't mean that it lets him off the hook. The discussion may run over several sessions, but the team should persist. When Mario attempts to criticize someone else who has taken a leadership role, it needs to bring him up short. It then needs to make clear to Mario that the way he earns the right to criticize others is to take the risks of leadership himself.

Remember that though the team keeps pushing Mario, its goal is to persuade him to try his hand at leadership. Peer pressure, particularly in a team, is a powerful force. Once Mario is willing to take a leadership role, the team should fully support him. The worst step the team can take is to set him up for failure as a leader. It needs to back him just as it would any other member.

If Mario habitually criticizes leaders:

If this appears to be the case, the team needs to confront Mario with his behavior. Look at the section above for some suggestions. In this case, though, the team is trying to help Mario break a long-standing habit. He needs to understand how a team is different from a traditional work unit and that his habit of criticizing leaders has no place in a team.

Together with this, of course, the team needs to nudge him into taking a leadership role and then supporting him in that role.

If Mario is unhappy with the team:

Chapter 3 discusses several situations where an individual's behavior is the result of his or her dissatisfaction. Look back at it for some ideas on how to handle Mario's actions.

As the cases in Chapter 3 stress, the team's goal is to get Mario's real dissatisfaction out on the table where he and the team can deal with it. This requires sensitivity and patience combined with persistence. The team must first work with Mario to identify the real problem, then work with him to resolve it.

Team Strengthener

Because traditional organizations so often concentrate on blaming individuals, it's hard for a team to realize that confrontation doesn't have to mean blame. Confrontation is a necessity for team effectiveness. When an individual is behaving in a way that handicaps the team or makes it harder for members to work together, the team must call the person on his or her behavior. But it must do it without accusation or blame. Instead, it poses the problem and then enlists the individual's help to solve the problem. The goal is always to remove the problem but integrate the individual even more closely into the team. It can be done, and a good facilitator can be invaluable in helping it happen.

The Problem
The team won't accept leadership from anyone

The Scene

"Look, I'm not ready to make a decision yet."

"But, Freda, we have to do something. I know it's not perfect, but I do have a plan for getting started on the project. We can always change it later if it doesn't seem to be working."

"Art, I thought this was supposed to be a self-managing team. Well, I'm managing myself and I don't think this is a wise step . . ."

"Yes," Carlos interrupts, "I don't think we should do anything unless we all agree on it. And we sure don't agree on this."

For the third time in two weeks, the team is paralyzed because the members won't accept another member's attempt to resolve a stalemate and provide leadership. How do you and the team get around this increasingly serious problem?

Possible Causes

Different members of the team are thinking of leadership in different ways.

Some members, such as Freda, are thinking of leadership as based on everyone's agreement. Art is more directive: He thinks that if an individual takes a "strong" approach, the others ought to follow him.

Attempts at leadership are caught up in status and power issues.

Art, Freda, Carlos, and others are struggling for influence on the team. To let someone else have influence, each of them thinks, is to lose it for oneself. They're carrying over to the team the picture of leadership they developed in their previous jobs in more traditional organizations.

Team members don't trust one anothers' motives.

This is even more fundamental than the cause above, because it reflects an underlying distrust that makes it impossible for the team to perform effectively.

Hints

The causes don't exclude one another. One, two, or all three could be underlying the problem. None of the causes are easy to correct, but until the problem is solved it will continue to paralyze the team. In other words, get to it!

Cures

If different members of the team are thinking of leadership in different ways:

This is probably the easiest cause of the three. It is also the best place to start because you can use it as an entryway (if necessary) to the next two causes.

This topic is important enough to schedule a team meeting to discuss it. Perhaps the best way to begin is to state the problem and then let each team member describe how he or she understands leadership. You or another member can then condense the descriptions and put them on a flip chart or white board. When everyone has contributed, combine whatever definitions you can to reduce them to the smallest number that won't leave out anyone's ideas.

Then go through the list, one definition at a time, and ask: "If we all agreed on this definition, how would we act?" This should raise important questions not only of what the team does but how members treat one another. Once these questions are on the table, the team can begin to construct at least a tentative leadership model to use.

If the team can't make it to the last step, you will need to start exploring the next two causes.

If attempts at leadership are caught up in status and power issues:

When you begin the discussion described in the section above, "listen through" team members' comments, particularly if the team appears to be getting bogged down. Are members trying to build and defend their place in the team? ("Look, I spent eight years in Finance—frankly, I think I ought to be the leader for any financial projects we have.") And are they trying to establish alliances? ("I really think Carlos, Wendy, and I ought to be in on all the new product discussions.")

You might call this the "scarcity model of leadership": We each have to fight for it because we can't all have enough of it. Successful teams find that there are abundant opportunities: Everyone can have enough. How do you get from scarcity to abundance? Only by having the team start spreading leadership around. Find a shared leadership model that everyone is willing to try temporarily. If possible, have someone from another team that has successfully solved the problem explain to the team the way they exercise leadership. Get your team going so they can start to get some experience.

If team members don't trust one anothers' motives:

If this is the core cause, you are in the midst of a life-and-death issue for the team. Either the trust develops or the team falls apart.

Unless you are extremely well versed in team dynamics, find a good facilitator to help with this. It will take time to get the issue of trust on the table, and the first few sessions at least are apt to be stormy.

If you can't get a good facilitator? Can you and the team attend a team-building course together? If not, look through the many cases in this book that deal with trust—beginning with Case 1–1.

Team Strengthener

The situation this case describes is harmful enough on its own. It is also harmful because it invites one or even both of two other undesirable situations. First, as the second section above suggested, it can lead to cliques as a way of dealing with the scarcity of leadership opportunities. Second, it can lead to a collusion between you and the rest of the team that keeps you permanently in the leadership role. The two may combine in a clique forming that encourages you to exercise leadership and depend on them as your right-hand people. Needless to say, for the sake of the team, these tendencies need to be chopped down as quickly as possible.

8–9

The Problem
The team has a very rigid approach to leadership

The Scene

"All right, Carla, you need to ask everyone how they feel and then we'll take a vote."

"Gee, Sol, I think it's pretty clear that we're all in agreement on this. Checking with everyone and then voting seems like a waste . . .

"Now, let's not hurry, Carla," Harriet interrupts. "It's never a waste of time to follow the right leadership procedure."

And so it continues. A relatively simple matter that should have been resolved in minutes is dragging on and on. There must be some way to get the team to loosen up.

Possible Causes

The team is inexperienced as a team and is using approaches that they've used in clubs or read about in books on teams.

The team may not have had useful training in team leadership roles, or they may not have had any training at all. So it's using what it knows.

The team has gotten burned by leadership behavior in the past and is attempting to prevent its happening again.

Perhaps someone in a leadership role ran roughshod over the rest of the team. The team has concluded that the best way to prevent a recurrence of this is to adopt and insist on rigid procedures.

The team doesn't trust itself to relax and let leadership roles develop.

In traditional organizations, no one does much ad-libbing where management is concerned. So why expect it to happen in teams?

Cures

If the team is inexperienced as a team and is using approaches that they've used in clubs or read about in books on teams:

Since this most likely results from lack of training, training appears to be the best solution. Talk with your training department and have them arrange it. If that doesn't work, find a commercial provider or a local community college to provide it.

Just be sure that team members get the chance to practice what they've learned as soon as possible after they've learned it. If they don't start practicing, they'll forget the new ideas and go back to what they're familiar with.

If the team has gotten burned by leadership behavior in the past and is attempting to prevent its happening again:

Having fixed leadership procedures may be a good idea for a while. It may still be a good idea. But it's a temporary one, which the team needs to move beyond.

When you believe that the team needs to move beyond its rigidity—and you are hoping it is ready to do so—make it the topic of a team meeting. See where everyone on the team is with the issue. Remember that the procedures arose because of a painful experience; help team members deal with their emotions on the matter. Then help them move beyond emotion to a rational decision on the subject.

If the team doesn't trust itself to relax and let leadership roles develop:

This largely requires team maturity and team members gaining confidence in one another. But there are steps you can take to expedite the process. For instance, if a team member comes up with a simpler way of handling something, call it to the team's attention as an example of how it might begin depending on itself and its members to find creative new ways of exercising leadership.

Another thought: If the team is coming along and maturing, you might be able to intervene in situations such as the one in this case and ask whether the particular procedure is even needed in the current circumstance. This may help team members begin to ask the same questions on their own and thus start loosening up.

Team Strengthener

This book makes many recommendations that the team do this and the team remember that. So does every book on teams. Study these recommendations and use them where they help. But your goal is helping the team find the way to operate that it's most comfortable with and that works for it. This requires confidence, and one sure sign of team maturity appears when it develops this confidence. Make the development of this confidence one of your basic goals as team leader and team member.

CHAPTER 9

Problems With Your Team's Mission

The team's mission is the key to its success. When the team possesses a clear, unique, important mission, it will most likely succeed. But when the mission isn't clear, or isn't unique, or the team doesn't believe it's important, problems begin. And when the team has problems with its mission, no amount of positive attitude and hard work can make up for them.

The cases in this chapter all deal with problems a team can have with its mission. Your team will almost certainly encounter one of the problems, and it may encounter several. Don't worry; organizations often create teams and assign missions to them without thinking through what the missions are. And even when an organization is careful about the way it assigns missions to teams, missions change.

Review the cases in this chapter occasionally, even if the team doesn't have one of the problems the chapter describes. Mission problems can sneak up on a team, particularly if the team has been concentrating on day-to-day problems or on accomplishing a major project. Don't let that happen to you and your team.

A team often has trouble dealing with mission problems because it often needs at least its next-level manager's permission to change its mission. This chapter doesn't try to explain how to "get around" your manager. It does provide a variety of recommendations for taking the initiative and making it easy for your manager to approve mission changes.

The Problem
The team's mission isn't clear

The Scene

"Whatta ya mean, that's not our job?" Tal virtually yells into the phone. "If it has to do with networking, it's our job." There's a long pause while he listens intently to the individual at the other end.

"We're gonna have to find someone to settle this," he says finally. "That's our business and we're the ones who're going to do it!" Without waiting for an answer, he hangs up.

The incident would be bad enough if it were the only one, but the same kind of thing has happened three times in the last two months. You thought you knew what the team's mission was, but now you're confused. Somehow, you and the team have got to get this cleared up.

Possible Causes

The organization didn't think through assignments to different teams.

In traditional organizations, units and individuals are usually given specific duties and tasks to carry out. The job of a voucher examiner, for instance, is to look at a certain number of vouchers in a day or week and decide what can and can't be paid. If anyone worries about a mission, it happens at higher management levels.

Not so with teams. Teams outproduce traditional units only when they have clear missions that team members can commit themselves to. If the voucher examiner in the paragraph above is part of a team, she needs to understand just what the team as a whole must accomplish and what she contributes to it. The more the team operates as an integrated whole, the more she may be performing duties that go beyond her role as a voucher examiner. She can do this successfully only if she has a clear focus on the overall mission. When the mission is fuzzy, neither she nor any other team members can develop this focus, and this seriously limits her performance.

The organization doesn't understand how to establish effective boundaries.

This may have produced the situation just above: The organization can't think effectively about how to draw lines among the various teams. If so, the problem probably carries over from the previous traditional organization. Lines between units may not have been very clear then. In fact, managers may have spent much of their time negotiating who does what. If that sounds familiar, your team has a serious problem on its hands.

Teams don't work together closely enough.

No matter if one or both of the causes above are part of the problem, this one almost certainly is both a cause and an effect. It helps cause the problem because the teams spend time arguing instead of clarifying missions. And it's an effect of the problem because the fuzzy missions push the teams to defend their turf, which can easily take precedence over working with one another.

Hint

None of these causes excludes the others. One, two, or all three of them may be contributing to the problem.

Cures

If the organization didn't think through assignments to different teams:

If this is the cause of your team's unclear mission, the team needs to start to work to change the situation. If possible, get other teams that have the same problem involved (see the last section in this case for some suggestions). Identify the conflicts specifically. Also identify what appears to be, or should be, the team's core mission and the responsibilities that go with it, so the team has a clear alternative to suggest to the current situation. Then present your case to your next-level manager and enlist his or her help.

Don't let your enthusiasm to get your mission clarified make it appear that the team is trying to aggrandize itself at other teams' expense. If what you propose looks like a power play on the team's part, it will probably backfire, particularly if the teams don't work well together. You're not trying to expand; you do that by producing efficient, high-quality work. You're simply trying to get a clear mission everyone on the team can concentrate on.

If the organization doesn't understand how to establish effective boundaries:

How does the team go about solving this problem? The best avenue is to work with other teams; the next section goes into that alternative. At the same time, see if you can enlist the team's next-level manager. Does he or she understand the situation and give it enough priority to be willing to work on it? If so, start collecting the data on where the conflicts occur.

Then identify the one or two other teams with which these conflicts most often occur and try to enlist their help. It may also be effective to concentrate on other teams reporting to next-level managers that your manager has good relationships with. Take the highest priority conflicts to your higher-level manager, so he or she can begin working with other managers to resolve them at their level. This will probably be a slow process, but it will bear results.

If teams don't work together closely enough:

No matter what, your team needs to get to work immediately to change this. Every team member probably has friends or at least connections on other teams. The team should assign a mission to every member to begin building up these relationships. The team may want to visit every other team that is a customer, supplier, or colleague to discuss any issues that are causing problems in the relationship.

In the meantime, the team has a specific problem with a specific other team. Start working on this. You or someone else on your team needs to meet with a representative of that team. The goal: to lay the groundwork for a joint team that will clarify the missions of both teams, especially as they impact one another. If the other team isn't interested, back off for the moment, but only for the moment. Take every opportunity to work with that team and keep suggesting that both teams would be better off if they jointly clarified their missions. Patience and persistence pay.

Team Strengthener

A team should have a formal, written mission statement. This should be one of the first pieces of paper a new member receives, and it should be carefully explained to the individual. Whenever conflict occurs with another team, your team should examine its mission statement to see how it bears on the conflict. And it should review the mission statement as often as necessary, but at least once a year, to make sure it still fits the organization's and team's current operations.

9–2

The Problem
The team doesn't think its mission is important

The Scene

"Mickey, we're not going to meet tomorrow's deadline unless we really get to it," you say. You try not to sound like a boss but you're concerned about the team's performance.

"I know I ought to worry about that, but you and I both know no one cares whether the report gets out of here then— or ever. What's it been, two months, since we did the space utilization study? Have we heard a word? Does anyone care? The only thing we've done all year that anyone cared about was the revision of the executive suite—and I sure don't want to go through that again!"

You won't admit it out loud, but you know Mickey is right. The organization apparently consolidated all the responsibilities that didn't fit any other teams' mission and gave them to your team. You could live with that, except none of the responsibilities seem to matter to anyone else. But how can you change the situation?

Possible Causes

The team or its members (or both) have a poor reputation.

This is a hard question to ask, but is the team made up not only of unimportant duties but of individuals who weren't wanted elsewhere? (Doubly hard: Is this true of you?) After all, from the organization's point of view it makes sense to combine unimportant responsibilities with inefficient workers.

The team's responsibilities used to be important, but aren't in the current team-based organization.

This cause seems similar to the one above, but there's one critical difference. Your team wasn't assigned these responsibilities because no one thought well of you. That means you can count on the team to want to solve the problem and do worthwhile work. And these responsibilities may have been important when they were assigned to the team. But time has passed and—without anyone intending it—the responsibilities have become unimportant to the organization.

The team hasn't taken the initiative it should.

Teams cannot wait passively for the organization to correct their problems, even a problem so fundamental as an unnecessary mission. Your team needs to actively seek new missions. And it needs to actively seek new customers.

Cures

If the team or its members (or both) have a poor reputation:

What do you do? How much energy and perseverance do you have? Some other members of the team are probably more than happy to do work that doesn't tax them. They may have spent the last number of years doing just that. You may have an ally or two who are willing to do real work. If so, your job will be easier. And it is a job, because you're going to have to find real work for the team to do and then persuade them to do it.

If you decide that you really want to do worthwhile work and that you're willing to lead the team in that direction, look at the next section for suggestions on how to proceed.

If the team's responsibilities used to be important, but aren't in the current team-based organization:

Don't wait longer. You and the team need to change the situation before someone else notices that your mission is unimportant. Take a two-pronged attack. The next section describes how to find customers; it's the first prong, and it's the key to the entire problem. But it needs to be supplemented by another approach. If your next-level manager is sympathetic to the team and has confidence in it, you need to enlist him or her as an ally to get your formal mission changed.

How do you do this? First, get the facts together on what you're doing now. Show how no one uses the team's products. Summarize the impact that this has on the team's morale and willingness to work hard. Then take all of the information to your next-level manager. Show him or her how wasteful the team's mission is—both in terms of its usefulness and in terms of all the talent that's underemployed by the organization. Then suggest what mission the team might assume. This takes us to the next section.

If the team hasn't taken the initiative it should:

How do you go about finding a new mission, or new responsibilities that together might make a full-time mission? Can you expand what you provide your current customer or find new customers? Team members need to fan out throughout the organization. If the team has good relationships with the units it provides products to, ask them what would have been useful instead of what the team provided. Ask other teams and units what you might be able to do for them that no one else is doing. (Two qualifications here: First, you're not trying to replace other teams. Second, be sure to concentrate on work the team can do; this isn't the time to volunteer for duties no one has the skills to perform.)

As you find work that's needed but not performed, start looking at all the work together. Find the most logical groupings of products you can, then find the most logical overall mission you can create from the groupings. Keep at it, no matter how long it takes, until you've found appropriate work and appropriate new customers. Then package this new mission and take it to your next-level manager.

For more suggestions, look at Cases 5–1, 5–2, 5–3, and 5–6.

Team Strengthener

Your organization may not have trained itself or its teams to think in terms of a chain of customers. What does that mean? It means that everything your team does is done for an internal or external customer. And what it does is only as important as its customers believe it is. Every team should know all its customers and understand exactly what they need. And every team member should keep his or her eyes and ears open for ways that the team can provide more value to its customers. At times, these customers may suggest other customers. ("We like your expedited service so much that we told the Division administrative unit about it. You need to talk to them; I think they're interested in it.") Know your customers. Know their needs. Meet these needs. Then look for opportunities to meet the needs better or to meet other needs. This is the world's best defense against becoming unimportant.

The Problem

The team's mission overlaps that of another team

The Scene

"I thought we were supposed to work up all the promotional materials for the SuperSystem fall rollout?"

"That's the way I understood it," you answer. "What's up?"

"I was just visiting Emelda in the Scarlet & Grey Team and they're working on it. She was amazed to find out we thought it was ours, and she suggested that we get together as quickly as we can and iron the situation out."

"Good idea," you respond, nodding. "Set it up and tell me when."

Fortunately, your team has good relations with the Scarlet & Grey Team, so you're confident you can work the problem out quickly without anyone getting upset. But the deeper issue is why this happened in the first place, and that's what you need to find out and solve.

Possible Causes

The organization didn't set realistic boundaries among the teams.

Either through neglect or lack of competence, organizations may fail to divide missions realistically among teams. For instance, the delegations to different teams may be so broad that it's difficult if not impossible to tell what team is responsible for what. This leads to exactly the kind of overlap depicted in this case.

The missions of the two teams have converged since the missions were first assigned.

The organization may have done a completely adequate job of separating the missions of the two teams when they were first established. But things change, and team missions change with them. Without either team intending to infringe on the other, their responsibilities have begun to overlap.

There should be an overlap at this point.

No matter how hard they try, organizations can't banish all the potential overlap among teams. It may really be the case that doing the work on the SuperSystem is genuinely part of the mission of both teams. For instance, your team may be responsible for all initial promotions, while the Scarlet & Grey team is responsible for all seasonal promotions. It just happens that the rollout of the SuperSystem is also a Christmas promotion, so that both teams have a valid stake in the event.

Hint

The causes listed assume that the overlap was unintended. It also may be the other team's attempt to take over part of your mission. If this seems to be what's happening, look back at the cases in Chapter 7 for suggestions on how to handle the situation.

Cures

If the organization didn't set realistic boundaries among the teams:

The team needs to take the initiative and clarify the boundary between itself and the other team. Begin by meeting with the other team to see if the two teams can negotiate a boundary acceptable to both. If the teams can, the problem is taken care of.

Suppose the two teams can't resolve the situation on their own? You need to get higher management to resolve it. Look at the first two sections of Case 9–1 for suggestions.

If the missions of the two teams have converged since the missions were first assigned:

If the relationship between the two teams is as good as the relationship sketched in this case, the solution is clear. Representatives of your team should meet with representatives of the other team and work out boundaries that both teams can agree upon. Then when it's hammered out, the teams should jointly present the resolution to higher management. (This assumes that higher management is flexible and committed to realistically supporting teams. If it isn't, the two teams might want to reach agreement and then go on about their business.)

What if the relationship between the teams isn't so good? First choice is to begin working on the relationship, to build it to the point that the two teams can work the problem out themselves. If the other team isn't interested in this, your team has no choice but to take it to your next-level manager and ask for his or her help to resolve it. It's hoped that the manager has the kind of relationship with the manager of the other team that they can work out an amicable solution. (It's also possible that your next-level manager is also the next-level manager of the other team, which further simplifies matters.)

If there should be an overlap at this point:

You'll hope that your team and the other team have developed a good working relationship, because you'll need it. Both teams will need to work on the project, and each will need to cooperate with the other. If the relationship is there, you can both make this happen quickly and painlessly.

But what if the relationship isn't that good? Well, each team had better make establishing an effective relationship a top priority. It doesn't matter how your team feels about the other team or that team about yours—you have a major project to accomplish together. This tests the maturity of both teams. If the teams spend their time focusing on team turf issues, the project is in deep trouble. On the other hand, if the teams can concentrate without undue fuss on working with each other to achieve the result, you can get it done. With luck, the teams will have a strong relationship by the end, and this will serve both of you well in the future.

Team Strengthener

This book stresses the importance of effective relationships among teams. When teams work together well, the organization benefits, and so do the teams. In a number of cases the book presents, the only effective solution for the problem is for the teams concerned to solve it, with or without support from higher management. Every team should spend part of its time and attention on developing and maintaining the broadest and most effective relationships possible with other teams. One of the best ways to accomplish this is to concentrate on being helpful to other teams and making clear to them how they can be helpful to you.

9–4

The Problem
The team's mission is too broad

The Scene

Wally walks up to you on break. "We're getting snowed under. I'm ending each week with at least a dozen more problems to solve than I begin with. I know we're supposed to help out everyone with their personal computers, but we couldn't keep up with all the calls if we worked 24 hours a day. I'm burning out, and so is almost everybody else on the team. There's gotta be some relief!"

Yes, there does have to be some relief. Corporate assigned your team to "take care of any problems that teams have with their new personal computers." It would take an army to take care of the problems. If your team did nothing but install new software, it would probably be occupied full time. There has to be some solution.

Possible Causes

The organization didn't realize the scope of the mission.

Managers who assign a mission to a team may not be familiar with the work that's assigned. Personal computers require a lot more support than anyone expected in the beginning. But so may other areas: supplying or ordering equipment for teams, for instance. It's all too easy for a team to end up with more work than it can do well.

The team interprets the mission more broadly than the organization intended.

The team may actually be doing more than management intended. For instance, the organization may have intended it only to take care of hardware issues, or just to make sure that commercial help was available to computer users. Because the mission wasn't stated in clear, concrete terms, the team took the broadest interpretation and went from there.

The team isn't setting effective priorities.

Any individual, team, or unit that's overworked needs to take whatever time necessary to prioritize the workload. Unless this happens, the most pressing work will get done, and this may not be the most important work.

Cures

If the organization didn't realize the scope of the mission:

What does the team do now that it sees how broad the mission really is? It does its best to renegotiate its mission. Cases 5–2, 5–3, and 5–6 all deal with situations where the team may have too much work to accomplish. Look at these cases for suggestions on finding other teams that might be willing to pick up part of your team's mission. If it can find one or more other teams that will take over some of the mission, the teams can go to higher management with concrete suggestions on how the problem might be solved.

If no other teams can or will take over part of the mission, the team needs to carefully prioritize what it does (see the last section in this case) and then go to higher management with the alternatives laid out as clearly as possible. Why is prioritizing so important? The team wants to retain the highest-priority responsibilities, since these are the ones the team was presumably created to perform. They are also the ones that the organization most needs performed. If possible, the team should recommend how the other responsibilities can be handled; it will be easier for higher management to agree with the team's requests if the team has concrete recommendations for management to consider.

If the team interprets the mission more broadly than the organization intended:

If the team thinks that this might be the case, it should begin in the same way as in the section above, by prioritizing its duties as clearly as possible. Then, working through your higher-level manager, the team should raise the question of what management intended when it created the original mission.

If the team is asking management what it intended, why spend time prioritizing? Because what management intended may not take care of the highest priorities. In this case, management may have intended the team to perform simple hardware repairs and contract out more serious repairs. But the crying need may be for help with new software packages. The team owes it to the organization to make the situation clear, so that management can make an informed choice, not simply repeat a past decision.

If the team isn't setting effective priorities:

The team must decide what work it does that is most important to its customers. It can't decide this in a vacuum. Unless it knows its customers well, it needs to take time to have members visit with them and get a clear fix on their needs. Once the team has this picture, it can make decisions about its priorities.

Then it's time to use the priorities. If not all work can be done, the team needs to decide what will happen with the work it can't do. Most likely it will decide to work with its customers and help them perform some of the work the team previously performed for them. The team might even decide that its basic mission is to train customers to perform all but the hardest support work themselves. Whatever the outcome, the team needs to ensure that it concentrates on the work its customers need that it can best perform for them.

Team Strengthener

Some things in life are important, some are pressing, and a few are both pressing and important. Whenever an individual or team has more work than it can do in a reasonable period of time, it needs to look carefully at the work. It needs to spend a minimum amount of time on work that's pressing but not important. And it needs to ensure that it spends at least some time on work that's important but not pressing. In the case above, installing new software may be pressing for customers, but it may be more important to work out a training program that enables them to install it for themselves. The same principle applies no matter the kind of work: Don't get so swamped in the pressing but unimportant that you neglect the important but not pressing. Most of the time, if you spend at least some time on the important but not pressing work you will reduce the amount of pressing work.

9–5

The Problem
The team has trouble establishing short-term objectives

The Scene

"Okay, everybody understand? We need to cut our combined mail, fax, and phone bill by 20 percent within 90 days." Adrienne looks around to make sure everyone understands. "Now, the floor is open for suggestions."

The team discusses the matter for a few minutes and comes up with a number of practical ideas (and a few thoroughly impractical ones). "Now," Adrienne says, "what do we want to set for some interim goals?"

"Why worry about them," Orvie responds, "We all know what we have to do. And I think we have plenty of good ideas for doing it."

"Yeah," Nora offers. "I don't really see any need for anything else. Besides, I'm not sure what the right short-term goal would be. It seems to me that either we make the reduction or we don't."

The discussion goes on for a minute more, but the team clearly isn't going to establish interim goals. This is the way the team does business, and you are sure that it is going to get them into trouble sooner or later. But how to get them to establish short-term goals to support their longer-term goals?

Possible Causes

The team doesn't understand how to set short-term goals.

Goal setting has been popular for years, but that doesn't mean that many workers really learned how to set effective goals. For most workers in traditional organizations, goals were imposed by higher management, and units often played a variety of games to get around them. So too few workers learned what goals are really for or how they need to be set. This may be the case with most of the individuals on your team.

The team believes—wrongly—that it doesn't need short-term goals.

This gets stickier. Perhaps the kind of work the team has done hasn't required short-term goals. Perhaps it does, but the team has lucked out and succeeded without them. And many team members may believe, because of their experience in traditional organizations, that most goals don't really mean anything. Whatever the combination of reasons, it supports the belief of team members that they don't need short-term goals to succeed.

The team can handle longer projects without short-term goals.

This should be the last alternative you consider, and you should be deeply suspicious that it really is the case. It requires an extremely mature and intelligent team to handle longer-range goals without short-range goals to support them. There are such teams, but they are few and far between.

Cures

The team doesn't understand how to set short-term goals:

The solution is straightforward: The team needs to learn how to set short-term goals and then begin setting them. If your organization has an effective course in goal-setting, that's the place to start. If not, find a good course from a commercial vendor. Then, if possible, arrange for the team to take it as a group, so that everyone has the same background. Consider supplementing the course with a short workshop led by someone on another team that's particularly good at setting short-term goals. The workshop should focus on an actual project; in this case, it could focus on developing short-term goals to support the 20 percent reduction.

However the team members learn goal-setting skills, see that each of you applies them right away. Apply them on an actual project if possible. If worse comes to worse, make up a project and make up the short-term goals to support the final outcome. Once the team becomes comfortable with goal setting and sees the benefits that flow from it, you should have no more problems.

If the team believes—wrongly—that it doesn't need short-term goals:

One way to solve the problem, of course, is to let the team plunge ahead until the inevitable happens and it fails because it didn't develop effective short-term goals. You may be stuck with this alternative, if team members believe strongly enough that goals aren't necessary. If you're forced to take this option, at least do some advance planning so that when things fall apart you're ready with a specific plan to start using short-term goals immediately. The plan may also include training for the team, as in the section just above.

It's better if you can persuade the team to change. You may be able to, particularly if a few members of the team really believe that short-term goals would be useful. If you know of a situation in which another team got into trouble because they lacked these goals, perhaps someone from that team would be willing to talk with your team about what happened. Take any other reasonable steps you can to help the team see the problems it may cause itself and start planning to prevent them.

If the team can handle longer projects without short-term goals:

If you believe this is the case, help the team discuss it in depth. Ensure that everyone looks at what the consequences may be if the team isn't that good. Then let the team decide.

If the team decides not to use short-term goals, at least encourage a substitute for them. Try to persuade the team to schedule regular meetings on projects. Even though there may not be short-term goals and formal milestones, the team members concerned with the project can report on how they're doing. This will at least help everyone maintain a sense of how projects are going and whether any of them are beginning to encounter problems.

Team Strengthener

The last section, which seemed to be on nongoal setting, has an important clue in it for goal setting. When a team sets short-term goals, they should never be set just to set them. Instead, they should identify what the team needs to accomplish by a particular point in time. Then the team uses them to make sure it's on the right track and progressing at the necessary pace. In other words, short-term goals are an effective way to focus team discussion on the important issues. That should always be their primary purpose.

The Problem
The team isn't challenged by its mission

The Scene

"Okay, our next project is an internal audit of the Baton Rouge Office. Anybody got any questions?"

"Yeah—you know any good Cajun restaurants there?"

"Sam promised he'd have a list for us when we got there."

"I hope there are some good ones. I could do this audit in my sleep. In fact, I'd be willing to bet a dinner that I could write at least 80 percent of the report on the flight down."

The banter continues for a while, then tapers off. If ever there was a bored team, this is it. The audit work was interesting at first, but now everyone on the team is expert at it. If some employee or manager isn't engaged in outright embezzlement, an audit is about as challenging as a game of touch football. You know you have to try to find a way to change this, before the team gets sloppy and misses something important.

Possible Causes

The cause is clear: The team has learned to do its job too well. The question is how to find a solution.

Cures

If the team can get its mission expanded:

Start here. Are there other, related responsibilities the team might assume? For instance, if team members are skilled auditors, could the team perform some management audits along with its regular audits? Could it assume some consultation responsibilities and work with audited activities to help them improve, or even innovate?

Are there additional responsibilities that would require team members to develop new skills? Perhaps the organization would be willing to let the team take on these responsibilities on a trial basis if members get the requisite training and education. Not only would that be a good motivator for team members to improve, but learning new skills would be challenging in itself. Of course you want to talk to higher management about assigning additional responsibilities. But they're not your only source, not necessarily even your best one. Talk with the organizations you audit. What additional services might they want to see the team perform? Talk with other teams performing related work. Are any of them overloaded, so that your team might take on some of their responsibilities? Do a broad sweep, concentrating on how the team might use its skills to provide greater value to the organization.

If team responsibilities can't be expanded, look for a different but related opportunity. Are there several teams performing essentially the same work? Could your team swap assignments with another team? You'd be doing the same work, but you'd be doing it with different organizations. This helps you develop something of a fresh perspective and may help the team get back some of its edge.

If several members of the team can swap with other teams:

If the team is locked into its responsibilities, it doesn't mean that team members have to be locked into the team. Could the team work out a swap with another team or two that uses similar skills? Perhaps there is already a management audit team, and your team might swap a member or two with it. Perhaps there's a "tiger team" that provides short-term assistance to units in crisis. Someone with audit skills might be useful on that team, just as someone from that team might bring a new perspective to yours.

This alternative sounds potentially disruptive. It might be, if not carefully managed. If only one or two team members are swapped, though, the team should be able to manage the situation easily. It will stretch existing team members to see that audits are done on schedule and well while at the same time training the new members. And the new members will be challenged by learning new roles and skills.

Should the swaps be temporary or permanent? That's a team call, but here's a thought. If the missions and personnel of both teams are stable, you may want to work out a continuing series of swaps. Every year or eighteen months or so, individuals would return to their original teams, and one or two new members would be swapped. In a few years, the skill level of both teams would have increased significantly at the same time that members of both teams would have been challenged. That's a true win-win situation.

If members of the team could work for short periods with other teams:

Perhaps teams and missions aren't stable enough, or some other circumstance prevents teams from swapping members for extended periods of time. What about short assignments? They could be swaps, but for much shorter periods of time. Or they could simply involve a member of one team working with another team for several weeks to learn the basics of their mission and perhaps pick up limited skills in that work.

Short-term assignments like this always have a major drawback: The individual doesn't learn the work of the other team in any depth. In fact, the individual will probably feel that he or she is having to return just when the work is beginning to make sense. This is the price one pays for short assignments. But even a short-term assignment can have a major payoff: It gives the individual the chance to experience the *perspective* of the other team and learn from it. This different perspective can be a real asset to the home team when the individual returns.

Whether a member or two of your team can be assigned to other teams, your team can certainly encourage members of other teams to join it for short—or long—periods of time. Again, training a new individual is a break from the routine and a challenge in itself.

A final thought: If all the swaps are impractical, or if they're not enough of a cure, can several teams arrange workshops for one another so they can learn about each other's responsibilities? Particularly if there are a few other teams with responsibilities similar to yours, these workshops could help members significantly expand their horizons.

Team Strengthener

Most individuals produce best when they are continually challenged, and so do most teams. Work that was exciting at first can become boring when it's repeated over and over. Some teams find that their mission or responsibilities change frequently enough that boredom never sets in. Others may have such a high level of turnover that few individuals ever become expert enough to become bored. Yet others may have to work constantly to ensure that they have challenging work. This case has discussed some ways to accomplish this. There are many others. The key is simple. A team needs to have a "boredom early warning system." When tasks are beginning to become boring and "old hat," the team needs to search actively for ways to overcome or at least reduce the boredom and make work challenging again.

9–7

The Problem
The team doesn't get any feedback on how its doing

The Scene

"Hey, you guys, I've got good news and I've got bad news." Susan, Michael, Rowena, and you all turn to Pete as he walks in.

"The good news is that it turns out Accounting was satisfied with our breakdown of field expenses last quarter after all. And the bad news . . ."

"I know what the bad news is," Michael interrupts: "We've spent darned near a week revising the way we did it because we heard roundabout that they were dissatisfied."

"Yeah, that's it," Pete says wryly. "Of course, everyone knows we have all kinds of time to waste, so it doesn't matter—right?"

He's greeted by a chorus of "Yeah, right!" as the others ceremoniously tear up the material they've been working on.

No wonder they're so disgusted. The team doesn't find out for days and sometimes weeks what the units and teams that use them think of its products. It does the best it can to do a good job, but it certainly is hard in these circumstances. You wonder how you can change them.

Possible Causes

The organization doesn't think in terms of customers and feedback.

Traditional organizations operated for years without serious regard for either internal customers or feedback from them. Each unit "did its job" and produced what it was expected to produce. No one said anything about what they thought of the product unless it was really unsuitable. Then the unit using the product complained to its boss, who complained to the first unit's boss, and so on. Total Quality changed that way of looking at organizations. Organizations that have applied TQ think in terms of chains of internal customers and of constant feedback to producers.

The team has its own standards of what's a good product.

This, too, characterizes traditional organizations. Sometimes units have written standards for what constitutes the right outcome. There are engineering standards, programming standards, instructional development standards, and so forth. When a product fails to meet these standards, it automatically is not a satisfactory product. And there's nothing wrong with this. The problem is that traditional organizations tend to stop there.

Internal standards are never enough. The ultimate standard is always customer satisfaction. Either a team provides its customers with what they need or it doesn't. The team may believe it has done a tremendous job, but if its customers look at its output and think "That doesn't give me what I need," it has failed.

The team doesn't aggressively seek feedback.

No matter what else is true, this is the core of the problem. Most organizations have deficient systems for providing usable feedback—even many organizations based on teams. Teams can and must take responsibility for getting the feedback they need.

Hint

As in many other cases, the three causes don't exclude one another. And even if the first or second cause (or both) are part of the problem, the third cause is the most important.

Cures

If the organization doesn't think in terms of customers and feedback:

It may be that your organization hasn't gotten this message yet. Your team doesn't get feedback because higher management doesn't believe that it needs feedback unless it fails. So what does the team do? It can start quietly and patiently campaigning to change the organization. In the meantime, it should change its own work situation to see that it gets the feedback it needs. The third section suggests how to accomplish this.

If the team has its own standards of what's a good product:

Don't attack the team's standards head-on. First, this will provoke resistance and make it harder to get the change you (and your customers) need. Second, the team may need many of the standards to ensure that they do an effective job. Internal standards aren't necessarily wrong; they are necessarily incomplete.

The next section has suggestions for getting feedback. First, though, the team needs to decide that it needs the feedback, and that's the most difficult step. Do you have a good customer who's dissatisfied with at least some of your work and who will level with the team? Have him or her talk with the team and do what you have to do to get the team to listen to him. It may take several attempts, perhaps with several different customers. Just keep at it. When the team crosses the bridge and sees its output through its customers' eyes, it will be a different team.

If the team doesn't aggressively seek feedback:

And that's exactly what your team needs to do—now. Does it know who all its customers are? If not, it needs to find them out. Does it know what its customers want? Yes? How? If it doesn't know, or if it thinks it knows its customers' needs some other way than by asking them, it has work to do.

Your team needs to visit or survey its customers regularly, to find out what they need and how satisfied they are with what your team produces. In this case, the team could easily have made arrangements for one or two of its members to visit the Accounting Department a certain number of days after the department received the team's product. The team's representatives could then have found out clearly whether the product met Accounting's needs. Even if it met these needs, the team might have gotten a better idea of the needs, so that it could do an even better job next time.

The moral is simple. Don't wait for someone else to decide that your team needs feedback and how it will get it. Take the initiative. Stay close to your customers, whether they're inside the organization or are its ultimate customers. Ask them how you're doing at giving them what they need. Then use their feedback to improve.

Team Strengthener

Don't get the idea that all you have to do is ask a customer and he or she will tell you honestly and completely how you're doing. It doesn't happen that way. Customers level with you only when they believe that (1) you really want to hear the truth and (2) you will act on what they tell you. We often don't level with people who ask for our opinions because we don't want to "hurt their feelings," or because we're afraid they'll get defensive with us. Teams often act in the same way. We also don't level with people because we don't expect them to take what we say seriously and change how they treat us. Teams often act this way as well. Your team must prove to its customers that it wants to meet their needs, that it wants the truth from them, and that it will use the truth to improve its operations. Do that, and you'll get the feedback you need.

9–8

The Problem
The team's mission keeps changing

The Scene

"Hey there," Bernie calls as he walks up to you. "Did you know that we don't have to support Operations any more? Now they want us to take over for the Administrative Department."

"Sorry I hadn't told you yet, Bernie," you answer. "I just found out this morning, and I've been trying to get some more information on it."

"Do you realize," Bernie continues, "that this is the third change we've had in our mission in three months. I was just getting some relationships built up in Operations, and now I've got to start all over again in Administration. I don't know how they expect us to get our job done if they keep changing it every time we turn around!"

You've put on the best face you could, but Bernie's right. This constant change in the team's mission is really getting through to the team members. Something has to be done about the situation.

Possible Causes

The organization is unstable.

For different reasons, almost every organization goes through periods of instability. There may be rapid turnover in top management. Sales may be dropping, with the organization trying frantically to find out what's wrong. One or more important departments may be reorganizing. Or any one of a dozen other events may be causing it. Whatever the cause, the instability spreads throughout the organization and affects everyone.

The organization is having to deal with rapid change.

It may not be the organization that's causing the instability. It may be under pressure to find new markets, deal with rapidly changing customer requirements, develop products and get them to market faster, or otherwise respond to a super-heated competitive environment. Even if the organization is used to handling rapid change—and many aren't—it's still disruptive of many routines within the organization.

The team hasn't learned how to deal with rapid change effectively.

Of course, this is the question that the team must honestly ask itself. It may be that the team never had to deal with this degree of change before. It hasn't developed the skills it needs to cope with it. The change may be making it harder for the team to perform effectively, but its inability to handle the change may be making it even less effective.

Cures

If the organization is unstable:

What can you and the team do? About the overall instability, nothing. For now, you're stuck with it. Don't waste time trying to change it, because any change would probably make it even worse.

You and the team can work together to minimize its impact on you. What does that mean? Whatever else, it means that

- You don't let the stress get you down, individually and as a team. You don't sit around in your negative feelings as if they were a sauna. Yes, the situation is uncomfortable. But you have a job to do.

- No matter what happens, you don't take the additional stress out on one another. You may need to cut one another extra slack and accept that individually and collectively the team won't work quite as well as it has before, and will again. If each of you appreciates the problems that all of you share, team cohesiveness and ability to deal with change may actually increase.

- Above all, help one another keep your senses of humor. It's almost impossible to survive unstable situations such as this without an active sense of humor. But with a good sense of humor, you can not only survive them but grow from them.

If the organization is having to deal with rapid change:

It doesn't matter a lot which of these situations is driving the problem, the problem feels much the same. All the suggestions in the section above apply here, too.

You need to help the team understand that if it does its job as competently and smoothly as possible, it will make a positive contribution to the overall stability of the organization.

Take this one step further. Help the team work with other teams to maintain effective relationships and minimize the stress among teams. This magnifies the contribution your team, and each team, can make to organizational stability. The more that teams can work together without bringing the overall conflict into their relationships, the easier it will be for each team.

If the team hasn't learned how to deal with rapid change effectively:

Can you and the team attend a training course on change? Perhaps. If you can find one, though, don't expect it to make a major difference. It may help, but just learning about change is far different from actually going through it.

This means that the best action the team can take is to deal openly with the change. Take the time the team needs to discuss the change and its impact. Then start planning the specific actions the team can take to manage the change. In this case, Bernie was concerned because he had to develop a new set of relationships with a new customer. How might the team change its ways of building relationships so that it could build the necessary ones more rapidly? It might want to devote more concentrated time up front to getting to know new customers and their needs than it did before. But it also might want to look at its internal practices and processes, cutting out any unnecessary steps. And it might want to look for shortcuts that let it respond more quickly to customers (old or new) without cutting quality.

Team Strengthener

Rapid change is a fact of life for more and more organizations. While it harries and often frustrates those caught in it, it also acts as a powerful force for efficiency. In the midst of change, neither individuals nor teams can afford to waste time on "nice to have" activities and features. Everyone has to focus on the critical items, which is where everyone should have been focusing all along. And no one can afford to fight change. Specific changes may be mistaken or wrong-headed; your team may need to confront them and try to stop or channel them. But no one can stop or channel change itself. Has your team been getting bored with its mission (as in the sixth case in this chapter)? Just let the velocity of change build up and the challenge will be back, in spades. Treat it as a challenge.

9–9

The Problem

The team is consistently assigned special projects that detract from its mission

The Scene

"Trini, how much spare time do we have between now and the fifteenth of next month?" you ask.

"Like zero, maybe less. What's up?"

"I just got back from the departmental meeting, and they want us to do a quick project for them."

"Again? What do they think we are, supermen? Oops—superpeople? Don't they know we have work to do?"

Apparently not. The team's been given a string of special projects, all of them rush jobs. So far, it's been able to get its regular work done, but you're not sure how much longer that can last. Something has to be done.

Possible Causes

The organization believes the team can do anything.

Whatever the problems that the special projects cause, getting them is a high compliment to the team. The team gets them because higher management believes that, no matter how heavy the team's workload, the team can handle them. That's an enviable reputation.

The organization doesn't think the team's mission matters.

A very different situation! In this case, the team gets the special projects because the organization doesn't believe the team's fundamental responsibilities make a difference to the organization as a whole. Possibly, the organization doesn't even care how well these responsibilities are performed.

Somebody in the organization is lazy.

Does this sound like a strange cause? It may not be. Whoever handles special projects has found that your team delivers, so he or she simply give them to you. That way the person gets the work done, but doesn't have to go to any special trouble. Your team's ability is providing him or her the opportunity to take the easy way out.

Cures

If the organization believes the team can do anything:

What do you do? You might mention to your higher-level manager that the workload is getting tight because of the special projects, particularly if this is jeopardizing some of your primary mission. You might even suggest that he or she try to get the team a little breathing room. But, unless the mission is suffering badly, no more than this. The team may be a little pressed, but the reputation for being "the team that can do anything" is well worth the pressure.

One way to deal with the problem is for the team to get better and better at handling both special projects and its regular mission. Perhaps this is just the trigger the team needs to bolster its effectiveness so it can take both its assigned responsibilities and the special projects in stride. Remember, if the team is really that good there's no limit on what it can accomplish.

If the organization doesn't think the team's mission matters:

This sounds as if the organization is willing to keep the team's mission, regardless of what it thinks of it. If so, the team will probably have to select one of two basic courses of action. On the one hand, it can let its present mission be and find satisfaction in the special projects assigned to it. On the other, it can attempt to get its mission changed. It needs to consider the choice closely and then pursue the alternative it selects carefully.

If it chooses to let its mission be, it needs to routinize it as much as possible. The goal is to spend the minimum amount of time and effort on it. Then do the special projects well. If necessary, go in search of more of these projects, and more interesting ones. Over time, you may get a reputation for doing special projects well, so that you get to concentrate more and more of your time on them.

Suppose you really want to get a mission that the organization cares about. Look back at the early cases in this chapter, especially 9–2. These cases deal with problems with the team's mission, and they'll give you some suggestions you can use here. You may also want to look at Chapter 5, especially the first three cases there, which deal with attempts to get the mission changed.

If somebody in the organization is lazy:

Does this have any payoff at all for you and the team? Find the answer to that question first. If whoever is sending you all the projects is tied in with significant higher-level managers and tells them how capable you are, you may want to keep the projects. But this probably isn't what's happening. Instead, whoever is doing it is probably doing his or her job off in a corner, and no one who really matters knows what the team can do.

If that's the case, you need to take the matter to your next-level manager. Get your facts straight and your arguments in line. The basic point, from your manager's point of view, is that the constant stream of special projects interferes with the team's ability to get its job done. Since the job is presumably being done for your manager, he or she has some reasons to see that projects are more equitably distributed. With luck, it won't take too long for the situation to change.

Team Strengthener

A team that's known to be effective often has a thin line to walk. On the one hand, it has to protect its primary mission and see that only a reasonable amount of work is demanded from it. On the other, being known as an outstanding team has its own rewards, in terms of individual promotions, team bonuses, even survival during "rightsizing." It should be a matter of pride with the team to accept every bit of work it can, as long as its primary mission never gets jeopardized. If you must try to turn work down, make a compelling case that the most important parts of your mission will suffer unless you do. If you can't make the case, take the work.

9–10

The Problem
The team doesn't have any customers or doesn't know who they are

The Scene

"Well, we're done the cumulative expense report and I've just sent it to Manufacturing," Amy says with a certain satisfaction.

Then she turns more thoughtful: "Does anybody know what happens to the report after it leaves us?"

They all shake their heads. "I can't even remember who assigned it to us," Marcus says.

"Well, I hope they like it," Amy adds. "It sure would help if we knew who used it and for what."

Yes, it would help. But what can you and the team do to find out?

Possible Causes

The organization still doesn't think in terms of a "chain of customers."

Traditional organizations seldom if ever looked on any internal units as suppliers or customers of one another. The only suppliers were firms that the organization bought from and the only customers were those who bought from the organization. Inside, there were just different units that had different responsibilities. Organizations that have adopted Total Quality have learned to think in terms of a "chain of customers" stretching through the organization to the final customer. But not all organizations think this way.

The team is responsible only for "nice to have" or obsolete products.

When there are no clear customers for a team's products, teams—and any other units—may end up producing products or services that aren't important to any one. It may be a "just-in-case" report that no one pays attention to. Or it may be a report that was important two years ago but doesn't matter now. Even worse, the team might be sending out evaluation forms that are carefully filled out and returned, only to be sent to a different unit that carefully files them away without using them for anything.

The team hasn't exercised the initiative it needs to.

It really boils down to this: It doesn't matter whether management understands the meaning of a chain of customers; the team needs to understand it. And the team needs to act on its understanding.

Cures

If the organization still doesn't think of a "chain of customers":

Apparently, your organization is one of those that doesn't think of itself as a chain of customers. It may not consider that teams really have "customers." If it does, it may not think it important that teams know who their customers are. This isn't good for the organization, and it's even worse for the team.

The solution is simple: Go find out who uses the team's products and what they use them for. This may take a bit of personal sleuthing. When the team finishes a product, have a team member take it to its next stop. There, the individual can ask what happens to it and follow it to that destination. Sooner or later, it will either go to someone who uses it—its real customer—or it will end up in a pile or a file of some kind. If it ends up being used by someone, talk with him or her to find out how it's used and how it might be improved. If it ends up piled or filed, go to the next section.

If the team is responsible only for "nice to have" or obsolete products:

You'll never know if this is the case if the team doesn't find out who its customers are. So follow the suggestions in the section above and find out.

Your team isn't just following good practice when it talks with customers, though it is doing that. It's also protecting itself against management's discovery that the team isn't needed. If the team really is responsible for products that aren't useful to anyone, it needs to find this out for itself, so it can take preventive action.

Now, what do you do if in fact no one cares about much of what the team produces? It's time to act! First, find out whether all of the team's output isn't important or only some of it. List the unimportant output carefully and document that no one cares about it. Then go to your next-level manager and ask for his or her help to get those duties taken away and have new, more useful ones substituted for them. Be persistent; your job security may be at stake.

If the team hasn't taken the initiative:

Actually, the team needs to look in two directions. First, it needs to look upstream and understand the teams or units that provide the input it needs. If it creates reports for someone, who provides it the data it creates the reports from? It should know who all of its providers are, what their problems are, and how it can be a good customer to them. Then it needs to look downstream, to find the customers for its products and how they're used. This way, it can ensure that its providers give it what it needs and that its own products are as useful as possible to its customers.

As the last section mentioned, this is a form of self-preservation. Especially during cutbacks or downsizings, teams and units that don't clearly add value to the organization's bottom line are sitting ducks for the ax. Conversely, teams and units that produce necessary products have much better job security. Your team needs to make sure it falls in this latter group. If it doesn't know who its customers are, it needs to find out. If it doesn't know how its products are used, it needs to find out. And if no one uses its products, it needs to go in search of a new mission. (Several cases in Chapter 5 have suggestions on how to develop new missions.)

Team Strengthener

The strongest possible justification for the existence of any team, unit, or organization is this: Its customers need what it gives them. While a team can always hope that management gave it a mission that fills an important need, it can't count on it. To ensure its survival, it must make its mission its own. It must know its customers and know their needs—not through an annual visit or a written survey, but through regular personal visits, perhaps supplemented by even more frequent telephone calls. ("Tom, did the package get there on time?. . .

Good—was it what you needed?. . . Excellent. Now give us a call if you find any problems.") Remember, job security is spelled "c-u-s-t-o-m-e-r—s-a-t-i-s-f-a-c-t-i-o-n.")

9–11

The Problem
The team is caught between its customers and its next-level manager

The Scene

"I need your help." Virgil does sound as if he needs it.

"What's up?" you answer.

"I know what the Sales Support Team needs from us, but Ms. Armstead won't let us give it to them."

"I'm listening."

"You know they want us to give them a sales summary by product for the last two years. That much is okay. I talked to them, and they would like us to break the data down by region. With our new database, that's a snap. But Ms. Armstead says that's not what they asked for. She says that they asked for it for the whole United States, and that's how they're going to get it."

Here you go again! The team has been practicing staying close to its customers, and it has a clear idea of what most of them want. But Ms. Armstead has a clear idea of what they *should* want, and she insists that the team do it her way. This has got to stop—but how?

Possible Causes

Ms. Armstead isn't customer oriented.

Cases throughout the book have stressed how important it is for teams to know their customers (and their providers as well). But Ms. Armstead may not have read the book. She's still thinking in terms of the organization as it was, when her primary responsibility was to see that the units that reported to her did their job the way she required them to.

The organization isn't customer oriented.

If the entire organization is still stuck in a more traditional approach, your problem is even worse. Ms. Armstead isn't just acting like a traditional manager because she wants to, but because that's what higher management expects of her.

The organization doesn't understand how self-managing teams need to operate.

Organizations often decide to become team based without fully understanding the basic changes that this requires. For instance, your organization may see teams as nothing more than a slight modification of traditional work units. It may believe that as a team leader you're essentially a traditional manager, though perhaps a bit more of a coach than most managers have been. And it may believe that your next-level manager should continue to function as she always has.

Cures

If Ms. Armstead isn't customer oriented:

I don't need to tell you how sticky this situation is. Ms. Armstead is probably quite comfortable managing as she's always managed and considers herself the authority on what the team should give its customers. You may find that there's little or nothing you can do in the short run to change her.

Don't give up, though. If you can get the cooperation of the next-level manager of one of your customers, try this: Have that manager call Ms. Armstead (or visit her) and talk with her about what he or she needs. If this manager understands the "chain of customers" concept, he or she might also suggest some new ways that Ms. Armstead might deal with the team— as a supporter, mentor, and coach, for instance, rather than as a boss. If this comes from another manager, Ms. Armstead may begin to realize that she needs to change.

Other cases in the book have looked at situations where a team's next-level manager is still operating in a traditional "boss" role; Cases 10–3 and 10–8, among others, deal with this problem. You may find some of the suggestions in those cases helpful.

If the organization isn't customer oriented:

If the organization is still trying to maintain a traditional management approach based on control, this approach and team self-management are going to run head-on into each other at some point. In situations such as this, the organization's need for control wins, unless teams can show that they're clearly more productive than traditional work units are. Your team needs to concentrate on demonstrating this level of productivity. It also needs to enlist the help of other teams, so that every team is as productive as possible. Then, when the teams' need for autonomy runs into the organization's need for control, the teams will be in the best bargaining position possible.

In the meantime, of course, the team should take advantage of every opportunity to point out to Ms. Armstead the advantages of having and satisfying customers. After all, she has a stake in the team's succeeding. The better the team does, the greater the chance that she may begin to change. If enough other next-level managers do the same, the organization itself will begin to change as well.

If the organization doesn't understand how self-managing teams need to operate:

The basic plan of attack for the team in this circumstance is to do the best job possible. If it has to change what it believes it should do to satisfy Ms. Armstead, it needs to do so while still focusing on satisfying its customers. (See the Team Strengthener for more on this.) But it must avoid, at all costs, falling into the trap of seeing her as its primary customer. That way leads back into the traditional organization—and there go the teams!

Yes, it's hard trying to please her and your customers when they don't agree. For the time being, though, there's no alternative. But don't get caught in the time being. Work with other teams to see that all teams work as effectively as possible. And work with them to set up an intelligence network that identifies the managers that are most likely to come around to the kind of management that teams need. Then work with these managers, so they in turn can try to move the organization in the direction it needs to go.

Team Strengthener

When a team is caught between its next-level manager and its customers, it's caught indeed. If it's possible to give your next-level manager what he or she wants and still satisfy customers, spend the extra effort to do this. But what if your next-level manager directs the team to take actions it knows are not what its customers want? Then you seriously need to consider producing two products—a visible one that gives your manager what he or she wants and a not-so-visible one that gives your customers what they want. Don't take this approach lightly; it's almost a last resort. But don't rule it out. If the contradiction between customer needs and higher-management requirements gets serious, this may be the only way to reconcile it.

9–12

The Problem
The team can't control the factors critical to its success

The Scene

"Well, anyone for a game of chess—a long game of chess?" Mikel says dejectedly as he sits down.

"Uh oh—what's happened now?" Teresa sets down the report she was marking up.

"You know that we need some high-level graphics for our presentation. Well, first of all, the graphics department is snowed under and can't help us for at least three weeks. They said they're sorry for us, but we have to deal with them and can't contract it out. And we can't order the software that might let us at least design something in time to meet our deadline. Right now, I'd like to find the guy who decided we were a self-managing team and strangle him!"

So would you. This isn't the first time that your team can't control one of the factors necessary for its success. The situation is demoralizing the team, and there's got to be something you can do about it.

Possible Causes

The organization didn't think through what self-managing teams need.

When an organization decides to base itself on self-managing teams, it makes a deeper commitment than it often understands at the time. Unless it stops to think through the implications of the commitment, it often makes minimal changes in its structure. This structure then remains the way it was when the organization used traditional management methods, which means that it doesn't fit well with the needs of teams. The most important need of any team is the ability to control the factors critical to its success. The organization is most apt to overlook this need, because in a traditional organization *no* operational unit ever controls these factors.

Support units don't want to give up their control.

Sometimes it's not that the organization hasn't thought how it needs to change to accommodate teams—it's that it's made a positive decision to maintain control in traditional ways. Accounting, Purchasing, Human Resources, and other staff offices have managed to maintain their control responsibilities with the blessing of the organization. In this case, the organization has caught itself in a serious bind. It is, as the old saying goes, neither fish (it can't swim effectively as a traditional organization) nor fowl (it can't effectively use teams to fly).

The team isn't taking enough initiative.

When an organization creates self-managing teams, it intends—at least in theory—for these teams to take the initiative to get their missions accomplished. If the organization builds the appropriate support structures, it supports the teams' initiative. But what if it doesn't build these structures? It doesn't matter. The team must exercise continuing initiative in either situation.

Hint

None of the causes exclude the others.

Cures

If the organization didn't think through what self-managing teams need:

That's how your team got here, but what does it do now? If your next-level manager is sympathetic, enlist his or her help. Try to raise the concern as far up in the organization as possible. But take care; if the concern gets raised too strongly or in the wrong way, the organization may begin to question whether it really wants self-managing teams. If the teams have proved themselves, you have greater freedom here. If not, don't back off, but tread softly. You may be caught on the horns of a dilemma: The team can't prove itself if it can't control its critical success factors, but the organization won't give up control of these factors until the team has proven itself. Ouch!

Remember, though, that if this is the case the organization hasn't made a positive decision to retain control. Instead, it has not looked as hard at its existing policies and structure as it needs. This provides far more opportunity than the situation in the next section. If your next-level manager believes that something can be done, by the way, you probably want to enlist other teams and their next-level managers in the effort.

If support units don't want to give up their control:

Once again, if you can get the support of your next-level manager, you need to raise the problem in the organization. And you need definitely to get the cooperation of other teams. The caution in the section above about pushing too hard is doubly applicable here. If the teams push too hard, they may force a confrontation that they are not yet strong enough to win.

Watch for any opportunity to make the point with higher management. In the meantime, read and use the material in the next section.

If the team isn't taking enough initiative:

In this situation, it becomes doubly important for teams to seize the initiative. They may have to fight staff offices. Or, often more effective, they must find ways around the existing control structure. This is one reason why this book so consistently stresses the need for teams to work together. If they do, they can help one another develop and maintain the autonomy needed for team success. Consequently, part of what it means to take initiative is to maintain close relationships with other teams. If you haven't done so yet, do so now. This chapter contains various suggestions of ways to build and use these relationships.

Don't ever forget the adage: It's easier to ask for forgiveness than for permission. The team has a job to do; it needs to find the best way to do it and then do it. If that requires bending policy a little or finding ways around the organization's various controls—well, so be it. In fact, if the team does this intelligently and in genuine concern for its mission, not its comfort or convenience, it may help raise issues that the organization must deal with for its own success.

Team Strengthener

From the beginning, the team must anticipate what it needs to accomplish its mission and then must see that it can control the factors that make the accomplishment possible. This case concerned a relatively minor factor: the ability to get graphic support when it needs it. Suppose, though, that the issue was its ability to make a commitment to a customer—say, that the team would provide immediate and free modification of a product that met specifications but wasn't just what the customer needed. Could the team do it? Could it perform its mission successfully if it couldn't? These are vital questions, because they go to the heart of the team's ability to succeed.

CHAPTER 10

Problems Caused by Higher Management

While a self-managing team may have tremendous freedom and authority, it still reports to a higher-level manager. It must satisfy this manager if it is to retain this freedom and authority. (In other words, some things don't change in organizations.)

The cases in this chapter present problems that a team may have with higher-level managers. The problems range all the way from a manager who insists on rating all team members with no input from anyone but you to a manager who's talking about disbanding your team. In other words, problems with higher management can be quite hazardous to the health of the team!

No team ever resolved the kind of problem this chapter describes by fighting higher management. The team's job is to show how it can help management achieve its goals better than any other alternative could. Each case concentrates on ways that the team can convince higher management of this.

Never think, though, that the problem is simply with higher management. Before it can convince anyone of anything, the team must make sure it has its act together and is performing effectively. So the cases stress what the team can do to ensure that it is effective and *then* what it can do to persuade higher management to support it.

The Problem

*Higher management gives a project to another team
that you think should have been yours*

The Scene

"Sit down—I need to talk with you." Marsha Boren motions you to a chair.

"I don't think I like the sound of this," you respond as you drop into the chair.

"You can probably guess what it's about. After a lot of thought, we've decided to assign the Werner project to Martin Leddeker's team."

The conversation continues for another minute or two, but it isn't important. Your team should have the Werner project. What went wrong?

Possible Causes

Your team has a reputation for poor performance.

When bad things happen to your team, the first question is always what the team did to help cause them. When higher management compared your team to the other one, they may have seen a performance difference, and it favored the other team. Even if the project really fit your mission better, management may have decided that the other team was more dependable and would produce a better result.

Another team worked smarter to get the project than yours did.

Notice that this doesn't say the other team worked *harder* than your team. It may or may not have. But it did work smarter.

Logically, your team shouldn't get the project.

You were disappointed that you didn't get the project, but perhaps your team shouldn't have gotten it. You may already be overloaded with important work. It might fit your mission, but fit the other team's mission even better. It may be in an area your team already has expertise in, and higher management wanted the other team to develop this same expertise. There are any number of reasons why—even if your team believed it should have the project—it should have gone to another team.

Cures

If your team has a reputation for poor performance:

If that is the case, management made the right decision. Your job, of course, is to see that this is never the right decision again.

Bring up the performance issue with the whole team. Be prepared for them to be angry and disappointed and help them work through it. Then help them face the performance deficiencies that led to the management decision. This may not be a quick process. If the team has never been told before that it was a poor performer, it will probably take time for it to accept that it is. Spend the time.

Once the team can look objectively at its performance, it can decide what to do to correct the performance and then do it. You'll find suggestions on how to accomplish this throughout the book, but the most relevant material is probably in Chapter 5. Use it and anything else to help the team turn around its performance.

The team can prevent situations such as this one by reviewing its performance on a regular basis. See the Team Strengthener at the end of the case for more information on this.

If another team worked smarter to get the project than yours did:

These are some of the steps the other team might have taken:

- It made presentations to higher management that were more effective than yours. (Perhaps it emphasized the payoff to the organization if it performed the project, while your team just emphasized that the project "belonged" to it. Or perhaps your team just assumed it was getting the project and didn't even talk with higher management.)

- It developed good relationships with the other teams that would be involved in the project; in turn, these teams supported its attempt to get the project. (Has your team not developed these good relationships, or did it not think of using them to support its bid for the project?)

- It performed particularly well on its last few projects, to establish a reputation that would help it get this project. (How was your team's performance on the last few projects it completed? It was probably okay, but did it stand out?)

While team-based organizations work best when there is a high level of cooperation among teams, competition can play a valid part at times. Higher management may choose to assign particularly interesting projects on the basis of team performance as a way of motivating teams to do their best. If your organization is like this, you need to watch your performance at all times. And you need to take the smart actions described above.

If your team shouldn't logically get the project:

Is this really the case? The team needs to review its own performance, and it needs to do some intelligence work. Is there really a hidden agenda? Does higher management think that the team doesn't perform well, but has tried to sugar-coat their decision by giving another reason? Is there some other hidden reason? It's extremely important that the team know the real reason so that it can respond realistically in the situation.

If the project should validly have been assigned to another team, don't waste any more time worrying about it. The team needs to concentrate on the projects it has now and perform them expertly. Then perhaps next time it will get a project that "really should have gone to another team."

No matter what the cause is:

If the project is one that the team wanted, you might volunteer to help the team that got it. Be careful; you must be clear that you're not trying to take over but just to get involved in something that interests you. If you're familiar enough with the project, you might even suggest specific tasks your team might perform, making sure that these are clearly subordinate—but still challenging—tasks.

Team Strengthener

An effective team reviews its performance regularly. If something goes wrong, the team looks for both *why* and *how* it went wrong. Even if things went well, it still looks to see if there were problems that might have had serious consequences. (For instance, the overall job may have been completed on time, but you got the draft to another team for coordination three days late. If that team hadn't agreed to finish its review in two days instead of a week, the whole job would have been late. Why was there a delay in getting the draft out to be coordinated?) The surest way to maintain both the team's effectiveness and its independence is to be expert at identifying and solving performance problems on a day-to-day basis.

10–2

The Problem

Higher management won't let you increase the size of the team, even though the workload is increasing

The Scene

"I'm sorry. You may need more people on your team, but I just don't see it. Instead of adding more members, you need to make better use of the people and the time you already have. You can get the new work done if you just work smarter. Your team's been operating for quite a while now; it ought to be able to perform more work now than it could at first."

You walk away from your next-level manager with slumped shoulders. You understand about your team being more experienced now, but it's already beginning to fall behind in its workload. What are you going to do?

Possible Causes

Your team needs more effective work processes.

As individuals and teams mature, they become more expert at performing the tasks assigned to them. But they must become more expert in another way: improving the processes that control the flow of the work. For instance, when a draft needs reviewing, is it done right away or does it sit in an in-box somewhere for days waiting for action? Processes that were once streamlined and effective become outmoded and even sloppy over time.

Your team has settled into a comfortable, easy work pace.

Your team began with a particular workload. Now that the team has matured, the workload is much easier to handle. If this has been the case for some time, the team has probably settled into the work pace that lets it get the workload done without anyone having to stretch. Probably no one really has to work a full eight hours a day. But you're used to this pace, so it seems as if the workload you have is the "normal" workload.

Your team needs to stop "goldplating" its outputs.

If the team has been able to handle the workload comfortably, it may have fallen into the trap of "goldplating" what it produces. In other words, it has been producing products that are far more polished and fancier than customers want; reports with elaborate covers that take time to design; reports that contain more figures than the customer uses or that take sixteen pages to cover what could be adequately covered in four pages.

Hints

These three causes are just a brief sample of what might be creating the team's inability to perform more work. The team can find a cure for each of the causes without adding to its size. You should also look at the cases in Chapter 5, to see if your team has one of these performance problems. If so, the case will suggest how you might solve the problem—again, without adding new team members.

This case won't deal with another possible cause: You really do need more members on the team, but you failed to persuade higher management. See the Team Strengthener at the end of the case for some suggestions about this.

Cures

If your team needs more effective work processes:

Has the team had training in continuous process improvement? If not, get it. If it was so long ago that you've forgotten it, get it again. Learn how to diagram processes, so you can see what's happening to the workflow. It will take some time up front, but if you really do need to improve your processes the time will be paid back manyfold.

This needs to be a team effort, but it also needs to be an individual one. You and others may have developed sloppy, inefficient individual work processes of your own. A simple example: Have you and others disciplined yourselves to handle each piece of paper only once? When you get a piece of paper, do something with it; don't put it in your hold basket with the thought that you'll handle it when you get time. Such a simple thing, but it can have a significant impact on workflow.

If your team has settled into a comfortable, easy work pace:

If the team has fallen into this comfortable rut, it's time to climb back out of it. The pace may seem comfortable, but it's also deadening. The team is probably stagnating; it's not facing new challenges or acquiring new skills. As this continues, the team becomes less and less effective, usually without even being aware of it. And it could end up with a reputation as a poor producer.

Because the team probably isn't aware of its comfortable rut, it may be difficult to shock it out of it. You're going to have to take the initiative. You may even want to bring the team's next-level manager in and have him or her make the situation clear: The team can do the work and is expected to do it. No matter how you handle the situation, expect serious griping and complaining. Don't give that much credence; just help the team work through it.

Combining this cure with the one above may pay off significantly. If the team is working at a comfortable pace, it probably has time to work on its processes. Start there. You'll hope this will begin to provide enough of a challenge to the team that it will gradually (and perhaps unconsciously) increase the work pace.

If your team needs to stop "goldplating" its outputs:

How did the goldplating start? Probably because the team got to the point where they became proficient at their mission. It had more time than it takes to complete its core jobs. Fortunately, this provides an easy way to find more time for other tasks.

If possible, members of the team should talk with the team's customers. They should explain about their increasing workload, then ask what's absolutely necessary for the customer to be satisfied. If the team hasn't talked to customers lately, it will almost certainly find that it can reduce its work and still give its customers what they need. Even if it's been meeting regularly with customers, it may find that they're quite willing to do without goldplating to help the team.

The team also needs to devote meeting time to the problem and try to develop a consensus about what's really necessary in what they produce and what's really goldplating. It's always best, of course, if this happens after talking with customers. But it's worth doing even if you can't talk with some or all of your customers.

No matter what the cause is:

If the workload really may be too much for the team to handle, have you thought about getting new technology as a way of improving the team's productivity? If you haven't, you might want to explore this approach. Organizations often treat getting new technology differently from hiring more workers. In other words, it may be easier to get new computers, for instance, than new team members.

Team Strengthener

Every successful team takes responsibility for seeing that higher management understands its current workload and challenges. Suppose the team's workload has been growing but no one has said anything to higher management. Then the workload requires additional team members. When the team goes to higher management, management is surprised because it's had no prior warning. The cure is to make sure that higher management knows of changes in the workload and of any other significant problems that may be facing the team. *Don't* present them as excuses or as complaints. The team simply wants to make sure higher management knows what's happening and knows that the team can handle most of the situations itself. Then, if workload really does increase or another problem arises that requires higher management's help, no one is surprised. And the team will have a better chance at getting what it wants.

10–3

The Problem

Your next-level manager insists on rating all the team members without input from anyone but you

The Scene

"Isabel, this is what I think the ratings ought to be. I'd like to get the team together, though, and give them the chance to come up with ratings for each other. If they do, you can always change them if you want."

"I appreciate your concern for your team, but that's just not how a leader operates. You don't ask the people you lead to come up with ratings. You know the overall picture, they don't—so you do the ratings."

You argue a little longer, but Isabel has her own ideas and she's the boss. You leave, wondering what you can do to change her mind.

Possible Causes

Isabel still looks at life as a traditional manager.

In a traditional organization, authority is specific. A manager is always responsible for a specific operation, and he or she is the one specifically responsible for it. If something goes wrong, he or she is the person on the spot. To a manager brought up in this type of organization, having teams rate themselves can easily seem like a total loss of control. Apparently Isabel looks at the situation this way.

Isabel wants to use you to control the team.

Though her actions are the same, Isabel's motive is different. She personally needs to maintain control. It's much easier for her to maintain this control of the team if she has only one person—you—directing it.

Isabel has specific reasons to think the team won't rate itself fairly.

This, of course, is the worst case. She may know of cliques in the team, long-standing friendships or hostilities, perhaps even discrimination that would keep team members from validly rating one another. She's afraid that if you let them rate one another she'll have to deal with a completely distorted pattern of ratings and perhaps a deluge of formal and informal complaints.

Hint

There's no short-run solution. Isabel has made it clear how things will be this time around. Your strategy should be aimed at the next rating cycle.

Cures

Isabel still looks at life as a traditional manager:

Depending on what Isabel's higher-level manager wants from her, you may not be able to change anything. Her manager may be the one insisting that you do the ratings with no input from or discussion by the team. But you can't assume that nothing can be done; if you do, you guarantee that the situation will never improve.

But what do you do? You and the team must demonstrate, repeatedly and consistently, that the team can manage itself successfully. You need to emphasize to Isabel, as subtly or as strongly as the situation permits, that the team is able to take responsibility for itself, and that it doesn't need an official "leader" to direct its actions. You also need to find out if the organization has a policy on the issue. If the policy is to involve team members in ratings, bring that to Isabel's attention when you get the chance. (If Isabel is following a policy of having team leaders do the ratings, see the last section in this case.)

If Isabel wants to use you to control the team:

Many managers exercise tight control over the people who report to them initially. Then, after they get to know the strengths and weakness of the individuals, they may loosen up. You can hope that this is the case with Isabel. If you and the team demonstrate that she can trust you, that you will keep her informed, that you are responsible, she may decide she can delegate more to you and the team.

But what if she intends to maintain control, period? You're in a very sticky situation because teams don't thrive in that kind of environment. You do your best to buffer between her and the team, satisfying her that you're maintaining control while giving the team as much freedom and responsibility as possible. And you encourage her and recognize every step she takes, no matter how small, to give you and the team more freedom.

If Isabel has specific reasons to think the team won't rate itself fairly:

Here, you take the initiative, and you take it strongly and quickly. If Isabel really believes there are severe interpersonal problems within the team, it's critical for you to talk with her and understand what she believes these problems are. What you want is information.

Isabel has a view of the team somewhat more objective than yours; she may see problems you are too involved with to recognize. Or she may be working from old information; you and the team may already have found and solved the problems. No matter what the truth is, you will be better able to deal with it if you understand *how* she sees the situation and *why* she sees it that way.

Now you and the team can get to work. If Isabel's information is dated, plan what you need to do to demonstrate how things have changed. Then show her how they have. If the problem she sees is real, it may be one of those addressed in Chapters 1 and 2. Whether it is or not, you and the team need to identify the problems within the team and then resolve them.

Team Strengthener

Team members on teams often rate one another's performance and may even determine the merit increases they each will get. Sometimes teams decide to give everyone the same rating, particularly if the team is relatively new and/or the members are evenly balanced. At other times, teams want to distinguish between members who produce consistently good results and those who don't, or between those who make a major contribution to the team and those who add relatively little. When a team gets the freedom for its members to rate one another, it picks up a serious responsibility, the responsibility to be just and fair. It needs to understand this responsibility, accept it freely, and then exercise it carefully. When it does all this, it will take another step toward increased maturity and effectiveness.

The Problem

Your next-level manager has unreasonable expectations for the quantity or quality of work the team can produce

The Scene

"You know I have great confidence in you, and I want to have the same confidence in your entire team. But I don't. You're producing far less than I expected, and the few times you've gotten your production up your quality has fallen."

"I understand how you feel, Ms. Tolkein, but these are good people. They work hard, and they really care about their work."

"I'm sure that's true, but it's not enough. If your production doesn't get up to what it should be in the next ninety days, we're going to have to talk seriously about disbanding the team."

"Wow!" you think to yourself as you walk away. You believe the team is really good, and here your boss is telling you that it has ninety days to improve or else. Now what do you do?

Possible Causes

Your team really isn't very productive.

What standard is Ms. Tolkein using? It may be more objective and realistic than the standard you and the team are applying to yourselves. You may not be as productive as you think.

Your team doesn't use processes that support both quantity and quality.

You don't automatically get either quality or quantity. You get what your processes will support. Your team may be using inadequate processes that make it impossible for it to produce high quality, high quantity, or both.

Your boss's expectations are too high.

Sadly, self-managing teams are often sold to organizations as ways to dramatically improve productivity and quality. They can accomplish this, though the evidence for higher quality is much stronger than for higher productivity. And teams won't produce either unless they are properly managed. Ms. Tolkein may be expecting major improvements in quality or quantity that aren't possible in the current situation.

Cures

If your team really isn't very productive:

As the book repeatedly stresses, when others are dissatisfied with your team's performance, the place to start is by looking at that performance. In this case, all you have to go on is your next-level manager's dissatisfaction. That doesn't give you much information.

Where do you begin? Ask your boss to get as specific as possible about what she expects. Don't appear defensive—a real danger here; make it clear that you're honestly looking for information. Get as little or as much information as she'll give you.

Are there other teams with missions similar to yours? Are they producing the quality and quantity that higher management expects? How? If you can't find a valid comparison, look at the cases in Chapter 5 and see if any of them help you understand your situation. Better still, spread the responsibility around. Can a different team member look at each of the cases in Chapter 5? Let them, then have a meeting to let everyone share what they found.

Once you've identified the problem, use what you learn from your next-level manager, other teams, and the suggestions in Chapter 5 (or even the suggestions in the next section) and begin to change the situation. It's not enough just to change. The team needs to develop a plan for changing: what it will do and by when it will have it done. Take this plan to your next-level manager, be sure she understands it, and commit the team to it. Even if your manager doesn't ask you to report on your progress, make sure you do (even if it's just a note every week or so). If you don't have the problem solved in ninety days, you want your manager to believe that you *will* solve it and give you the time you need.

If your team doesn't use processes that support both quantity and quality:

Several cases in the book have looked at this problem; the latest one was the second case in this chapter. Because of the Quality movement, we now know that effective processes can produce high output at the same time they produce high quality. You *can* increase both the team's output and its quality at the same time.

If you and the team haven't been exposed to the basic teachings of quality and continuous process improvement, now is the time to get exposed. Get training. If your organization has internal quality consultants, try to get one to help you. Read. Watch videos. Find other teams that understand how to improve processes and ask them to help you. Do whatever you have to do to learn and then apply sound quality principles to your processes.

While you're waiting to be trained, here are a few basic ideas:

- Keep all your processes as simple as possible. Don't let individuals handle a document twice if you can revise the process and permit them to do everything in one step.

- Don't uses processes that "goldplate" what you produce— that add features your customer doesn't need. A spreadsheet that summarizes expenditures down to the branch level when your customers need them summarized only to the division level is goldplated. If you aren't producing what your boss believes you should, identify exactly what your customers need, then produce that and no more.

- Don't involve the whole team in a task that an individual or subteam can perform. This is a key part of keeping processes simple. You and other team members may enjoy working on projects together, but it's *always* less efficient to have several people do what one person could do well by himself or herself.

If your boss's expectations are too high:

First question: How do you know? Do you produce at the same level as other, similar teams? Can you compare the team's production with that of a relevant workgroup before the team was formed? How do you know? You must begin by answering that question before you can go any further. But there's another, equally important question: How does your next-level manager know? Where did he or she get the idea of what your quality and quantity levels should be?

You need answers to both sets of questions to go further. Now suppose you've gotten them. You know why your next-level manager believes you're underproducing, and you know your production compares well with other teams. Now you can design a strategy to change your manager's mind.

What should the strategy be? One that addresses the specific concerns of your manager. Suppose she expects that because your work has been assigned to a team your productivity should go up 20 percent. If you want to be persuasive, you have to show why this expectation isn't realistic. How do you show this? By carefully organizing and presenting the data that support it. Have other teams like yours not produced this increase in productivity? Use that data. Select the data carefully and point out how your team is in the same situation. One word of warning: Don't fudge or exaggerate. If the data as they are don't support your claim, go back to the first or second cause in this case and work from there.

Team Strengthener

We talk constantly about customer satisfaction, and we ought to. But we need to talk about *boss satisfaction* as well. In progressive firms, bosses are satisfied when customers are satisfied. But all firms aren't progressive, and bosses don't always know when customers are satisfied. So the burden falls on you and your team to keep your next-level manager satisfied. How do you do that? Whether for bosses or customers, satisfaction equals expectations minus performance. If your boss expects a level of performance from you that you don't meet, he or she will be dissatisfied, even if you are the best team in the organization. The reverse is also true: If you're mediocre but your boss expects even less—well, you'll look good. So an effective team not only performs well but manages its boss's expectations so that it also *looks* as if it's performing well. That's what this case is really about.

10–5

The Problem

Higher management refuses to support team decisions that are controversial

The Scene

"But, Mr. Voinovich, we spent a lot of time coming up with this."

"I appreciate your time, but I still can't go along with it. I can't begin to tell you the problems this might cause us. Surely you can come up with something a little less controversial."

"We know it's controversial, but we're sure it'll work, and it'll work a lot better than what we're doing now."

"Maybe—but we can't take the risk. I want you to go back and have the team work the problem again. This time, come up with something that doesn't make waves for everybody."

So much for the hours of work the team spent analyzing alternatives and coming up with the one with the greatest potential. How can you get higher management to support anything that isn't in the same old rut? Or how can you get them to leave the team alone so it can do its job?

Possible Causes

The team has "gone off the deep end."

Nothing guarantees that a decision made by a team is a good one. While teams may prevent some of the wilder ideas that individuals can come up with, they may also come up with wild ideas themselves. This may happen particularly if the team is relatively new and wants to demonstrate its independence or creativity. After all, management may well have encouraged it to "think outside the box" and take risks. Unfortunately, there are real pitfalls outside the box, and not all risks are worth taking.

The team doesn't understand how higher management evaluates decisions.

In this case, your next-level manager may be speaking for management in general. The team's decision doesn't reflect higher management's values or priorities. The team's decision may have been very good in the abstract. It may have reflected the best current management thinking, or the best practice in the field, or just the solid ideas of its members. None of this matters if the decision didn't fit in with the values of the organization as a whole.

Higher management is still operating traditionally.

This isn't incompatible with either of the two causes above. Higher management may have a traditional approach, so that it expects teams to come up with the decisions that it would have come up with. It may also expect that when it questions a team's decision the team will immediately turn to and come up with a more acceptable decision. In other words, it may expect teams to operate independently and take risks only to the extent that the teams conform to higher management's conservative expectations.

Cures

If the team has "gone off the deep end":

The team begins by evaluating the decision it's made. Why does your next-level manager believe it's unacceptable? (It will be helpful, of course, if you asked this question and got all the detail you could in your talk with your manager.) Take this analysis as deeply as the team is capable of. The better you understand what seems wrong about the decision, the better your chance of coming up with a good decision next time.

Now the team has a choice to make. Does it work out a new decision or does it modify this decision to make it less controversial and more acceptable? That's a difficult question, but here's a suggested criterion. Is the decision as a whole really wild? If so, it's doubtful that any amount of tinkering with it will make it any more palatable to your next-level manager. Or is the decision as a whole fairly well in accord with past decisions in the organization? If so, you may be able to modify it to be acceptable to higher levels. The next section will give you some suggestions on criteria to use when making these decisions.

If the team doesn't understand how higher management evaluates decisions:

Your first step is obvious. While the team works out a new decision it also takes the time and effort to find out what higher management's decision criteria are. Does the organization always go with safe decisions? With ones that follow past precedent closely? With ones that produce the minimum disruption? If the team wants its recommendations to be accepted, it has to know what criteria higher management will use in judging them.

Now the team can plan and decide realistically. Not that it will always come up with the decision most acceptable to higher management. Not that it should. But it will be able to tell if it is on somewhat shaky ground and prepare accordingly. Besides, if most of the team's decisions clearly fit in with the organization's overall approach it will have a better chance of getting a few more adventurous decisions accepted.

If higher management is still operating traditionally:

What does the team do in this circumstance? In the short run, it delivers what higher management expects. In the long run, it does what it can to change higher management's expectations. It probably can't accomplish much alone, but it can work with other teams to develop a "united front" and a united approach to the problem.

Here's an example of one action the team might take. Even if higher management is very traditional, it might consider meeting quarterly with representatives from operating teams. These quarterly meetings might provide a forum in which both management and teams could speak effectively to one another. If sufficient trust develops, the teams might explain how they see the traditional structure handicapping them and make suggestions on how they would be more effective if management gave them more freedom. Don't expert miracles, and don't expect management to change the first time the issue comes up. But if the teams are being successful, higher management may begin to reevaluate its approach. Over time, it may be willing to give teams much wider latitude in making decisions.

Team Strengthener

What happens when we, either as individuals or teams, run into problems? Our first reaction is often to find a quick solution, so we can get on about our business. Some problems, though, can't be solved quickly. This book has discussed a number of these problems, scattered through the different chapters. Management attitudes are certainly among the problems that can't be easily solved. After all, managers seldom think that they are the problem. No matter how bad things may seem at the moment, though, significant change can happen over time. New managers may succeed previous ones and bring more open attitudes. Or existing managers may come to see teams in a new and more flexible way. Just follow three rules: (1) Do a consistently good job; (2) Be patient and persistent; (3) Expect higher management to come around to your way of thinking eventually and act accordingly.

The Problem

Your next-level manager keeps overruling your team's decisions

The Scene

"We're going to have to have a serious talk. I don't think your team has come up with a good decision in the last two months."

"But Mr. Tobin, our decisions haven't been that bad. And every one of them would have worked if you had let us try it."

"Now, now—don't get defensive. I know you and your team are trying hard, but you're just not doing the job you ought to be. I've been trying to support you, but I don't know how much longer I can do it."

The conversation doesn't last much longer, and it certainly doesn't get much better. It's clear—either something changes or the team is in serious danger of going out of business.

Possible Causes

Mr. Tobin doesn't like teams.

When organizations aren't very careful (and sometimes even when they are) second- and third-level managers believe that teams are usurping their authority. They often believe that teams will put them out of a job, and sometimes teams do just that. How does a manager handle this situation? One way is to keep overruling the team because it isn't making good decisions and then making sure that higher management knows that the team is "failing." This may be Mr. Tobin's strategy.

He thinks that the only way he can maintain control is by overruling the team.

In Case 3 of this chapter, the manager used performance appraisals as a way of maintaining control (and you might want to look back at it). Overruling team decisions is another way that a manager might attempt to preserve his or her control over the team. It could be a way of continuing to "show who's boss" in a team situation.

He doesn't feel as if he's managing if he "goes along" with the team.

This is a different situation, with much more potential for resolution than those in the two sections above. Mr. Tobin was evidently a supervisor in a traditional organization, and he thinks of supervision in terms of directing workers. He can't direct the team as such, since he's now at a higher level. But he can still act like a boss and do his job by overruling the team's decisions.

Hint

The case before this one contains a cause that might be relevant here: not knowing the criteria higher management uses to evaluate decisions. If you think that might apply to your situation, look back at that cause and cure.

Cures

If Mr. Tobin doesn't like teams:

The team needs to examine the decisions it's making very closely, to make sure they are solid. If the team remains convinced they are, you and/or other members of the team should talk with Mr. Tobin and ask him to explain why he believes they're wrong. Don't challenge him; if he's afraid he'll lose his job that will just make the situation worse. If you believe that he doesn't like teams and may try to get the team dissolved, though, it's time to act.

This is one of the few situations where you're justified in going to Mr. Tobin's higher-level manager. That person needs to know what's happening, but make it clear that you're not trying to "get" Mr. Tobin. You might ask the manager to reassure him that his job is safe (if it is) as long as he supports the team. If nothing else looks as if it will work, you can try to get the team assigned to another manager, one you'll hope is more sympathetic. At this point, you're justified in doing almost anything reasonable to preserve the team.

If Mr. Tobin thinks that the only way he can maintain control is by overruling the team:

Case 3 had a specific suggestion that's relevant here: Earn Mr. Tobin's confidence so he doesn't feel the need to exercise control this way. One way to accomplish this was suggested in the section above; find out *why* he believes the decisions need to be overruled. You might find, for instance, that if the team were to check each decision with him before it's final—so that he could make "suggestions"—you could begin making decisions that he would then approve. With good work on the team's part, his suggestions might get fewer and fewer, so that the team is in reality making the decisions.

Unless the situation gets desperate, don't even think about going to Mr. Tobin's manager in this circumstance. If you do, go with the single aim of being transferred out from under his control. If you go around him, don't get moved, and he finds out, he will make life far tougher than it's been. And it might be enough to push him into the situation mentioned in the section above: He may attempt to get the team disbanded.

If Mr. Tobin doesn't feel as if he's managing if he "goes along" with the team:

Evidently he doesn't understand his new role. The team's best strategy is to start asking him to act as the coach and counselor the manager of a team should be. The team might ask him to train it in budget procedures or in some other topic he's familiar with and the team needs to know. Several individuals, or perhaps the team as a whole, might ask him to help them plan how to advance in the organization. But you don't want to ask him to do anything that would look or feel like actually supervising the team. You don't want to ask him, for instance, to resolve an argument between two members of the team.

As he performs duties more like those of a coach or counselor, he may begin to understand what his role needs to be. In fact, he might even want to get training in how to do these duties, and that training might stress what his new role needs to be. The key should be clear: Don't try to *force* him to act differently. Just help him see and begin to act in the role appropriate for a higher-level manager in a team-based organization.

Team Strengthener

Many, perhaps most, workers were brought up to do what they were told. When it seemed wrong, or there was a problem, there often was no way to bring up the situation. Managers often considered that if a worker questioned them the individual was challenging their authority. So workers griped and talked with one another about the manager's "dumb" requirements and then went on about their business. Fortunately, many managers have changed today, especially in team-based organizations. When a team carefully builds a good working relationship with its higher-level manager, it becomes possible to ask "why?" You and your team should work at developing this kind of relationship; in the long run, it will make the team much more effective and its life more pleasant.

10–7

The Problem

Your next level manager "micromanages" the team and won't delegate

The Scene

"Well, if you and the team make just these few changes I think you'll have a good work plan. Then the next thing for you to do is get the research done and let me have a look at that. Now let's go over your budget for the next quarter . . . ."

These weekly meetings are draining you and discouraging the team. Mr. Senn wants to have a hand in every decision the team makes. No one on the team feels as if the work is really his or hers. They all feel as if they're just flunkies, carrying out Mr. Senn's directions.

Possible Causes

The team is new and Mr. Senn is supervising it closely only to get it started.

No effective manager lets a new workgroup perform without supervision, even if the workgroup is a team whose goal is to be self-managing. If your team is new, Mr. Senn may be supervising it closely for this reason.

Mr. Senn doesn't trust the team to manage itself.

What if the team isn't new, but Mr. Senn is still micromanaging it? The first question to ask is: Does he not trust the team to work independently? Perhaps the team made some mistakes that are on his mind. Or it had serious problems with a project that he had delegated fully to it. If anything such as this happened, his micromanaging may be his reaction to what he sees as a problem situation.

Mr. Senn doesn't know any other way to manage.

A manager used to a traditional role may overrule the team's decisions. Or he may exercise the role by managing so closely that no one ever has a chance to make the wrong decision. In both cases, the problem isn't with the manager's intentions but with his misunderstanding of how to manage an independent team.

Hint

The team needs to make sure that its performance is effective enough that Mr. Senn can afford to delegate to it. If you're not sure the team measures up, look at some of the cases in Chapter 5.

Cures

If the team is new and Mr. Senn is supervising it closely only to get it started:

What do you do? You accept Mr. Senn's close management. As time goes on, you and the team make more and more suggestions about what should be done. When you believe the team can complete part of a job, or even an entire small job, bring this up to Mr. Senn and ask him to let you do so. Don't fight him. In fact, you want to let him know that you appreciate the guidance he's giving. But you want to keep communicating that the team is growing and becoming more competent to work on its own.

What if you're not quite sure that Mr. Senn wants to draw back and give the team more independence? Unless you have a good reason to believe otherwise, act as though you believe he will delegate more. If he isn't really sure that he wants to let go, your acting as though he's willing to do so may help him decide to do that. Be sure to express your appreciation whenever he delegates more responsibility, and, of course, be sure that the team performs effectively.

If Mr. Senn doesn't trust the team to manage itself:

The first step? The team needs to analyze what happened. What mistakes did it make, why, and how? Or if the team doesn't believe it made mistakes, why does Mr. Senn believe that they were mistakes? (Even if the team doesn't believe there were mistakes, it still needs to have as clear an idea as possible why Mr. Senn thought there were.)

If the team believes it did make mistakes, this is an excellent opportunity to check its understanding with Mr. Senn. Start the conversation off by explaining that the team thinks it was mistaken and why, then ask Mr. Senn to explain any factors to the team that it might have missed. This demonstrates that the team is learning from its experience and that it's actively seeking his help. Both of these should help him loosen up and try delegating more fully again.

What if he brings up something that the team doesn't think was a mistake? An excellent opportunity has presented itself. Ask him why he believes it was a mistake. He may persuade you that he's right. If he doesn't, ask him to listen to your understanding of the situation. The worst outcome will be that you understand his way of thinking much better. And you may in fact persuade him that what happened wasn't really a mistake.

Mr. Senn doesn't know any other way to manage:

If this seems to be the situation, follow the suggestions in the third section of Case 10–6 and ask Mr. Senn to start performing as a coach and counselor. In this case, you might say to him that what the team needs is this kind of support, not close management. The clearer you can make the role of coach and counselor to him, and the more you can help act in that role, the more willing he will be to let the team begin managing itself.

Be careful about trying to force a higher-level manager to change his or her style. If that's all the individual knows, that's the only way he or she can act effectively. Instead of forcing, you want to encourage, suggesting a direction the manager might move in and asking for support that requires him to act in that role and then recognizing him whenever he provides that support.

Team Strengthener

If you work for a higher-level manager, and you almost certainly do, one of your responsibilities is to manage your relationship with that individual. The same goes for the entire team. This doesn't require you to be sneaky or to try to force the manager to be different. It does require you to find out what's important to him or her and then do your (and the team's) best to provide that. Here's a specific tip: Most managers have to feel comfortable before they're willing to delegate significant responsibilities to individuals or teams. So a primary job of yours (and the team's) is to find out what makes your higher-level manager comfortable and then act in ways that demonstrate he or she can be comfortable with you.

The Problem

Your manager is pressuring you to tell her who made the mistake that resulted in the team's missing a deadline

The Scene

"I want to know who ruined our productivity last week."

"Mrs. Moreland, I told you—the team was responsible for it. We've already looked at what happened and made sure it won't ever happen again."

"Don't give me that. I know it wasn't the team as a whole. It was Sheila Lockhart, wasn't it?"

"Mrs. Moreland, you keep telling us we should act as a team. Well, we are. The team made the mistake."

The conversation continues a minute or so longer, without getting anywhere except making Mrs. Moreland angrier. As you leave, she makes it clear that she is still expecting you to tell her who made the mistake. You know that's not how a team is supposed to work, but what are you going to do?

Possible Causes

Sheila often fails to perform, and the team covers for her.

There's a double issue here. First, the team is covering for a poor performer, which is causing problems with its next-level manager. Second, the team apparently continues to put up with Sheila's poor performance. Each problem makes the other worse.

Mrs. Moreland is uncomfortable with team instead of individual responsibility.

Many managers face this problem when organizations decide to become team based. Responsibility is almost always an individual matter in traditional organizations. The rule is that someone is responsible for every task, and when something goes wrong an individual is the cause of it. You may not believe that your organization operated that way, or that the view is realistic. But that was the official theory, and most managers are taught it. When something goes wrong, some *individual* caused it, and that individual needs to be identified.

Mrs. Moreland wants to control the team by dealing with individuals.

This means Mrs. Moreland still operates in her traditional "boss" role, but with a difference. She wants not only to supervise the team but to control it. You may already have found out, and so may she, that it's very hard to control an entire team. If your goal is control, one way to accomplish this is by breaking the team into individuals and trying to set them against one another.

Hint

The three causes don't exclude one another. Two or even all three of them may be at the root of the problem.

Cures

Sheila often fails to perform, and the team covers for her:

Why is Sheila failing to perform as she should? Is it a temporary matter, because she's going through a divorce, has problems with her teenage son, is recovering from surgery? In cases such as these, the team should "carry" her until she gets back on her feet. If she's been a productive member of the team, she's earned this.

But what if there's a continuing performance problem? The team does no one a service by carrying her. It has every right to confront her with her performance in a team meeting and negotiate with her how she's going to improve it. (See the cases in Chapter 4, which deal with this in several different ways, and Case 5–8.) And it has every right to insist that she improve. If she's a perennial underperformer and the team has been carrying her, it's no wonder Mrs. Moreland is suspicious that she's the one responsible for the problem. But she isn't the one responsible. The team is responsible for permitting it. The team needs to get *its* act together.

But the team also needs to deal with Mrs. Moreland's pressure to know who made the mistake. If this is a constant pressure, look at the next two sections. If it's a one-time thing, brought on by her perception that you're refusing to deal with Sheila's performance, it requires an entirely different approach. It may be best to admit that the team has been carrying Sheila but is now taking positive steps to have her improve her performance or else. Follow this up with the specifics on how Sheila will improve, once she and the team have worked out an improvement plan. But consider this approach *only* if you're sure that this is an isolated incident.

If Mrs. Moreland is uncomfortable with team instead of individual responsibility:

Mrs. Moreland is continuing to manage the way she was taught. The problem will be solved only when Mrs. Moreland learns her new role and chooses to operate in that role.

The team can help. First, it needs to understand what Mrs. Moreland's priorities are and ensure that it deals with them. She needs to know that the team is fully supporting her, even when she can't place responsibility individually. You and other team members need to express your appreciation every time she responds as a manager of teams should, for instance, when she supports consensus team decisions or acts more as a coach than a boss. And you need to ask her to provide the team what an effective coach provides: counseling, guidance, support, and so forth. You want to encourage her to move into her new role, even though she may not quite understand what the role is. As she sees that she can operate in this role and still get effective performance, she will become more comfortable with it. (There are further suggestions on dealing with a manager stuck in an old role in Cases 10–3 and 10–7.)

If Mrs. Moreland wants to control the team by dealing with individuals:

The key here is simple: The team can't allow its next-level manager to carve it up into individuals.

How do you accomplish this? You get support from other teams if you can. You get support from other next-level managers if you can. If someone on the team has a good relationship with someone above Mrs. Moreland in the chain of command, he or she uses this relationship to call attention to what Mrs. Moreland is doing. Through it all, the team insists on remaining a team, no matter what. It remains as responsive as possible to all of Mrs. Moreland's requirements that it can meet as a team, then draws the line. (And, as so many of these cases point out, it can do this best when it knows and responds effectively to her most important concerns.)

Team Strengthener

This case illustrates how important it is for the team both to be responsive to its managers and to see itself always as a team and never as a collection of individuals. Teams don't become teams because someone calls them that. Nor do they cease to be teams because someone calls them something else. More than anything else, a team is a team when it thinks of itself that way. Nothing else is more important than this. As a team leader one of your most basic responsibilities is to ensure that the team always sees itself as a team. How? In many ways. One of them is to ensure that the team takes responsibility for everything it does—even when a specific individual was the one who dropped the ball.

10–9

The Problem
Two unnecessary members have been forced on the team

The Scene

"But, Carlos, we don't need anyone else on the team." The frustration is obvious in your voice.

"Now calm down. Suzanne and Pauli are fine workers. We just don't have a place for them, and they've done the kind of work your team does. It won't be forever; if they don't work out, we'll find another spot for them."

"But. . ."

You try to continue, but it's a done deal. Suzanne and Pauli are going to join the team Monday.

Just what the team needs. You've achieved a good balance of workload and individual skills, and the team has learned to work together effectively. Now what do you do?

Possible Causes

Suzanne and Pauli are good workers who don't have jobs.

Even very good team members may need new jobs. Their team may have been broken up, through no fault of their own. They may have been surplus members of an effective team. Whatever the reason might have been, start with the assumption that they will be a valuable addition to the team.

The organization wants to see if the two can become effective team members.

This situation resembles the one in the section above, but with one difference. The organization has reason to believe that Suzanne and Pauli may *not* be good team members. Perhaps they've both been excellent as independent workers, but the team no longer has independent jobs for them. Perhaps they didn't fit into the team to which they were assigned.

The organization is "dumping" Suzanne and Pauli on your team.

They might be able to work effectively as part of a team, but they haven't so far. For whatever reason, the organization is giving them to you.

Hints

You will make sure the team knows what's going to happen, of course. But the team needs to decide, with or without encouragement from you, that it won't take out its unhappiness over the new members on them. It needs to genuinely welcome them. And it definitely is not going to try to drive them away; that's a last resort and a dangerous one.

The team needs to begin from the working assumption that Suzanne and Pauli have been assigned to it because it has a good reputation. In other words, take the situation as a compliment. That doesn't make solving it easier, but at least the team won't muddy the waters by worrying about what higher management thinks of them. Besides, whether management thinks highly of you or not, handling this situation well is going to make the team look good.

Cures

If Suzanne and Pauli are good workers who don't have jobs:

Can you turn the situation into an opportunity? Has the team been wanting to pick up an additional mission but been handicapped because it didn't have enough people to handle it? Can you increase the level of service to one or more of your customers now that you have two new members? Are there other goals the team has been wanting to work on but lacked the staff to do so? Okay, now's your chance. Integrate Suzanne and Pauli into the team's operation and take advantage of their presence. One caution: Make sure that they quickly become full participants on the team. Don't give them the jobs no one else wants. If you do that, and they're really good, you'll lose them quickly, and then there go your plans.

If the team can't change its mission or increase its services, get with other teams performing similar work to determine whether other teams can use one or both of your new members. If so, work out a joint presentation to higher management with the teams and attempt to get Suzanne or Pauli reassigned where they will be more productive. (Don't even think of this alternative, though, unless you're persuaded both are good workers.)

Will neither of these alternatives work? Well, perhaps this is the time to see that everyone gets trained in a wide variety of skills the team can use. Identify individuals—including Suzanne and Pauli—for company training courses and send them. If the organization will support this kind of course, send them to local community colleges or universities. Give them time to read up on useful topics. Balance the training around the team members (taking some yourself); you don't want anyone to OD on it. But this could be a great opportunity, and you might get new ideas from it that would enable the team to expand so that it genuinely needs its new members.

If the organization wants to see if the two can become effective team members:

How do you treat this situation? The team begins by attempting to integrate Suzanne and Pauli into the team's operations, to make them full members. This means giving them real work and creating situations where they have to work closely with others. It may be a little rocky at first, but the team will begin to find out if they want to be part of it. Many of the cases in Chapters 1 and 3 describe situations where independent workers cause problems for teams. If problems arise, you might want to look through these chapters for ideas.

If Suzanne and Pauli do turn out to be good team members, go back to the section above and follow its suggestions. However, not everyone is an effective team player. Suzanne or Pauli or both of them may not be comfortable having to work closely with others (though don't assume this, of course, until they've had plenty of time to do so). If they genuinely don't want to be part of the team, it's time to return to higher management and discuss a productive future for them.

When you do so, though, make it clear to them and to higher management that the two of them are good workers. If possible, make specific recommendations about the kind of work they can most effectively do. And take full account of what they want to do and believe they are most qualified to do.

If the organization is "dumping" Suzanne and Pauli on your team:

Ow—this is the one that really hurts! No matter how good your team is, having to carry two individuals who are not only unnecessary but nonperformers to boot is going to handicap it.

You may need to meet with team members individually or in small groups, but you need to develop a consensus that the team will insist that the new members are fully productive. You also need to get agreement that team members will devote the time and effort necessary to give them every chance to do so. Then you make clear to Suzanne and Pauli that they are full team members and are expected to perform as such.

Then keep that resolve. You may find that one or even both of them begins to perform effectively. Perhaps they never had anyone expect this level of performance from them. But one or both also may not perform, and you can count on excuse after excuse for why they don't perform. Let them make all the excuses they want. Help them whenever it's appropriate, but keep insisting on performance. If they don't deliver, get them off the team in any appropriate way. But once they've demonstrated that they won't perform, don't carry them a moment longer than you must.

(You might get some helpful suggestions from Cases 4–1, 4–6, and 5–8.)

Team Strengthener

All of us face problems, at work and at home. What distinguishes successful and creative individuals, teams, and organizations from others is that they look for the opportunities hidden in the problems. A problem points out that something being done now isn't working. When it's seen as no more than a problem, the proper response is to "fix" it as quickly as possible and then go back to what was being done. When it's seen as an opportunity, though, it can point us in a new direction that not only solves the problem but makes us more effective than we were before. This case has provided an example: By treating the two new members as an opportunity, the team may now be able to do important work that was impossible before. You can't avoid problems, so make it a habit to look for the opportunities hidden in them.

The Problem

The team wants to change its mission and your next-level manager won't consider it

The Scene

"The way you look, Ms. Babcock must have turned down our proposal to change our mission."

"She didn't just turn it down, Lou—she absolutely refused to consider it. She handed me back the folder and told me that we had our mission and it didn't need discussing any further. That was it."

"Wow. We need that change. What do we do now?"

You're wondering the same thing.

Possible Causes

Ms. Babcock wants to avoid change.

Many organizations go to a team-based structure to deal with change, because self-managing teams can often manage rapid change more effectively than more formal workgroups can. That doesn't mean that everyone in the organization, or even everyone managing teams, deals well with change. Ms. Babcock may be someone who doesn't like change. She made the change to manager of teams, but she wants to preserve as much stability as possible in her new job.

The organization doesn't want to change established team missions.

The resistance to change may go deeper than your next-level manager. Ms. Babcock may not want to consider the change because higher management has told her not to make changes. Needless to say, this situation is even harder to deal with than the one above, because she's carrying out only what she's been told to do.

Ms. Babcock is unhappy with the team, and this is a way of showing it.

Unpleasant as this is, it may be the easiest situation to deal with. For some reason, Ms. Babcock is upset with the team. Perhaps she believe it ignores a "suggestion" she made. Or didn't follow her directions. Or made an important decision without consulting her. Whatever the reason, rather than dealing with the situation directly she's expressing her unhappiness by refusing to consider the mission change.

Note

In a number of cases throughout the book, one of the recommended cures is to have the team's mission changed. In this case, the manager has no interest in letting it change. That may make it particularly important to understand this case.

Cures

If Ms. Babcock wants to avoid change:

Just what does this mean? Unfortunately, it means that Ms. Babcock probably won't be any more open to change in a week or a month than she is now. There's no profit in trying to deal with the issue directly. Instead, you and the team need to concentrate on gaining her confidence. Find out what she wants and, to the extent you can, give it to her. Raise her comfort level with the team by building up her confidence in you. Then, if she begins to be more open to change, bring the issue up again.

But what if the situation won't wait? What if the team's existing mission is becoming irrelevant? Or contains different duties that don't mesh well with one another? Or doesn't mesh well with other teams? Or you want to make the change so you and another team can trade duties to produce better missions for both of you? Can you do some or all of this informally, without getting official approval? If you can, you have a choice to make: Is it worth running the risk of being caught in order to change the mission? On the other hand, if you do informally switch duties with another team and Ms. Babcock finds out, the situation may provide the chance to bring the problem to higher management levels.

If the organization doesn't want to change established team missions:

The last paragraph in the section above raised the question of whether the team should take a risk and make the mission change informally. Is it possible that Ms. Babcock might be willing to see the change happen as long as it was done informally? Did she oppose it only because of her own higher management? If the team's relationship with her is very good, you might solicit her tacit agreement to let you change informally. You need to talk with her, unofficially, to let her know what the team wants to do. You also need to assure her that you will take the heat if anyone discovers and complains about the change. You just want her to know about it and give you the informal latitude to do it. It all depends on her relationship with the team, but if the relationship is strong it might work.

What if the relationship isn't that strong? Then the team can either wait for the relationship to improve and/or the organization to change its policy, or take the risk and go ahead and make the change informally.

If Ms. Babcock is unhappy with the team, and this is a way of showing it:

If you've read many other cases where an unexpressed problem was showing up in a different area, you already know what to do. Find out what she's really upset about and deal with it. Maybe this should be a team project. Does anyone on the team or on another team know what made her unhappy? And why it did? It's hoped that the team can find the answers to these questions. Then you and other members of the team can go to her with what it has found and hope that she will discuss the problem openly with you and commit to resolving the problem.

What if you can't figure out the real problem? You've no choice but to go to her and ask. One approach might be: "We have the feeling that you won't consider the mission change because of something we've done. I'm sorry, but we don't know what it is. Would you help us understand what happened so we can discuss it and see that the problem never happens again?" Even if the team's relationship with her isn't the greatest, this straightforward approach may work. If it does, it will certainly strengthen the relationship.

Team Strengthener

In an organization based on self-managing teams, a team may confront the problem of when to go off on its own, without organizational approval of what it's doing. Should it? There's no easy answer. On the one hand, teams need to be coordinated by higher management to keep them in sync with one another and working toward the same overall mission. On the other, self-managing teams exist to identify and solve problems quickly and effectively. Most of the time, the need for a common direction should prevail. Sometimes, though, a team has to commit itself to the course it believes is right and hope that the organization will ultimately accept it. It takes a mature team to evaluate the situation effectively and reach the right conclusion.

10–11

The Problem
Your next-level manager doesn't think much of the team's performance

The Scene

"I guess you and the team are pretty proud that you got everything done on time and still produced 10 percent over standard last month."

"Yes, Mrs. Veracruz. We had a really good month."

"Well, I don't think so much of it. I think you could easily have done another 10 percent. I don't know how you managed it, but somehow you've gotten your standards down to the point that you could meet them if you worked only half days."

You try to discuss the matter further, but to no avail. Mrs. Veracruz obviously has her mind made up. You believe that the team had to push to get 10 percent over standard; now, how are you going to persuade Mrs. Veracruz of that?

Possible Causes

The standards really are too low.

It's very easy for a team to get into a comfortable groove and decide that what it can produce in this groove is satisfactory. (See the second cause and cure of Case 10–2 for another example.) It feels good, so what's wrong with it? For a short while, nothing. It helps for a team to be able to cruise on automatic for a while. But in the long run it kills the team's edge. More important, it prevents it from developing further. In short, a comfortable groove is a temporary reward, not a place to do business month after month. (A comfortable groove month after month becomes a rut.)

Mrs. Veracruz was a top performer and expects the same from everyone else.

Very often, individuals get promoted to management positions because they're expert performers. It's not that this is the best criterion for promotion, it's just that it's the one that's often used. Perhaps this is the situation with Mrs. Veracruz. She was a superb performer, much better than the average. So she expects the team to match her performance, or at least come close to it.

Mrs. Veracruz doesn't like teams.

Oops—another manager who's dealing with teams only because she has to. That's a real danger, because she has a vested interest in proving that the team isn't productive enough; if she can, perhaps the organization will forget about teams and go back to its traditional structure. (It probably won't, but if she believes it will she'll act accordingly.)

Cures

If the standards really are too low:

Does it appear that your team is working under soft standards? Bring the matter up to the team. Is everyone comfortable? Can each team member do his or her job without thinking much about it? If the consensus is "yes," even a grudging and painful "yes," it's time for the team to stretch itself.

How far? This depends on lots of factors, but one is most important. Discuss the situation with Mrs. Veracruz. Get her thoughts in as much detail as you can. How are the standards soft? What must they be to convince Mrs. Veracruz that the team is really serious about performing?

Take the revised standards back to the team. Try to get a consensus that these will now be the team's minimum goal. Plan how you're going to achieve that goal, then achieve it (making sure that Mrs. Veracruz knows you've achieved it), then make the new standards the level that the team consistently meets or (preferably) beats.

If Mrs. Veracruz was a top performer and expects the same from everyone else:

If you and the team are convinced that this is the case, your next move is simple. Ask Mrs. Veracruz to help the team. You don't need her to spend a great deal of time with you. Instead, you want her to share with the team how she performed at such a high level. Perhaps she can do the actual work for a brief period of time, showing the team how she handled each part of it. Perhaps she can explain her general strategy. But make it clear that the team wants to learn from her, and do so.

Then build on this. Use her methods until they're routine. But don't stop there. If you want to persuade her that the team is really exceptional, it will have to do more than just match what she did. Build on what you've learned from her. Improve on her methods. Beat her performance. Wow her. Then thank her for helping you make this improvement.

If Mrs. Veracruz doesn't like teams:

What do you do in this potentially dangerous situation? To begin with, the team makes sure that it's consistently productive. Use all the suggestions in the sections above that are relevant. Find out how other teams are performing and ensure that your team performs at least as well. She may continue to complain about your productivity, but if it compares favorably with other teams the organization won't pay that much attention to what she says.

You also try to find ways to convert her. Why does she not like teams? Does your team threaten her authority? Does it feel to her as if she's lost control, or that she can't really be a manager any more? Previous cases in this chapter have dealt with all those problems. Look back at them and use the suggestions that fit. No matter how much she dislikes teams, the goal of your team must always be to get her on your side and turn her into a consistent supporter. It may be difficult, but don't for a moment give in and believe it's impossible. It's not.

Team Strengthener

Is there a real payoff if the team is exceptionally productive? Does the team get a bonus? Does it get meaningful recognition from the organization? Or does it just get to feel good about itself and set an example? If any of these reasons appeal to you and the team, you might consider trying to make a quantum jump in productivity. Is the team willing to increase its productivity 33 percent, 50 percent, even 100 percent? Does that sound ridiculous? It is, if you want to keep performing the way you are now. But if you want to "think outside the box" and push yourselves to find new and better ways—well, committing yourself to this kind of improvement will force you to do that.

10–12

The Problem
The team isn't recognized for its good performance

The Scene

You come in a few minutes late to the team meeting because of the big management-team meeting you just attended.

Joel can't wait. "Well, what did they say about us?"

"Nothing."

"What do you mean, nothing," Hilda chimes in. "We meet or beat every target for the last quarter, we completed two special projects in record time, and we had the highest customer-satisfaction rating we've ever gotten."

"Yeah," Joel adds, "and it's almost the highest rating any team has ever gotten."

"I know," you sigh wearily. "We've done a great job. But all anyone at the meeting could talk about was how everybody needs to use the fewest possible supplies and watch their budgets. In fact, no one even noticed that our budget for this coming quarter is 10 percent less than last quarter.

You sink into your chair, just as discouraged as anyone else and wondering how much longer the rest of the team is going to keep on doing a great job when nobody seems to care.

Probable Cause

Your next-level manager, higher-level management, and/or the organization as a whole don't understand the importance of recognition.

Cure

First, you and the team must accept that most organizations don't understand what recognition is, and few if any managers who understand it intellectually practice it. The prevalent view seems to be: "That's just doing the job right—why should I compliment anyone for that?"

You should have at least some sympathy with managers. The fact is that they often receive precious little recognition themselves. Many companies run on the basic idea that the fact that a manager still has a job, or got a bonus at the end of the year, is recognition enough.

Of course, along with this goes the idea that every mistake should be noticed and pointed out immediately. And how many thousands of managers hold the view that everyone needs a good chewing-out once in a while?

Every organization has a "recognition" program of some kind. Typically, rewards are few, don't amount to much money, make other employees (including managers) jealous, and come long after the act that earned them. On top of it, the performance that earns awards, such as supporting the New Quality Initiative, is too seldom the performance that gets you promoted or even the performance that makes higher management happy.

What does all that add up to? Your team and the others should do what they can to change the negative mind-set on awards. But that's not the critical point. This is: Make your team an absolute hotbed of recognition and appreciation.

Here's the absolute lower limit: You and everyone on the team should praise one another at least four times for each time you complain or are critical. Notice that this is the lower limit; if you praise ten or even twenty times for each criticism everyone will do even better.

What if no one is doing anything worth praising for? If that's the case, the problem is with you—you're not paying attention. Don't you appreciate it when others keep their commitments to you? Wouldn't you like them to appreciate when you work a little harder to keep a commitment to them? Every workday is full of actions to be grateful for. Just find them and notice them.

This may sound Pollyanaish, because you and most of the team probably came from an environment like that of the organization. Forget that. Concentrate for a month or two on identifying and recognizing all the positive aspects of team life and work. It may not transform the team, but then again, it may. And everyone will certainly feel better about working on the team.

When the team gets proficient at informal recognition internally, extend it out in every direction. Recognize and appreciate what other teams do for you. Recognize and appreciate your customers. Recognize and appreciate higher management (!) when their actions make the team's life easier and more productive. But be careful—you may end up infecting the whole organization with recognition and appreciation.

Will this wake up higher management, so it recognizes what the team does? Perhaps. And perhaps not. If you and the team and the other teams get into recognizing and appreciating one another, it won't matter as much.

Team Strengthener

This entire case will help you strengthen your team. Take it seriously.

10–13

The Problem

Your next-level manager doesn't believe in teams and won't support your team

The Scene

"What happened at the division meeting?"

"Well, to make it brief, Mr. Yowell sold us down the river. When a couple of other teams complained about our performance, he not only agreed with them but bad-mouthed us on his own. Then he complained to everyone that we weren't performing as we should. When some manager I've never heard of complained about teams in general, Mr. Yowell fell all over himself to agree with her. It was a mess!"

What's the use? The team works overtime to do a good job, and then its next-level manager does nothing but criticize it. What can you and the team do?

Possible Causes

The team isn't performing effectively.

Once again, the team is in trouble because it isn't performing as well as it should.

Mr. Yowell feels as if he's lost control.

When traditional mangers aren't properly prepared to work with teams—and sometimes even when they are—they don't understand that they are performing in a new role. They attempt to stay in the role they're familiar with, which means controlling the workgroup or team. Mr. Yowell may not have made a conscious decision that he wants to control the team. Instead, he's simply managing as he's always managed.

Mr. Yowell doesn't, and doesn't want to understand how teams work.

Mr. Yowell didn't want to work with teams in the first place and has little motivation to spend time understanding how they work. He doesn't know what the team needs from him to thrive, and he doesn't care.

Cures

If the team isn't performing effectively:

How do you tell that this is the case? The team needs to meet and evaluate its performance as objectively as possible. It might also be a good idea to talk with other, similar teams and compare performance with them. Your team wants to be *at least* as good as the average of the other teams. If it's not, the team's performance may be directly responsible for Mr. Yowell's low opinion of teams.

If there are any doubts about whether your team is performing at the same level as the others, get to work. What does the team need to do to improve? Talk with other teams. Talk with Mr. Yowell to find out, as specifically as possible, why he's dissatisfied. Then do what you need to do, and make sure that Mr. Yowell knows what you're doing. (You may find some useful suggestions in earlier cases in this chapter and in Chapter 5.)

Remember, as earlier cases in this chapter have pointed out, that the team needs to know what Mr. Yowell expects from it. No matter how well the team performs, no matter how much it improves, he will judge it by *his* standards. If the problem is his low opinion of the team, it can be solved only by understanding what he expects and then delivering it.

If Mr. Yowell feels as if he's lost control:

The team's first task is to reassure Mr. Yowell that he's still in control. This means keeping him informed; finding what kinds of decisions he's particularly concerned with and checking them in advance; and asking for his advice on matters that are important to him. Doesn't this infringe on the team's autonomy? Certainly, but if it's the price of remaining a team it's worth it.

At the same time, the team works on long-range solutions. It uses its short-range performance to increase Mr. Yowell's comfort level with teams. It tries gently to steer him toward a management role oriented less toward control and more toward supporting the team. If the opportunity arises, an offhand remark to Mr. Yowell's manager about his concern for control might influence the organization to provide Mr. Yowell training on the requirements of his new role. No matter how the team accomplishes it, it should work to develop its autonomy and freedom in the long run.

If Mr. Yowell doesn't, and doesn't want to understand how teams work:

In this situation, the team resigns itself to providing its own support. It does this first by performing effectively. He may want to agree with other teams that yours performs poorly, but he can't if other teams don't complain. Build up your relationships with other teams by helping them achieve their mission. In return, they may give you the support Mr. Yowell is unwilling to provide. If some member of your team has a good relationship with a manager at a higher level than Mr. Yowell, cultivate this relationship. Take every available step to gain support for the team from every source possible.

Does this mean you write off Mr. Yowell? Of course not. Once again, the team needs to establish and pursue the long-term goal of converting him to a supporter. Keep him informed. Take advantage of every opportunity to see that he knows what the team has accomplished. Find out what's important to him, then demonstrate to him that the best way for him to get this is to support you. (Example: Suppose he values stability and "not making waves." Gain his support by pointing out how the team acted to avert conflict with another team.) Don't quit. Keep working to get his support and you will quite probably get it, perhaps sooner rather than later.

Team Strengthener

When a manager won't support your team, it's easy to decide that this is how he or she is and accept it as a given. Don't! Managers, like everyone else, change. A manager who has no interest in your team this year may be an ardent supporter next year. (And remember that the reverse is also true, if the team's performance isn't up to snuff.) The key is simple: Find out what's important to this particular manager and see that the team delivers it. This requires the team to understand the manager, not just superficially but in depth. Does he want to avoid making waves, or is he concerned to be seen as an innovative manager? Does she want to get promoted, or does she mostly want to establish her reputation among her peers? An effective team finds the answers to these questions and then does its best to provide the manager just what he or she wants. In return, the team can expect to earn more and more autonomy for itself.

10–14

The Problem

Your next-level manager is talking about breaking up your team and reassigning its members

The Scene

"I've got something you've got to hear."

You put down what you are working on and give Vance your full attention. "Shoot."

"I was down talking to Chip Wozniak and one of his people heard Mr. Bernstein talking with their manager. According to him, Mr. Bernstein said he was thinking seriously about breaking up our team and reassigning all of us somewhere else!"

"You're sure that you heard this right? Mr. Bernstein really is considering breaking us up?"

"I asked him to repeat it, then asked him several questions. It looks as if Mr. Bernstein really did say it."

Just what you and the team need. You knew things hadn't been going well lately, but the team was concentrating on giving Mr Bernstein what he wanted. Apparently this isn't working. What would?

Possible Causes

The team has been performing very poorly.

If your team hasn't been up to the standard of other teams, it's no wonder your higher-level manager is thinking about breaking up the team. The organization will almost certainly get better overall performance that way.

The team doesn't understand what Mr. Bernstein wants.

It may be that Mr. Bernstein has expectations for the team very different from what the team expects of itself. Look at the earlier cases in this chapter where the team didn't know what the next-level manager expected. It doesn't matter how good the team believes it is, if it doesn't understand the standards its next-level manager is applying to it, it's courting trouble.

Mr. Bernstein has never liked teams.

Several cases in this chapter—the latest was the one before this one—have dealt with situations where the next-level manager's real agenda was to get rid of teams. That may be what's happening here. Mr. Bernstein believes that he can make a case for your team's poor performance and break it up. That may not get rid of all the teams, but it's a start.

Hint

Don't take any of the following steps until you've confirmed that Mr. Bernstein really did say that he was considering breaking up the team and until you've concluded that he wasn't just "blowing off steam." If possible, ask him. If not, ask around among other teams or even among higher managers you and other members of the team know.

Cures

If the team has been performing very poorly:

Is there time to prevent the breakup of your team? It depends on how poor the team's performance is and how quickly it can improve it. As so many cases have stressed, the team needs to analyze its performance objectively and identify where the weaknesses are. It may help to talk with another team or two and make some comparisons between how they perform and how you do. Whatever you do, find out as quickly as possibly what's wrong and then begin to fix it.

Make sure Mr. Bernstein knows that the team knows its performance isn't what it should be and that the team is working hard to improve—quickly. Also, if the team's relationship with Mr. Bernstein is strong enough, ask him if what you heard about his wanting to abolish the team is true. If he acknowledges that it is, then you can negotiate with him the improvement the team would have to make and when it would have to make it. That gives you and the rest of the team clear guidelines.

If the team doesn't understand what Mr. Bernstein wants:

If your team doesn't understand what's important to Mr. Bernstein, it needs to find out quickly. Does he believe the team doesn't produce enough? Fails to complete tasks as quickly as he believes it should? Doesn't get his approval when it needs to? There could be all kinds of reasons, but what's important is to find out what *his* reasons are. Exactly what does he expect, and exactly how is the team falling short of this? Find this out by asking Mr. Bernstein directly if this is possible. If you can't, as a poor second choice talk to other individuals and teams that have worked with or for him. But find out.

Then the team can act. It should meet and see that everyone knows and understands what Mr. Bernstein wants. The team as a whole should develop the strategy to give it to him. Explain to Mr. Bernstein just what the team is doing and its timetable for doing it. As the team completes each step of the plan, it should make sure that Mr. Bernstein understands what it has accomplished. And the team should continuously check to see that it's understood correctly and that it's genuinely moving in the direction Mr. Bernstein wants. If not, it revises its plan and goes back to work.

If Mr. Bernstein has never liked teams:

The best defense, as always, is a good offense. For a team, the best offense is consistently effective performance. It can't do anything in this circumstance unless it produces that.

If you do perform well, can you change Mr. Bernstein's mind? It's worth a try. See if he will admit having made the statement, then ask him for the reasons why. Then, if he truly seems determined to break up the team, go around him to his next-level manager. Make your best case. And try to get the team reassigned to another manager. If it fails, Mr. Bernstein will certainly do his best to break up the team, but that's about where you started, so you haven't lost very much.

Team Strengthener

Work, like life, is a matter of timing. Sometimes you can prevent a manager from taking an action detrimental to the team by using some of the suggestions above (and throughout this chapter). But sometimes you can't, for whatever reason. If you see that there's no chance, it's time to change focus. Instead of fighting the decision, begin planning how to make the best of it. In this case, start examining the possibilities for reassignment to other teams. Then if Mr. Bernstein goes through with his plan, the team can at least suggest how it believes its members can best be used. It can also smooth the transition of the members into other teams. Sometimes it's worth fighting what appears to be a losing battle, if the stakes are high enough. It's virtually never worth wasting time fighting a lost battle.

The Problem

The team is expected to act as a traditional workgroup

The Scene

"Is it really that bad?" Marty asks.

"Yes, it really is," you reply, sinking into a chair. "They expect me to be the full-time team leader, and from what I can understand I'm just a traditional supervisor with a different title."

Mary slams down the magazine she's reading. "You mean all this team building and stuff we went through was just a farce?"

You nod. "Oh, they used all the buzzwords—I think they used 'teamwork' in every other sentence. But it was all window dressing. What they want is for us to do what we've always done, but work closer together and be more committed to our jobs."

Nobody says anything. What is there to say? And all this had to happen just when the team was beginning to jell. What now?

Possible Causes

No need to speculate a lot on the cause. In all probability the organization jumped on board the team bandwagon without thinking through the consequences. As soon as teams began exercising autonomy, managers felt that they were losing control. So they decided to "rein in" the teams.

Cures

Become a self-managing team—just don't tell anyone.

Does this sound foolish? In two circumstances, it isn't. First, how close is your next-level manager geographically and how much does he or she interfere in your team's activities? He may care primarily that your workgroup not cause problems and prevent unpleasant surprises. Other than that, you may be largely free to manage the way you want. So help your workgroup become a self-managing team, but create all the paper required to make it look like a traditional workgroup.

The second alternative is even better. Does your next-level manager support self-managing teams, or is he or she at least willing to let you experiment with one? Bingo—now you have a buffer between the team and the organization. Go to it; help the team be as self-managing as it is capable of being. But make sure the team looks out for your manager's interests and concerns at every point. You want to make him or her look really good, so that if someone discovers that the manager permitted you to be self-managing he or she can say "Yes—and look how well it's worked."

Become as self-managing as possible and keep working the problem.

This situation is harder to manage, but there are some steps you can take:

- Most organizations pay at least lip service to delegation, and their management training encourages it. Is it written anywhere that you can't delegate to small groups rather than to individuals? With a little work, you can get many of the workgroup's tasks done by a series of relatively self-managing subteams.

- The organization expects you to select new workers. But if you let other workgroup members talk with them and then give you their comments, you could get close to the kind of group selection that most self-managing teams practice.

- You're expected to plan your group's work and then to review how well it's being done. Is there a reason why you can't link planning with the review, so that the group gradually gets more involved in the planning?

The point isn't any of these specifics—it's to look for every opportunity to spread leadership around in the group. Be careful, though, and never use "team" language. We're all too accustomed to reacting to the way people describe what they do rather than what they do itself. If you and your workgroup are careful to use "orthodox" workgroup language, you will have a surprising amount of freedom. Use team language, though, and the freedom will begin to vanish.

If you can use either this alternative or the one in the first section, try to create a network of other workgroups that are attempting to be as self-managing as possible. You will all need the support. And remember that the organization may change its mind (and perhaps its top management). If it decides to use real self-managing teams, having at least a few teams who are used to working together will facilitate its decision.

Give up.

Needless to say, this is a lousy alternative. If you really want to try working with a self-managing team and you can't in your current organization—well, you catch my drift.

Team Strengthener

If you and your team run into the kind of situation this case depicts, you will almost certainly be angry and disappointed. You may even feel betrayed. That's normal, but get the emotion out of your systems. Then think carefully about your alternatives, draw up a plan of action, and go. The first two cures in this case involve deception to some degree. That's regrettable, but if you and the team genuinely concentrate on performing effectively then the deception is just the cost of reconciling what the organization wants with what the team wants.

CHAPTER 11

Problems With Computers and Support Systems

This chapter contains cases that describe problems a team can have with the technology that is supposed to support it (primarily computers) and with organizational support systems.

Most organizations' computer systems were designed to operate effectively with traditional organizational structures, processing routine financial transactions (such as payrolls) and generating regular reports for higher management. They don't fit the way a team has to work. This chapter recommends ways that a team can deal with and even overcome some of the most troublesome aspects of inefficient computer support.

Be warned, though. As you may already know, it's time-consuming and expensive for an organization to modernize its existing computer systems. You may be able to persuade your organization to make some changes, particularly if the changes are relatively quick and easy and you can show how they will increase productivity. (Don't take "quick" too literally, though—it usually means a much longer period of time to the people making the changes than it does to you and your team.) Too much of the time, you will simply have to find ways to work effectively despite the problems the computer system causes you.

But computers don't pose the only problem. Teams require support systems: They need to get supplies, get training, fill jobs quickly. All too often, the organizational systems to accomplish these goals don't fit teams well either. Several cases deal with the problems this can cause.

The Problem

*The computer system ties the team into rigid,
inefficient work methods*

The Scene

"Okay, who's going to stay late and put the data in?" Arlynn asks.

"Hey, don't look at me. I did it the last three times," Benito responds clearly and firmly.

"I'll do it," Sarah volunteers after a short pause, "but I won't do it happily. Why in the world do we have to work with a system we can only get onto a half hour before normal human beings get to go home?"

"I sure don't know," Hallie joins in. "We can get data in only by staying after hours, the reports we get are almost too late to do us any good, when we get them we have to dig through a hundred pages just to get about a half-page of data we can use, and on top of all that we can't implement the process improvement we came up with because it's not compatible with the record structure. It's awfully frustrating."

It is, and you know it. You and the team sometimes wonder whether the computer system is there to help the team or just to provide it with one more challenge. Is there anything you can do about the problem?

Possible Causes

In this case, no one has to look far to find the cause: an outdated computer system that wasn't created to support a team-based organization. Unfortunately, it costs both money and time to fix "legacy" systems such as these. And many times fixing them isn't a priority for the organization. The situation is difficult; it may not be hopeless.

Cures

If the organization might consider changing the system:

Obviously you explore this alternative quickly. Try to find out from the Management Information Systems Department if there are any plans to change or update the system. If it happens that there are and the anticipated completion date isn't several years off, the team's best strategy is to encourage the change however it can and see if it can use either of the next two cures in the meantime.

What if there are no plans to change the system? Does it present a problem for teams other than yours? For other parts of the organization? If the problem is big enough and if enough affected individuals are willing to try to change it, it won't hurt to try. Get as much support as possible, then calculate the wasted time caused by the system. Also consider factors like the process improvements that can't be made because of the system's rigidity. If higher management sees that the system is raising costs significantly, the organization may decide to spend the time and effort required to change the system.

Remember, while higher management may regret that your team and others are inconvenienced by the system, they won't make changing it a priority just for that reason. If you and the team want to get it changed, you need to make the business case that it's causing lost production and/or wasting assets in some other way.

If the team can stop using the system:

If the team gets little benefit from the system, can it opt out of using it? Exactly what is the system designed to do? Who really benefits from the information in it? What would happen if it ceased to exist?

It may be that the data you provide aren't necessary, so the team stops its input. If this seems to be the case, get with other teams and see if they would be willing to take the same step. If they are, it's time to take the situation to higher management. Even if management isn't willing to try to change the system, it might be willing to let some parts of it go unused if they cause more trouble than they're worth.

If the team must live with the problem:

Does the team have personal computers or access to them? Can someone on the team, or someone from outside, write a short program to make the data input to the system automatically? Then the data could be put into the personal computer, which could transmit it to the computer system whether team members were present or not. There might even be a payoff for the organization in this. A personal computer can transmit data dozens of times faster than an individual can enter it, so that the time used to send the data could be cut sharply.

If this won't work, would it help the situation to get several teams together and have one person input the data for all the teams? It would mean someone would have to stay even later, but far less often. That might make it much less disruptive to individual team members.

If it looks as if none of the solutions will work, your only choice is to spend as little time and attention as possible fighting the problem. Make the data input as efficient as possible. Don't bother to get the data from the system unless the information the team gets clearly outweighs the time it takes to get it. Look for process improvements that don't conflict with the way the system works.

Team Strengthener

If you and your team have to work with this kind of outmoded, rigid computer system, make it a point to understand how the system works in as much detail as possible. Where does it get all of its data? Who uses its outputs? Are there parts of the report that would be useful to the team if you knew what to look for? What are its update cycles? Perhaps most important, what would happen if the team was late getting its data in or didn't get it in at all? The more you and the team know, the greater the chance that you can find ways to work around the system and keep it from causing quite so much of a problem. Of course, having to use "workarounds" is a problem in itself, as the next case shows.

The Problem

The team constantly has to use "workarounds"
to accomplish its work effectively

The Scene

"Hey, Clarence, did you get the order through for the new color printer?"

"Yes, no thanks to the procurement people!"

"What do you mean?"

"You know it cost a little over $12,000. Well, I took the order down and asked them to expedite it. Charlie Gomez took one look at it and gave it back to me. Told me that they can't handle anything over $10,000 unless the MIS Department signs off on it. So I went there. No matter how I pleaded, they said it would be the end of next week before they got it to me. I wasn't going to leave the order with them, 'till I suddenly remembered that the Red Knights have a printer just like it. I went to talk to them—anyhow, to make a long story short, they agreed to give us theirs if they get the new one *and* we buy them a dozen reams of coated paper. Then they got all softhearted and agreed to deliver it here this afternoon and set it up for us."

How many times have you heard stories like this? It seems that every time the team needs to get something in a hurry it has to fight its way through a bureaucratic maze. There must be some other way!

Possible Causes

The organization doesn't have the support systems that teams need.

When organizations commit themselves to widespread use of teams, they may not realize just how far-reaching the commitment is. Systems (accounting, supply and capital equipment, for instance) that worked adequately in the traditional structure may be major problems for a team-based organization. The

389

organization may not realize this or may decide that it's not a high priority to develop new systems. When new systems aren't created, teams must develop a series of wasteful workarounds.

The organization is still trying to maintain control in traditional ways.

It can be scary to traditional managers when an organization becomes team-based. Their roles change, teams and individuals have much more autonomy; it feels as if management is losing control. This may be particularly true of the remaining departments (usually support departments) who feel that their authority and influence are being bled away. Their all-too-human reaction may be to maintain the controls they have, perhaps even to implement new ones.

The organization doesn't understand what teams need.

This may be the deeper cause of either or both causes above, or may be the cause of the problem all by itself. Unless the organization begins to focus on teams and what they need, it continues to handicap them. And, once again, it forces them to develop a wide range of wasteful workarounds to get their jobs done.

Hint

As in many other cases, none of the causes are exclusive. All three of them may be part of the problem.

Cures

If the organization doesn't have the support systems that teams need:

What do you and the team do? You enlist the help of other teams to develop a picture of how the traditional systems are standing in the way of effective team performance. Then you turn the picture into a presentation for higher-level management. Remember, as this book has often stressed, to concentrate on the problems that the inadequate systems cause the organization, not the inconvenience that they cause the team. If you have to, your team can go it alone, but it will be much less effective.

Then make the presentation. Remember, we're assuming here that teams don't have the proper support systems because the organization hasn't yet realized the problem or how serious the problem is. You're attempting to wake up higher management, to get them to acknowledge the problem and begin solving it. Treat them as potential allies and demonstrate that you are allies of theirs. And use the suggestions in the next section as well.

If the organization is still trying to maintain control in traditional ways:

If this appears to be the case, you and the team need to pursue several strategies at the same time. One of them is the strategy in the section above: Get the facts together and demonstrate to higher management how the controls are handicapping the teams. But that by itself isn't enough.

The team needs to demonstrate, and to have been demonstrating since it was formed, that it uses resources wisely. Take the color printer in this case as an example. Does the team really need it? Did it consider other alternatives, such as using the Red Knight's printer? Using a commercial color service—much more expensive than a printer for a few copies, but much less expensive than buying a printer for a few copies? Buying a lower-priced color printer? Controls will never be relaxed unless your team and the others demonstrate that they can use resources wisely.

If the organization doesn't understand what teams need:

Look at the two sections above this one; the suggestions in them are applicable here. What makes this cause different, though, is that it requires primarily an *educational* solution. The organization needs to learn what its teams need before it can meet these needs. So presentations to higher management, while they need to be persuasive, also need to provide proper education.

How do you help higher management become educated? Here's one way. Are you and your team familiar with process mapping or some other technique for showing what happens in a process? If you are, do a process map of one of the support systems (such as supply or data processing) that interferes with the team's performance. Whenever you can, put time on it, especially if the system delays the team's performance of critical activities. Then map out the process as it ought to be. Make these two charts the cornerstone of your presentation, remembering that you will get someone to acknowledge a problem more quickly if you also suggest a solution to the problem.

Team Strengthener

When organizations establish controls such as having the MIS Department approve computer-related purchases over a certain amount, why do they do it? No matter how wrongheaded you may believe the control is, it has one basic purpose: to ensure that the organization makes wise use of its resources. How do you persuade higher management to relax these controls? By demonstrating that the team will consistently make wise use of its resources. This includes making wise use of time, of money, of supplies and equipment, of any asset it uses. When the team demonstrates to higher management that it can use resources carefully, it makes it much easier for higher management to relax controls. One final strategy: It may help to negotiate gradual relaxation of controls with management, rather than having all the controls lifted at once. This makes it easier for the team to demonstrate its responsibility and for the manager to begin lifting the controls without becoming uncomfortable.

11–3

The Problem

The computer system constantly makes mistakes that the team can't control

The Scene

Evie sees you stomping back into the work area. "What happened?" she asks.

"I was in Mr. McCorkle's office again, trying to explain to him that the 8 percent error rate on our records wasn't our fault. If we can't find a fix or show him exactly what's happening pretty soon, he's going to run out of patience. If this damned thing were just a piece of machinery," you add angrily, slapping the computer terminal, "I'd give it a good kick. At least I'd feel better!"

Evie has the good sense not to try to say anything more. Besides, she and the rest of the team are just as upset over the computer problem as you are. There's just got to be some way to deal with this situation.

Possible Causes

The team doesn't understand the computer system well enough.

Because computer systems are often "just part of the furniture," the workers who use them often don't take time to understand how they function.

As a result, they can't recognize when a problem can be fixed or at least ameliorated.

There's some sort of workaround the team can use.

We'd all prefer to avoid workarounds, gimmicks that get around the formal requirements of the system in ways the system's designers hadn't counted on. (For instance, a team might use the field for an obsolete data item to store workload information the system won't accommodate.) But sometimes workarounds are the only way to make the system useful.

Your next-level manager doesn't understand the computer system well enough.

Workers often don't understand enough about the computer systems they use, and managers often understand even less. Consequently, managers often don't realize how the system impacts a team's ability to get its work done, so it's easy for them to blame a team for problems caused by a computer system.

Cures

If the team doesn't understand the computer system well enough:

You ought always to consider this alternative first. Has the team been routinely using the system for months or years, without trying to find out exactly how it works? Does the team assume that what it knows is what there is and that nothing can be changed? If so, the time has come to quit sitting passively and find out in detail how the system works.

How do you do this? Whoever "owns" the system—probably the management information system people—can give you some details. Beware, though; they may not know some of the workarounds you could use, and they may not want to tell you about the ones they know about. Unless they're unusually responsive to customers, their primary concern is to keep the systems operating "properly." But learn all you can from them.

Then talk with other teams and individuals who use the system. You might even want to convene a meeting with individuals from several teams and pool everyone's knowledge. Is there an alternative way of operating the system that doesn't generate as many mistakes? Are there more efficient ways to use the system that avoid the mistakes? Try to develop an understanding of the system as a whole, using what everyone has learned from using it.

If you find more efficient methods, use them. Then be sure that your next-level manager learns about the improvement the team has made—from the team.

If there's some sort of workaround the team can use:

Suppose that after studying and learning the system the team can't find a better way to use it. Now what? It looks for workarounds. Workarounds take advantage of gaps in the system that permit its users to perform actions that the system doesn't formally allow. It's unfortunate when the team has to use workarounds, but reality is reality and you have a job to do.

Here the experience of other teams is particularly valuable. No one team may know enough to work around the problem, but if several teams pool their experience they may come up with an approach that works.

Your team may have to test a number of different approaches. Most of them probably won't work, and some of them may even make the mistakes worse. But be willing to experiment, taking as few risks as possible. If you can reduce or eliminate the mistakes the system makes, you can spend your time in the future on more important matters. You can also keep your next-level manager off your back on the issue.

If your next-level manager doesn't understand the computer system well enough:

The other two solutions are better than this one, but educating and converting your next-level manager may be the only one available to the team.

First, get the data. You may want to do a process map of what you go through to enter and then correct the data. If so, show in as much detail as possible the conditions under which the system makes the mistakes and what the team has to go through to correct them. If the process is complicated, simplify the map of it as much as possible without distorting the basic problem. If other teams are involved in the problem, try to involve them in mapping the process and designing the presentation.

Now it's time for the team to make the presentation to higher-level management. If other teams have the problem and have cooperated in developing the presentation, involve them in the presentation and give it to as many managers as possible. If you have to, though, do the presentation with your team alone and give it to your higher-level manager. You have two basic goals in the presentation, no matter whom it's given to. First, you want your next-level manager to understand your problem and stop blaming the team for something it can't control. Second, you want to enlist the help of as many managers as possible to get the system changed.

Team Strengthener

If your team has to put up with an old mainframe system that wasn't designed for today's fast-paced, team-based environment, don't put too much energy into getting the system changed. It's both expensive and time consuming to change large existing systems. Many organizations are moving their systems from large mainframes to more flexible "client-server" systems. This can materially help, but it's a matter of years to do it. Encourage any changes that will make the system more responsive to your team and to teams in general. But don't make that a major goal, because you'll probably be disappointed. Instead, as these first three cases have suggested, try to use the system as efficiently as possible when you can and work around it when you can't. Sure it's an irritation, but you and the team have more important problems to worry about.

11–4

The Problem

*The team has to reenter data it gets from
other teams*

The Scene

As you walk by, you notice Jill sitting at the computer terminal, frowning and digging through a pile of papers beside her. She finds what she's looking for, props the paper up beside the terminal, and enters a few numbers. You walk over and watch her for a minute as she repeats the same process over and over.

After entering a set of numbers, she turns her head slightly to look at you. "Well, how much longer are we going to have to do this? I've been digging out data from the reports from the three sales teams and plugging it in for an hour and a half so far. There's gotta be a better way!" Without even waiting for an answer, which she knows you don't have, she turns back around and picks up another set of reports.

How much longer is it going to last? Everyone on the team hates to do the data entry, particularly when most of the data they get came out of a computer in the first place. Jill's right; there must be a better way.

Possible Causes

Once again, the organization hasn't anticipated team needs.

In traditional organizations, moving data from one unit to another is often at least as frustrating as it is for your team. But traditional organizations are more accustomed to these kinds of frustrations, and organizations don't expect the consistently high level of performance from them that they expect from teams. Team-based organizations have to be more flexible, to enable teams to adapt to changing circumstances quickly. Apparently, your team is in an organization that hasn't yet realized this.

The teams have never thought about how they might resolve the situation.

The problem may not have been created by the computer system. The teams might actually be able to communicate data to one another by network or even by "sneakernet" (carrying or mailing a data disk from one team to another.) But no one has devoted time and attention to the problem.

The teams have never attempted to respond to one another's needs.

One of the real dangers of problem situations is this: When individuals or teams can't solve them in one try, it's easy just to accept them and stop trying. Perhaps the basic system can't be changed, or at least can't be changed in the near future. The core problem, though, is that the teams concerned haven't tried working together to find how they can better meet one another's needs within the system.

Cures

If the organization hasn't anticipated team needs:

Your team probably isn't the only one with this problem, so begin by enlisting the help of other teams. Don't exclude any team that has the problem. Form a team of teams to describe the problem carefully. You might be able to map the process, but that may turn out to be very complicated, and you want to keep the description of the situation as simple as possible. Use whatever method the individuals concerned are most comfortable with and most proficient at.

Once you have the data, create a presentation for higher management. (See the Team Strengthener in this case for a suggestion on the presentation.) If the project represents a number of teams, get all the higher-level managers to the presentation that you can. In particular, if the teams involve different functions, get managers from all the functions if possible. Then make the presentation. Focus on the extra time it takes to reenter the data and what this time costs; that's primary, particularly if the time creates delays in the cycle time for the teams' outputs. But don't omit the frustration that the data entry causes and the distraction it represents from the team's primary mission. You may not be sufficiently convincing the first time. Don't stop. For instance, you and/or the team of teams might submit a regular report to higher management—on your own initiative—of the number of hours wasted in that month. It will eventually get their attention.

If the teams have never thought about how they might resolve the situation:

Is this really the case? Start finding out. Talk with other teams. Where do they get their data, and how do they prepare the data they output? How do they know what the teams that use their data want? Can (1) the format be changed to concentrate on what the receiving team needs and (2) can it be transmitted as a file over the network or at least on a disk?

You'll hope that the teams working together can find a solution to their joint problem. If they can't go that far, they may be able at least to make some of the problem easier. Don't assume that once you and the other teams have looked at the situation that's the end. The teams may need to put together a special team to look into the matter more deeply; there may be solutions not visible at first glance. If the problem is as widespread and as frustrating as it appears, it's worth spending time trying to solve it.

If the teams have never attempted to respond to one another's needs:

Each team should know from the beginning who its internal customers are and what they need. And it should update this information constantly. If this hasn't happened, start now. You should know the needs of every team or other part of the organization to which you provide output. And you should know the input you get from every other team or part. Meet with your customers to determine exactly what they need from you. Then meet with your suppliers to make sure they understand just what you need from them. Use this information to work together better and more closely.

How can you do that if you can't change the situation? Consider these simple solutions. Can the team giving you the information rearrange the report so it's easier for you to find the material you need? If not, could they mark the information for you since they're familiar with it? Can they get you the report a day or two sooner, so it at least doesn't delay your own outputs? You can think of another dozen ways that small changes such as these will make life easier for your team. Then get together with your customers and identify the small changes your team can make that will make life easier for these customers. And keep working the problem on a regular basis.

Team Strengthener

When your team makes written or oral presentations to other teams and to management, does it routinely use an "executive summary"? We're often tempted to arrange a report or presentation to "tell a story"—history or background followed by the current situation followed by proposed solutions. Most readers and listeners don't want to be told this kind of story. They want to know what happening that's worth their attention (the problem) and what you want them to do (the solution). These should be summarized on the front page of the report or at the beginning of the presentation. Then everything in the report should tie into either the problem or the solution; at every moment, the audience should know exactly why the information it's getting is important. Do this carefully and thoughtfully, and you'll find that the effectiveness of your presentations and reports will increase markedly.

11–5

The Problem
The team can't get the data it needs from the computer system

The Scene

"Kim, do you know where Oscar went?" you ask.

Kim doesn't even look up. "Yeah—he's over at Manufacturing. He's trying to get the figures on the anticipated production for the next ninety days so we can see if we need any special marketing efforts."

"Why in the world is he over there? Can't he just get the data from the reports we get?"

"Nice thought," Kim answers. "What we need is buried in a summary section with four other products. That report's useless for us!"

One more report that doesn't help. What can you do to get the data to your people without their having to wander all over the organization?

Possible Causes

The team doesn't understand the reports it uses.

In this case, it's not critical whether the team doesn't understand the computer system well enough to use it effectively. The basic problem is the report rather than the system itself. Perhaps the report is new, the format has changed, or the team isn't familiar with this particular form of the report. Whatever the cause, the team doesn't understand the report well enough to use the data from it effectively.

Reports haven't been changed to fit the team organization.

Organizations cause problems when they don't change computer systems to support teams. Whether the systems change or not, organizations can still cause serious problems by not reviewing the way it gets and outputs data. Reports are still designed for the traditional organization that team-based organization has replaced.

The team or unit that prepares the report doesn't know what your team needs.

Have the teams and units that furnish you data ever asked you to tell them in detail the data you need and how you would like them presented? Has your team ever made it clear to them exactly what you need and how you use it? If not, this lack of communication may be a fundamental cause of the problem.

Cures

If the team doesn't understand the reports it gets:

This cause is easy to investigate. Meet with the team or unit that prepares the report and go over it with them. Find out if the data you need are in the report, but in a form you don't expect or can't find easily. If so, you've at least partly licked the problem.

If finding and/or interpreting the data is particularly complex, you might ask someone from that unit or team to come explain the report to your team. That way, your team gets an explanation straight from the horse's mouth. The team also gets a chance to discuss with the individual what it needs from the report (see the following two cures).

If reports haven't been changed to fit the team organization:

Changing the data and formats of reports is easier than changing the system itself, but don't get too optimistic before you look into the situation. It takes time and effort for someone to make the changes.

First, the team must make sure it understands exactly the data it needs, when it needs them, and how it needs them to be presented. The more specific and detailed the team can get, the more useful it will be and the greater the odds that it can actually get the report changed. As always, if other teams have the same problem involve them in the analysis. Be sure the analysis shows not just what you need but why you need it and the impact of not having it.

Present the information to your next-level manager (or the next-level managers of all the teams involved). Ensure that they understand why there's a problem and what needs to be done to fix it. If possible, you might brief an even higher level of management and ask for its support. Now it's time for the teams involved and their managers to meet with the Management Information Systems department, to go over the changes you need with them.

That may do it. Or it may not. If it doesn't, do whatever's needed to keep your higher-level manager and the MIS department aware that the problem is continuing. Don't give up and don't let them sweep your problem under some carpet.

If the team or unit that prepares the report doesn't know what your team needs:

In an effective organization, providers meet regularly with their customers to ensure they know their needs and are meeting them. Apparently this hasn't been happening in your organization, at least not where your team is concerned. Perhaps all reports are developed by the management information systems (MIS) department. Unfortunately, these departments many times don't check regularly with their customers to see how their products are used.

So you take the initiative. Your team needs to visit all of its providers to ensure that they understand what it needs. The team needs particularly to identify situations where it's not getting what it needs and then work with each provider to improve the situation. It's hope that at least some of the reports are being furnished by other teams, who will be more motivated to work with you to meet your needs.

Cases 5–9 and 5–10 deal with situations where teams don't get or use feedback from their customers. Review these cases. They may help you understand why some of your suppliers operate as they do. Then you need to work with the suppliers and help them become familiar with and more responsive to your needs. Then visit your customers. Find out if your team is giving them what they want. If it isn't, work with them to see that it does.

Team Strengthener

Cases earlier in this chapter and others throughout the book have emphasized working closely with other teams to solve problems. In traditional organizations, individual units often had to solve problems by going through higher levels or otherwise following authorized procedures. *That will not work in a team-based organization,* particularly if the teams are expected to be self-managing. To succeed, your team must work closely with other teams to solve mutual problems. Don't wait for someone else to solve them. In fact, unless something specific prevents it, teams ought to be meeting together on a regular basis to discuss and resolve their mutual problems. And teams should be meeting regularly with other teams that are their suppliers or customers to make their needs clear and to ensure that they are meeting their customers' needs. The more effectively teams do this, the greater the authority that higher management will give them to manage themselves.

11–6

The Problem
The team doesn't get the information it needs

The Scene

You storm into the team's work area, more than a little upset. "Why didn't anyone tell me about the change in the sales plan?"

"What change in what sales plan?" Arnie asks in his usual laid-back way.

"The Home Gem plan, that's what. And the fact that management moved the introduction date up two weeks."

"Hold it right there," Carmina says firmly. (One of Carmina's goals in life is to make sure you never get away with anything.) "Did any of you know about the change?"

Five heads shake. Carmina turns back to you: "That's why no one told you—we don't know a damned thing about the change. Now, would you please be so kind as to inform us." As she says the last words, her face relaxes into the famous grin that makes it impossible to get angry with her.

You have "informed" them. An hour later, you find out that the decision on the change had been made two weeks before. That's two weeks of time the team lost that it needed for planning and design. This has got to stop!

Possible Causes

Some other team or unit didn't coordinate with your team.

Is this a pattern? Is it just the one team, or do many of the teams seem to forget to coordinate with you? No matter which is the right answer, you have a problem. Someone thinks you don't need to know, or doesn't want you to know, or doesn't care whether they tell you or not.

The organization hasn't changed its coordination policies to fit teams.

When an organization makes the decision to base itself on teams, it ultimately must change virtually every one of its systems. It may take a long time for it to realize that who coordinates what with whom has to change, and perhaps change significantly.

Coordination is poor where teams are concerned.

Teams must show much more initiative than units in traditional organizations do. They can't just wait for someone higher up to solve problems, even when the team surfaces the problem and suggests solutions. Teams have to act to solve all the problems they can on their level. And this includes understanding how and when they need to coordinate with one another.

Hint

Note that all three causes might be true. None of them excludes the others.

Cures

If some other team or unit didn't coordinate with your team:

Whether it's one team or several, your team needs to act. Arrange meetings with the team (or with all the teams, if there is more than one). Ask why you're not getting the information you need. It's possible that the team doesn't know you need the information. It's also possible that it believes your team isn't giving it necessary information. Or it may result from a poor relationship in general between the teams.

When you find out why the coordination didn't occur, fix the problem. Make clear to the team(s) involved what information you need and why you need it. If your team is also guilty of not providing needed information, make certain you change that situation quickly. If the other team believes that your team hasn't been cooperating, identify what you need to do to change that and then change it.

If the organization hasn't changed its coordination policies to fit teams:

Are you the only team that doesn't get the information it needs? If you are, then you need to deal with the situation with your next-level manager. Explain clearly to him or her the problems that the team has been having. As always, suggest one or more alternatives to solve the problems. If your team has worked with other teams to resolve all the coordination problems it could, make sure your manager knows that too. If it's appropriate, volunteer that the team will contact the unit responsible for formal coordination policies and suggest the changes needed.

What if a number of teams aren't getting information? Follow the same procedure that several earlier cases in this chapter have suggested: Get the teams together, get the facts, then arrange a presentation for higher management (using the suggestions in Cases 11–1 through 11–4). Make sure that you show the impact of the lack of coordination on team productivity. If the presentation doesn't succeed, keep after the issue until the policies change.

If coordination is poor where teams are concerned:

This means, first of all, that your team must have good relationships with other teams. The teams, or representatives from them, need to meet and share information. They need to build up trust among themselves. They need to understand one another's needs and orient themselves to meeting these needs. And they must be constantly proactive, jointly looking for, identifying, and then solving problems.

Depending on the organization and its history, building relationships may be difficult. If that's the case, don't try to build relationships with everyone at once. Select one or two teams because you feel an affinity with them or because you're dependent on them. Work to develop a close relationship with them. Then work outward from that core, including more and more teams. This will take time, but the results will be worth it.

Team Strengthener

Actually, this tip repeats what's been said both in previous cases and in this one: Team-based organizations can't function effectively unless teams constantly take the initiative to identify and solve problems and develop strong relationships with one another. Individual teams can't function effectively either unless they do both. Whatever the rest of the team's goals, the twin goals of initiative and strong relationships need to be included.

The Problem

The team has to keep its own production records because the formal system isn't accurate

The Scene

"Hey, got a minute?"

You turn around to see Vic, computer printout in hand. "Hey—do you have the new program working?"

"Not completely, but well enough to give us what we need. I've gone through three months by hand and compared it with what the program produces. I think I know where every discrepancy is, and I've taken account of it. I can justify every point where our figures are different from the report. We finally have accurate data."

"Good," you reply half-heartedly.

One of the team's best members has just spent the better part of two weeks working out a spreadsheet to track the team's productivity. Why? Because the organization's production reporting system consistently underreports what your team does. You doubt that you can do anything about the organization's system, but now it doesn't matter as much.

Possible Causes

The organization's system wasn't changed to work with teams.

So many of the problems throughout the book have this same cause: The organization didn't think through the changes it needed to make to support teams before it committed itself to teams. Now it has a production-tracking system that won't work with its team structure.

The organization's work has changed but the system hasn't.

This has nothing to do with teams. Today's competitive environment changes very rapidly. Products and services become obsolete, or they change constantly. Internal processes change just as rapidly; the way we do things today isn't necessarily the way we'll do them next month. If the production system was built for a more stable operation, it may still be stuck in the way things were done then. It's always useful to remember that computer systems change more slowly than operations do, unless the systems are being created and run by the same people who are responsible for operations.

The organization's system has never been accurate.

In many ways, this is the worst problem of all. The system may have been designed by a staff office that didn't really understand operations. It may have concentrated on quantity, while the organization has been stressing quality for the last several years. It may have taken so long to design and field that it was obsolete by the time it was working. Still, it's what the organization has, so it's what the organization uses.

Cures

If the organization's system wasn't changed to work with teams:

You need to bring this to higher management's attention. Your team probably isn't the only one with the problem. Get with other teams and compare notes. (You might also offer to let them use your production-tracking system.) Use the suggestions in Cases 11–1 through 11–4 to develop a joint presentation on the problem. Then make the presentation to higher management.

Why bother, when you now have a production-tracking system of your own that gives you what you need? Because higher management may still be getting reports from the old system that distort what the team's production really is. Other teams may not have been able to develop their own systems, or may not even have recognized the problem, so that they're still living with the old system. Higher management needs to know that the data it's getting aren't accurate. For its own sake, it needs to see that the old system is modified or replaced, so that it provides the information it needs. And it needs to keep in mind that your team may run into similar problems in the future.

If the organization's work has changed but the system hasn't:

This time you really need to let higher management know what's happening, and let them know quickly. It costs money to operate the old system, but the system isn't producing any useful information. It may be producing something much worse— misleading information. Managers need to understand this, and you have a stake in their understanding it. If the old system is erroneous enough, it may lead them to believe that teams aren't productive, and you don't really want your team abolished.

Once again, you need to arrange a presentation to higher management. Use the suggestions in Cases 11–1 through 11–4. Include the most specific data you can in the presentation; if higher management realizes how misleading the old system is, they'll take it from there and change things.

If the organization's system has never been accurate:

Do you bring this up to higher management? You probably should, though it's not worth doing unless you can make clear the problems the system causes. Perhaps no one believes in the system; everyone keeps his or her records on the backs of envelopes or on his or her personal computer. In this case, management may not want to bother with changing it. That may sound like a poor solution, but often it's not. Some problems are more expensive to fix than to live with.

How strongly do you feel about pointing out that the system doesn't work? On the one hand, your new system works for you, so you don't care about the old system. On the other, the organization is wasting time and money keeping the old system going. You and the team need to discuss the situation and perhaps discuss it with other teams. Then you decide what's best and pursue it.

Team Strengthener

Personal computers are one of the great inventions of the last quarter of the twentieth century. Too often, they're used to duplicate what large computer systems should be doing because these large systems aren't responsive or are out of date or don't work very well. Your team needs to ensure that it has the personal computers it needs and that it uses them to meet its information needs. If it can network its computers with those of other teams, so much the better. E-mail isn't just another version of written mail. It's something different and much more effective. And sending files over a network is much faster and more effective than sending written documents or carrying computer disks around. More and more, team success depends on the right kind of computer support. And, unfortunately, centralized computer systems are seldom effective at providing this support. So make sure you have personal computers or some other close-in computer support you can depend on.

11–8

The Problem
The team can't get the supplies it needs

The Scene

"Connie, have the binders come in?" you hear Felicia call.

"Not a chance. I called Supply again today. Frank wasn't there, so it took them ten minutes to find our order. Frank's going to try to place it tomorrow morning, they say, if he isn't still sick."

"Why don't you just go ahead and order the binders yourself? At least that way we'd be sure of getting them."

"Boy—I'd like to. But Supply won't let us because they say that we'll pay too much if we buy them ourselves."

"Yeah, but at least we'll have them before next year's Christmas party! If they don't get here in the next two days we're going to have to use the old, ugly binders we've got. You can figure how happy that'll make the team."

And so can you. Ever since it began, the team has had problems getting even fairly routine supplies and even worse problems trying to get equipment. The team could be so much more productive without this constant hassle.

Possible Causes

The organization is still using old support systems.

Support systems designed for traditional organizations don't support teams well. Teams exist to provide quicker response than traditional workgroups can. They can't accomplish this when they're handicapped by unresponsive support systems.

The Supply Branch isn't customer focused.

Whether or not the support systems have changed, the Supply branch may see itself first as a control organization, whose basic function in life is to ensure that everyone abides by company policy. Then, when the branch is sure that has happened, it takes care of the needs of its customers. We associate this kind of rule-based behavior with government organizations, but there's plenty of it in large organizations of any kind.

Teams aren't doing all they could to change the situation.

Teams can't succeed without showing significantly more initiative than traditional workgroups do. This initiative is an intrinsic part of self-management.

Hint

Note that none of these causes excludes the others. All three could be causing the problem. If the first cause exists, though, it's by far the most important one.

Cures

If the organization is still using old support systems:

Your ultimate goal is to get rid of these kinds of systems. Obviously, your team can't do that by itself. Get the affected teams together and start planning a killer presentation to higher management about the situation. Cases 11–1 through 11–4 contain basic suggestions on how to do this.

Take your time, as much as the current problem may hurt (and pursue the courses suggested in the next two sections in the meantime). You want to build the strongest possible case, because the organization probably still thinks in terms of the control/support systems its had for so long. It will not change them or give them up lightly. Consequently, when you finish your presentation you want higher-level managers to know down to their toenails that these systems are a problem they must address and begin solving immediately. Just convincing them it's a minor annoyance will get the teams nowhere.

If the Supply branch isn't customer focused:

The traditional cure is to complain to higher management. Forget it! That just reinforces the old, control-oriented system, and it will certainly get you on Supply's list of troublemakers. Instead, go to Supply and offer to work with them. If they don't seem interested, insist. You have a carrot—if they'll work with you, you *won't* complain about them to management. Unless you really have to press, though, keep the tone positive. You want them to be a better provider, and you want them to help you become a better customer.

Take the point about being a better customer seriously. Operations that aren't customer-focused often don't spend time and energy helping their customer become more effective as customers. (For instance, an effective customer knows when a supplier can make an exception and when it can't and plans accordingly.) The more your team knows about the policies Supply (or other support activity) works under, the better the system will work for you. You still want to be clear with Supply about what you need from it; just combine this with a genuine concern for what it needs from you.

If teams aren't doing all they could to change the situation:

To reach their potential, teams need to work closely together. Of course, most serious problems can't be solved by teams alone. Teams can generate the momentum, however, to bring problems to higher management's attention (as in the first section of this case). And when they work together, teams can go a long way toward trimming any problem to manageable size.

When it's difficult for any organizational unit to get supplies, the unit usually overorders and overstocks. This overloads the supply system, so the organization establishes priority codes. Before long, the only way to get anything is to use the top priority, so the priority system fails. There's an endless circle, and nothing ever gets any better.

How do you escape it? If you and other teams get together and start looking for solutions, you'll find some. Here's a suggestion: Identify all the common supplies the teams use. Now, instead of everyone trying to order everything at one time, set up a coordination system. This is easiest if the teams are networked and have access to a good spreadsheet or database program. Even if they don't, but at least some of the teams use personal computers, you can make a start. Identify the most important supplies; don't even think about trying to control all of them. Then devise a program to keep track of them. When one group of supplies begins to run low, such as the binders in this case, *one* team orders binders. Of course, it orders enough for all the teams. Yes, this is extra trouble for teams. If they stick to it, though, they will at least reduce the damage that the problem causes.

Team Strengthener

Don't skip lightly over the idea of being a good customer. Total Quality advocates and many others have stressed the importance of being customer oriented and giving outstanding customer service. No one with experience seriously denies the importance of this. But that's only half the equation. Individuals, teams, and organizations need to be effective customers. They need to understand what their suppliers can and can't accomplish. They need to be responsive when their suppliers face problems just as they expect their suppliers to be responsive to them. And this requires one more step: A basic responsibility of every supplier is to help its customers become good customers—in other words, to *educate* them. Customer satisfaction equals customer expectations compared with what they actually get. If they expect more than your team can deliver, they will always be dissatisfied, no matter how good the team is. So, make sure you educate them so that what they expect is realistic. Then deliver at least that every time.

11–9

The Problem
The team can't replace members quickly enough

The Scene

"I guess we'd better have that meeting to decide who takes over Vonda's projects, and we might as well start planning to do the same for Yves when he leaves next month."

"Sounds like things didn't go very well at Human Resources."

"They didn't go very well anywhere, Hank. I'll bet it's at least three months before we can fill either of the jobs."

Three months! The team is pushed hard enough now with Vonda gone. It'll be in real trouble if it can't add at least one person when Yves leaves. But is there anything you can do?

Possible Causes

The organization is trying to control costs by limiting hiring and promotions.

When costs seem to be too high, organizations make many different kinds of responses. One of the responses is to impose a freeze on hiring, and perhaps even on promotions, for a few weeks or months. (This often happens during the last quarter of the organization's fiscal year.) Exceptions may not be permitted; if they are, they normally require approval high in the organization.

Vacancies require several approvals before they can be filled.

You're caught in a problem the book deals with over and over: The organization hasn't changed its traditional support and control structures to accommodate teams. (It's a way that support offices can maintain their status and control, even with teams.) It expects rapid, responsive action from teams, but doesn't provide them support in the same rapid, responsive way.

The team hasn't built the network it needs to get resources quickly.

Regardless of any other factor, each team needs a network of other teams and individuals it can call on for support.

And it needs to take the initiative to create and maintain this network.

Cures

If the organization is trying to control costs by limiting hiring and promotions:

In this circumstance, your team has two alternatives. The first is to try to get an exception. But don't attempt this unless you can show that the unfilled vacancy is going to produce significant, measurable impact on productivity and/or costs. Does the vacancy mean that the team will have to work significant amounts of overtime to meet a critical deadline? Does it mean that an important project will be finished late, causing delays for teams down the line? If you can't find an argument at least as compelling as these, don't ask for an exception. On the other hand, if you do have a compelling argument, make it—and make it as quickly as possible.

If you can't justify an exception, or if the organization doesn't accept them, you need to plan work for the team members still available. Here's the chance to look critically at how the team does its work and cut out all the slack. The team may also discover that it's been "goldplating" its products and that customers will be just as happy without the goldplate. At the same time, make sure that whatever the team needs to do to be ready to recruit is done. Generate the paperwork. Get it through any approvals it has to have and to the Human Resources office. Get it as close to the front of the line as possible so it will get immediate attention when hiring begins again.

Perhaps you can take a little satisfaction in the fact that every unit, team or not, has to put up with the freeze.

If vacancies require several approvals before they can be filled:

What does the team do? If it can spare the time, it should select one member to expedite the filling of the vacancy, no matter what it takes. The individual should walk the requisition through, sweet-talking, pestering, cajoling—doing whatever it takes. Be sure to select someone who won't take "no" for an answer and doesn't discourage easily. Push the system for all it's worth. Stop only when the job is filled.

Several earlier cases in this chapter have provided suggestions for how to change management policies that don't work. Cases 11–1 through 11–4 in particular describe a good strategy. Use these. Mount a major effort to persuade management that the policies aren't meeting the team's needs. And in the meantime read the next section carefully.

If the team hasn't built the network it needs to get resources quickly:

It doesn't matter why you're having trouble getting vacancies filled promptly; this strategy will help no matter what. And it will help you get other resources, operate more effectively with other teams, develop support in management. The book has hinted at it throughout this chapter. The strategy? Build a network of friends throughout the organization. Your team has several members, more than enough to build an effective network.

How does networking begin? Whenever any member of the team has a contact with anyone else in the organization, *one of the basic purposes of that contact is to build or strengthen a relationship.* You need to do more, but this is where you begin. Everyone who deals with the team should go away from every encounter thinking "They're easy to deal with" or "I can trust these guys" or "They really looked out for me and what I need." When you do that, and do it consistently, you lay the groundwork for a powerful network.

Then the team makes a point to establish strong relationships with the individuals, teams, and units it doesn't deal regularly with, but which it nonetheless needs to have strong working relationships with. That's where filling the vacancies comes in. Do they have to be approved higher in the organization? Whoever does the approving should know at least one member of the team and through him or her have a high opinion of the team as a whole. A member of the team, the same one or someone else, should have established a strong relationship with key people in the Human Resources office. And everyone on the team should have a strong relationship with the team's next-level boss.

Isn't this manipulative? It doesn't have to be if you try genuinely to be helpful to those you deal with. This means that the team always has a double goal: It wants to build a relationship of high trust and credibility, and it wants to do this by being truly helpful to everyone whom it deals with. Neither goal is adequate by itself; together, they are a powerful combination.

No matter what the cause is:

Don't ever let yourself and the team get so pressured that you choose a questionable candidate. Poor selections normally remain with organizations for a long time, providing repeated opportunities for regret. No matter how pressing the need to fill the vacancy, take the time necessary to get the right person in it.

Team Strengthener

The previous cases in this chapter have covered aspects of effective networking. All this case did was draw these aspects together and put a name to them. You might want to scan back through the cases, then reread the section above to get the whole picture. Remember this: A successful team always attempts to be useful and by doing so to build strong relationships throughout the organization. The more effectively it does this, the more effective both it and the organization as a whole will be.

The Problem
The team can't get the training it needs

The Scene

"I'm sorry," Killea says, interrupting you, "I just don't understand what this section of the manual means."

You look up, making it a point to smile. Killea is one of the newest members of the team, a very conscientious and motivated person. But she hasn't been able to get the training she needs. You're glad to help her, but it's going to take time you need to spend on something else. "Put it down here, and let's look at it together."

Killea needs training at the moment more than anyone else, but she's not the only one who needs it. And if the big system change goes through as scheduled next month *everyone* is going to need significant training to use it effectively. How are you ever going to get the team the training it needs?

Possible Causes

The organization doesn't understand the need for training.

Not very long ago, training was an easy process for organizations to manage. Most training was gotten on the job. Since jobs didn't change rapidly, an individual could use for years with little modification, what he or she learned. For team-based organizations, those days are gone gone. But organizational systems and attitudes often don't keep up with the changes that teams require. That may be what's happening here.

The organization doesn't know how to provide training effectively.

Because the organization gave so little training in the past, it hasn't established an effective system for getting and delivering training to teams, or to anyone, for that matter.

Requirements are changing so fast that the organization can't develop training fast enough.

This seldom happened in the fifties, the sixties, or even the seventies. Beginning in the late seventies and accelerating until now, though, organizations discovered that they had to change rapidly to survive. One way many organizations chose to deal with change was to develop and use self-managing teams, which not only constantly deal with change but accelerate it.

If the organization has a traditional approach to training, even a motivated and effective one, it can't keep up with change that's this rapid. Typically, an effective training department would survey the organization annually, asking for the training that everyone needed for the coming year. Then it would arrange the training, or at least as much of it as it could fund. But in today's environment, your team may not be able to anticipate the training it needs a year ahead of time, perhaps not even three months ahead of time.

Cures

If the organization doesn't understand the need for training:

If the training need is widespread throughout the organization, the team should get together with other teams in the same situation and present the case for change to higher management (see Cases 11–1 through 11–4). It's unlikely that it's confined to your team; if it is, the team needs to prepare the best case it can and take it to your next-level manager.

This probably takes time. So, in the meantime, exercise initiative. Assuming that the problem is broader than your team, meet with the other affected teams and determine what training is needed. Some of it can probably be gotten through commercial training organizations, some more of it through local community colleges. Some of it may have to be developed. But identify the training that's needed clearly and then pay a visit to the organization's training department. They may be delighted to help you; after all, they probably don't like the organization's attitude toward training any better than you do. Even if they're not enthusiastic, they'll have to respond to your requests, and the subtle suggestion that you may need to go out and get training on your own if things don't get better may help them become even more cooperative.

If the organization doesn't know how to get training effectively:

With luck, there's a competent—though probably understaffed—training department. If so, make it a top priority to develop a strong relationship with them. You may not be able to change anything to get Killea training in time, but you can lay the groundwork to see that the problem doesn't recur. And don't dump the issue on the training department; make your goal for it and the team to learn together. You can help by identifying sources of training. You'll hope that the training department will be enthusiastic that someone really cares about training. If not, use the subtle suggestion mentioned at the end of the section above.

Suppose there's no effective training department or it doesn't care or (worst of all) it's incompetent. Then you start identifying where you can get the training your team needs. Some of it is already available through commercial and educational sources. But some of it will have to be specific to the organization. That means that (1) the teams will have to develop it themselves or (2) some part of the organization will have to develop it or (3) the organization will have to contract for it. Now that you know the training needed and the alternatives for getting it, take it to higher management. And keep pushing until things start to turn around and the organization builds an effective training operation.

If things are changing so fast that the organization can't develop training fast enough:

There's no quick and easy solution. To begin, create a team formed from all the teams or a representative example of teams whose function is to identify coming needs for training. Then get this team working with the training department. It wants to help the training department, of course, but it also wants to see that the training department becomes responsive to the teams' needs. You'll hope that the team and the training department can develop a true partnership, one that can find how to develop training rapidly enough to deal with rapid change.

In this circumstance, the organization and the team will have to rely increasingly on on-the-job training. Make sure your training department understands how this needs to be done; then get training for the team in how to do it.

Team Strengthener

This chapter has presented an example of how teams need to take responsibility for all facets of their work existence. That doesn't mean that teams have to do everything for themselves. Not at all. Instead, they need to take the initiative in identifying the problems they face and then seeing that the appropriate parts of the organization provide them the support they need to resolve these problems. You and other members of your team probably spent years in a traditional organization thinking "If only they'd let me take care of that, I could do it a lot better!" Well, now that you're on a self-managing team you can "take care of that." Do it, and do it regularly.

11–11

The Problem

Team members are still being appraised as individuals, not as team members

The Scene

"Hey, Charlene, what kind of a rating did you get?"

"At the risk of seeming rude, Bernice, it's not really any of your business. But I will tell you that it's pretty good."

"Well, mine is 'pretty good,' too, but I think I did better than 'pretty good' this year. And I'd think you'd feel the same way."

"I really do. The team has done really well, but my appraisal certainly doesn't look as though we did. What irritates me most of all is that none of us got to say anything about other team members' performance."

You smile ruefully. You wanted to appraise the team as a whole and then give everyone a chance to decide what the appraisal should be and whether everyone should get the same rating. But you're not officially even a supervisor, so your next-level manager had to do the appraisals, and she insisted on doing the team members as individuals. Somehow, all this has to change before the next appraisal cycle.

Possible Causes

The organization hasn't updated its policies to fit teams.

One of the organizational systems that most needs to change when it implements teams is the appraisal and compensation system. Unfortunately, this is also a very difficult system to change.

The organization believes that only individuals can be appraised.

In the section above, the organization may not have changed its policies because it didn't see the need, or because it hadn't gotten around to it. Here, it hasn't changed because it doesn't want teams to be appraised or doesn't want individuals to be appraised for their contribution to the team. The attitude that individuals need to be appraised and that they need to be appraised on their individual performance runs very deep in most organizations.

The organization believes that only managers can give appraisals.

Appraisals have been part of the managerial and supervisory job for so long that organizations may not be able to think in any other terms. Since no team leader in a self-managing team is a supervisor, you can't give appraisals. That leaves only your higher-level manager to do them.

Hint

All three causes may contribute to the problem. They don't exclude one another.

Cures

If the organization hasn't updated its policies to fit teams:

Why is it so important to change this system? Because unless the team controls its own appraisals it cannot be fully self-managing. In a real sense, the team as a whole takes over the role that a supervisor used to play, and the power to give appraisals has always been a key element in a supervisor's job. Even if the team's next-level manager thinks well of it and tries to do well by it, it's not the same as the team exercising its own control.

Can you persuade the organization to change its policy? Maybe. Maybe not. You should try. But that's the long-range target. Your short-range objective is much closer. Feel out your next-level manager. If he or she is willing to give the team more autonomy, perhaps the team can develop its own appraisals. Then the manager can provide the signature that the system requires. What if your manager isn't open to considering that? Does anything prevent you from having a quiet meeting with the team and getting their input, and then presenting it your next-level manager as your own? It might be worth a try if nothing else works.

A final thought. If you and other team leaders make a strong enough case, the organization may be willing to consider changing the appraisal system. If that happens, you probably need to do your best to see that each team has two alternatives. On the one hand, all team members can get the same appraisal. That supports team spirit and avoids conflicts within the team. But it may be no more than a way station. Mature teams often want a second alternative: the freedom for the team to appraise each member differently when their contributions to the team are different. If the organization shows signs of changing the policy of individual ratings only, be sure that you and the team discuss the alternatives carefully and present your suggestions to your higher-level manager.

If the organization believes that only individuals can be appraised:

This may be a harder nut to crack than just the failure to update policies. That doesn't mean that you and the team shouldn't try, or that you shouldn't work with other teams to make a strong case with higher management for the change. Before you do, though, make certain that the teams are being successful and that you can show how changing the appraisal system will support this success.

While you're trying to create this change, use the suggestions in the section above. The team needs to do everything it can to make the ratings team ratings.

If the organization believes that only managers can give appraisals:

If this drives the organization's unwillingness to delegate appraisal responsibility to teams, your first move is to enlist your higher-level manager as an ally. He or she may already understand what the team needs and may support its appraising itself. If not, a little persuasion may produce the same result. (After all, exactly what does either the team or the manager get from the manager appraising it?) That means that the manager can campaign with the organization to delegate appraisals to the team. It also means that, in the meantime, he or she may be willing to let the team do the actual appraisals and then sign them.

Once again, the last alternative is for you to let the team develop the appraisals, then "sell" them to the manager. Don't do this if you're forbidden to do it, and don't get in a situation where you have to lie about it. But if no one has told you absolutely that you can't, think seriously about doing it.

Team Strengthener

"It's easier to ask forgiveness than permission." This phrase, almost a buzzword at times, is tailor-made for teams. This book stresses how important it is for a team to take the initiative. This often means doing something that's not authorized. On occasion, it may mean doing something that policy discourages or even forbids. In each situation, the team has to weigh the risks before deciding. Certainly, you don't want to disregard a policy because it's inconvenient or the team doesn't like it. But if the policy gets in the way of getting the job done—well, that's a different matter. And if the team continues to succeed, higher management will have an excellent excuse not to ask too many questions.

CHAPTER 12

The Final Problem

Here it is, the problem no team wants to face. And the discussion of it summarizes the four most important steps a team can take to prevent having to face it.

The Problem

The organization has just decided to abolish its teams

The Scene

Jon throws himself down in the chair and lets out a deep sigh. "Well, it's official—the CEO has decided to abolish all the teams."

"Oh, no, that can't be," Norma responds.

"They've been working so well."

"*He* doesn't think so. He's given the department heads a week to show him why he shouldn't, but it sounds like a done deal to me."

Stunned, you and the other the members of the team just stare at Jon and each other in silence.

Possible Causes

The teams haven't been as productive as the organization expected.

Teams are often sold as the solution to a variety of problems: quality, productivity, shortened cycle time, whatever. They can help achieve these goals, but it won't happen automatically. Whatever the reason, it didn't happen for your organization.

The organization feels like it's losing control and wants to reestablish its control.

One of the major problems with any form of worker "empowerment," such as self-managing teams, is that managers often feel as if they're losing control. If no one has prepared them how to handle the situation, they often deal with it by reestablishing the traditional, hierarchical system they're used to.

Hint

This is the worst of all team problems. The goal is not to solve it; it's almost certainly too late for that. The goal is to prevent it from happening in the first place.

That's what this book is really about. Follow its suggestions and you will minimize the chance that you will ever have to deal with this problem.

Cures

While this book deals with many problems, many causes, and many cures, it advocates a basic fourfold strategy for teams:

1. The team needs to perform effectively, day in and day out.

Of course, traditional workgroups need to be productive, but teams have a special burden. They must prove themselves to management, including top management. Too many members of management believe that teams aren't worth it and/or that the organization can't properly control them. As soon as teams appear to be nonproductive, they reinforce these views and play into their critics' hands.

The book repeatedly stresses how a team must first look to its own effectiveness. If a problem arises, it needs first of all to ensure that its less-than-optimal performance isn't helping to cause the problem. When a team automatically looks first at its effectiveness, it establishes a solid base for its survival.

2. The team needs to be sensitive to the issues of its next-level manager and of higher management in general.

In a traditional organization, a manager is judged by the effectiveness of the workgroups that report to her. In a team-based organization she is judged by the effectiveness of the teams that report to her. In each case the workgroup or team must be sensitive to the manager's issues and pay attention to them. In short, a basic goal of the team must be to make its next-level manager look good.

Because teams can have so much autonomy, they can forget this and concentrate exclusively on their own issues. That won't work. As a manager sees his issues being pushed into the background, his comfort level begins to drop. He may deal openly with the team and help them change. Or he may decide that teams are hard to control and become a potential voice against continuing them.

So a team must pay close attention to its manager's concerns and make them its own. When it does this successfully, it earns the manager's support, both for itself and for teams in general.

3. The team needs to network and to work closely with other teams.

When organizations become team based, much of the work of coordination moves from higher management to the teams themselves. For team organization to succeed, teams must develop the relationships that enable them to work closely together.

They can't do this by waiting around until they need to coordinate with one another. Each team needs to actively develop relationships with other teams. In today's jargon it needs to network—early and often.

When teams do this successfully, they increase their ability to manage their own affairs significantly. And the more they can identify and solve their own problems, the more successful higher levels of management will believe they are. One more point for teams!

4. The team needs to exercise constant initiative.

This is listed last for a good reason: If a team exercises constant initiative without consistently practicing the first three points, it runs the danger of being seen as out of control. Once the team has its act together on the first three items, though, this is the one that makes the whole process work.

When team-based organizations work, it's largely because the teams exercise constant initiative to make them work. Teams don't wait for someone else to solve their problems. They take positive steps—on their own or with other teams—

to solve them themselves. This is how they protect their autonomy and freedom. This is how they remain self-managing rather than other-managed.

Team Strengthener

If the team performs effectively, day in and day out; if it is sensitive to the issues of its next-level manager and of higher management in general; if it networks and works closely with other teams; and if it exercises constant initiative to identify and resolve its problems—well, it will have done its best to prevent the worst of all team problems.

May your team live long and prosper.

INDEX

A

Administrative work, avoidance of, 149-52
AIDS:
  team member with, 34-39
    and confidentiality, 37
    health risks posed by, 36-37
    and moral statement of others, 37-38
    and sense of betrayal, 38
Anger, at team member, 7-9
Arguments:
  among team members, 25-28, 51-53
  between teams, 248-51
Arrogance:
  and new work methods, 213-16
  of team, 242-44
Assignments:
  and mission, 290-93
    detracting from, 317-20
Autonomy of team, 189-91
Avoidance of work, 140-42

B

Badmouthing, 98-100
Balance of skills, wrong, 48-50
Behavioral problems, 79-111
  dogmatism/lack of compromise, 83-86
  hogging the credit, 80-83
Blame, 66-70
  action plan for, 68-69
  other team's, 252-55
  seeking source of mistake, 358-61
Blowing off steam, 77-78
Boundaries:
  establishment of effective, 291-92
  failure to set, 297-99
Breakup of team, 378-82, 427-30
Burnout, 153-55

C

Career progession, lack of, 191-93
Center of attention, team members seeking, 28-31
Chain of customers, 321-22
Challenge of mission, 307-10
Changes in mission, 314-17
Clannishness, 10-13
Clarity of mission, 71-72, 290-93
Cliques, 19-22, 340
Coaching, leaders, 273-76
Cohesiveness of team, 51-53
Commitment:
  lack of, 116-19
    and poor decison making, 153-55

Company procedures, refusal to conform to, 217-20
Competition:
  among team members, 41-44
  between teams, 239-41
Compromise:
  lack of, 83-86
  working problems through vs., 60-63
Computers:
  failing to see benefit of, 208-12
  fear of, 203-5
Computer/support system problems, 385-425
  appraisal of team members, 421-25
  coordination policies, 404-6
  incorrect data, 400-403
  lack of information, 403-6
  reentering of data, 396-400
  replacement of team members, 414-17
  supplies, 410-13
  team production records, maintenance of, 407-10
  team work methods, 386-88
  training needs, 418-21
  uncontrollable errors, 392-96
  workarounds, 389-92
Concentration:
  on mission, 176-79
  on mutual goals, 248-51

Confidence:
  criticality of, 134
  lack of, 87-90
    in leadership, 262-65, 280-81, 287-88
Conflict, 25-28, 54-63, 234-37
  avoidance of, 87-90
  managing, 235-36
Confrontation:
  skills, lack of, 162-65
  and teams, 282
Control, 270, 272, 359-61
  and breakup of team, 427-30
  of critical factors to success, 327-30
  managers,' 340-41
  and overruled team decisions, 351-54
  of support units, 328-30
Controversial team decisions, support of, 347-50
Controversy, avoidance of, 93-95
Cooperation:
  lack of, 159-62
    between teams, 239-41
Covering for another team, 255-57
Creative, unproductive team, 227-30
Criticism, 98-100
  of leaders, 280-82
Customer orientation, 324-27

Customers:
  feedback
    refusal of, 165-69
    refusal to accept, 170-73
  identifying for team, 320-24
  lack of satisfaction, 71-73

D

Decision making:
  by team, 63-66
  controversial, support of,
    347-50
  lack of support for, 63-66
  overruled team decisions,
    351-54
  poor, 153-55
  rejection of team decision,
    95-97
  team's fear of, 259-61
Deep interpersonal issues, 55,
    56-57
Deference to team member,
    266-69
Delegation, 354-57
Departing team member, 13-
    16, 99-100
Differences, discussing, 57-60
Disagreement, fear of, 86-87
Discipline, lack of, 228-30
Discouragement, 70-73
  and lack of career proges-
    sion, 191-93
Discrimination, 10-12

and cliques, 20-21
Dislike, of other team mem-
    bers, 44-47
Disorganization, 223-27
Disrupters, 119-22
Distrust:
  among team members, 2-4
  of motives, 284-85
  of new team member, 17-19
Dogmatism/lack of compro-
    mise, 83-86

E

Extremely difficult problems,
    and discouragement,
    71, 73

F

Facilitator, and conflict resolu-
    tion, 27-28
Fear:
  of computers, 203-5
  of decision making, 259-61
  of making mistakes, 263-65
Feedback:
  from customers, 165-69
  from organization, 310-14
Fighting, 25-28
  over trivial matters, 51-53
Follow-through, 224-27
Functional rivalries, 23-25

G

Goldplating of output, 336, 338, 345

H

Hidden agendas, 97, 334
Higher management problems, 331-84
blame-seeking, 358-61
breakup of team/reassignment of members, 378-82
changed mission, team's desire for, 366-69
lack of recognition, 372-75
micromanagement of team, 354-57
new members forced on team, 361-65
overruled team decisions, 351-54
quantity/quality of team's work, 343-47
and self-managed teams, 382-84
support of controversial team decisions, 347-50
team member ratings, input for, 339-42
team performance, 369-71
team size and workload, 335-39
work assignments, 332-35

Hogging the credit, 80-83

I

Immaturity, 119-22
and decision making, 260-62
Incentives, team problems with, 54, 56
Independence:
of individual worker, 17-19
of team, 221-22
Initiative of team, 294-96, 321-23, 328-30
exercising, 429-30
Internal standards, 311-12
Interpersonal problems, 1-39
AIDS, team member with, 34-39
anger at team member, 7-9, 96-97
blame, 66-70
cliques, 19-22
competition, 41-44
compromise vs. working problems through, 60-63
conflict within team, 25-28, 54-63
criticism/badmouthing others, 98-100
departing team member, 13-16
differences among members, discussing, 57-60

disagreement, fear of, 86-87
discouragement, 70-73
dislike among team members, 44-47
distrust, 2-4
failure to raise problems, 92-95
fighting, 25-28
    over trivial matters, 51-53
invasion of privacy, 104-7
lying, 108-11
malfunctional teams, 47-50
oversocialization, 74-76
prejudice/discrimination, 10-12
rejection
    of other's ideas, 90-92
    of team decision, 95-97
    of team's overtures, 17-19
serious disagreement, 54-57
sexual harassment charges, 31-34
shutting out team member, 5-7, 120-22
silliness, 77-78
team building skills, lack of, 22-25
team decisions lacking full support, 63-66
theft, 100-104
weird member, 28-31
Inter-team problems, 238-57
    arguments, 248-51
    blame, 252-55
    lack of cooperation, 239-41

lying for another team, 255-57
teams take over other team's functions, 244-47
team wants to work alone, 242-44
Invasion of privacy, 104-7

K

Knowledge workers, and administrative duties, 149-52

L

Lack of career progression, 191-93
Lack of confidence, 87-90, 266-68
    in leadership, 262-65
Lack of cooperation, 159-62
    between teams, 239-41
Lack of discipline, 228-30
Lack of quality work, 156-59
Lack of recognition, 372-75
Lack of support:
    for decision making, 63-66
    from next-level manager, 189-91, 375-78
    of leaders, 276-79
Laziness, 129-31
Leadership problems, 258-88
    coaching/mentoring, 273-76

criticism of leaders, 280-82
deference to member, 266-69
lack of confidence, 262-65
lack of support of leaders, 276-79
leaders as supervisors, 269-73
rejection of leadership, 283-86
rigid approach to leadership, 286-88
team's request for guidance, 259-62
Leaders as supervisors, 269-73
Lying, 108-11
for another team, 255-57

M

Malfunctional teams, 47-50
Maturity, 119-22
and decision making, 260-62
and leadership, 287-88
Member behavioral problems, *See* Behavioral problems
Mentoring, leaders, 273-76
Micromanagement of team, 354-57
Miscommunication, 252-54
Mission, 48-50, 289-330
assignments detracting from, 317-20
challenge of, 307-10

changes in, 314-17
team's desire for, 366-69
clarity of, 71-72, 290-93
and training/skills deficiencies, 143-45
controlling critical factors to success, 327-30
customer orientation, 324-27
customers, identifying for team, 320-24
expanding, 307-10
failure to concentrate on, 176-79
and feedback, 310-14
importance of, 293-96
lack of viable, 77
less-than-full-time, 140
and mismatched team, 228-30
objective setting, 303-6
overbroad, 300-303
overlapping, 297-300
and poor performance, 146-49
problems with, 74, 75
scope of, 301-2
and team creativity, 177-78
team not up to, 153-54
team problems with, 54, 56
and training/skills deficiencies, 146-49
Mistakes:
fear of making, 263-65
seeking source of, 358-61

Mistrust:
  of motives, 284-85
  of new team member, 17-19
  of other team members, 2-4
  of team self-management,
    355-57
Moral principles, 83-86
Motivation, and competition,
  41-44
Motives, mistrust of, 284-85
Multifunctional teams, performance problems with,
  179-84
Mutual goals, concentration
  on, 248-51

N

Networking, 429
New team members, and training, 363-64
New work methods:
  lack of approval of, 220-23
  refusal to use, 213-16
Next-level manager:
  breakup of team/reassign-
    ment of members, 378-
    82
  and change in mission,
    team's desire for, 366-
    69
  lack of recognition from,
    372-75
  lack of support from, 189-
    91, 375-78

micromanagement by, 354-
  57
overruled team decisions,
  351-54
and quantity/quality of
  teamwork, 343-47
and team member ratings,
  input for, 339-42
and team performance, 369-
  71
Nonperformers, handling by
  team members, 162-65

O

Objective setting, and mission,
  303-6
Obsolete products, team's
  responsibility for, 321-
  23
Overbroad mission, 300-303
Overconfidence of team, 242-
  44
Overlapping mission, 297-300
Overreaction, 7-9
Overruled team decisions, 351-
  54
Oversocialization, 74-76
Overwork, 142-46

P

Performance problems, 112-38
  administrative work, avoid-
    ance of, 149-52

and autonomy of team, 189-91

commitment, lack of, 116-19

customer feedback
refusal of, 165-69
refusal to accept, 170-73

disrupters, 119-22

going around the team, 125-28

and immaturity, 119-22

lack of career progression, 191-93

lack of cooperation, 159-62

lack of quality work, 156-59

laziness, 129-31

and mission, 146-49

mission, failure to concentrate on, 176-79

and multifunctional teams, 179-84

nonperformers, handling, 162-65

overwork, 142-46

poor decision making, 153-55

poor productivity, 113-16

shutting out team member, 120-22

split team suggestion, 197-99

status inconsistencies, 184-88

task preferences, 132-38

teamwork, lack of, 122-25

turnover, 173-76

unrealistic deadlines, 157-59

unreasonable amount of work, 143-45

violation of team norms, 199-201

workload problems, 140-42

Performance rating on individual basis, 67, 69

Poor decision making, 153-55

Poor initial training, 23-25

Poor performance:
and breakup of team, 379-80
lying to cover, 108-11
reputation for, 332-33

Poor productivity, 113-16

Prejudice, 10-12

Priority setting, 301-3

Productive, uncreative team, 231-34

Productivity, 343-47
and breakup of team, 427-30

Q

Quality work, lack of, 156-59

Quantity/quality of team's work, 343-47

R

Rapid change, dealing with, 314-17

Reassignment of team members, 378-82

Recognition, lack of, by management, 372-75

Rejection:
  of leadership, 283-86
  of others' ideas, 90-92
  of team decision, 95-97
  of team's overtures, 17-19

Reputation:
  for poor performance, 332-33
  of team, 294-95
  and turnover rate, 173-76

Resentment, 44-47, 99-100

Rewards, based on individual performance, 41-44

Rigid approach to leadership, 286-88

S

Scope of mission, 301-2

Self-management:
  higher management distrust of, 382-84
  learning, 325-27
  next-level manager's distrust of, 355-57
  stress of, 194-96
  and team needs, 328-29

Sexual harassment charges, 31-34

Short-term objectives, setting, 303-6

Shutting out team members, 5-7, 120-22

Silliness, 77-78

Splitting the team, 197-99
  drawbacks of, 198-99

Standards, 311-13

Status inconsistencies, 184-88

Stressful projects, recovery from, 74-76

Structural matters, team problems with, 54, 56

Subteams, use of, 197-99

Supervision, need for, 129-31

Swapping skills, 308-10

T

Task preferences, 132-38

Team, interpersonal problems within, 1-39

Team assignments, and mission, 290-93

Team building skills, lack of, 22-25

Team creativity, and mission, 177-78

Team decisions, 63-66

Team discipline, lack of, 74-76

Team member ratings, input for, 339-42

Team organization, failure in, 26

Team size, and workload, 335-39

Teamwork, lack of, 122-25

Technology:
    avoiding use of, 203-5
    refusal to use, 209-12
Theft, 100-104
Total Quality Management
        (TQM) programs, 156-
        57, 167-68
Training:
    deficiencies, and mission,
        146-49
    and new team members,
        363-64
    and turnover rate, 175-76
Turnover problems, 173-76

U

Unrealistic deadlines, 157-59
    agreeing to, 253, 254
Unrealistic expectations, of
        team member, 14, 16
Unreasonable amount of work,
        143-45
Unstability of organization,
        314-16
Uptight organization, new
        team member from, 17-
        19

V

Violation of team norms, 199-
        201

W

Weird team members, 28-31
Wheeler-dealers, handling, 2-4
Workarounds, 389-92
Work assignments:
    given to other teams, 332-
        35
    and mission, 290-93
        detracting from, 317-20
Workload problems, 140-42
    and team size, 335-39
Work practice problems, 202-
        37
    company procedures, refusal
        to conform to, 217-20
    conflicting team members,
        234-37
    creative but unproductive
        team, 227-30
    disorganization, 223-27
    new work methods
        lack of approval of, 220-
        23
        refusal to use, 213-16
    productive but uncreative
        team, 231-34
    technology
        avoiding use of, 203-5
        refusal to use, 209-12
    work improvement meth-
        ods, avoiding, 206-9
Work processes, improving,
        336-37
Wrong balance of skills, 48-50